STREET SPEAK 3

THE COMPLETE COURSE IN AMERICAN SLANG & IDIOMS

Front cover:

fit like a glove (to) *exp.* said of a piece of clothing that fits perfectly.

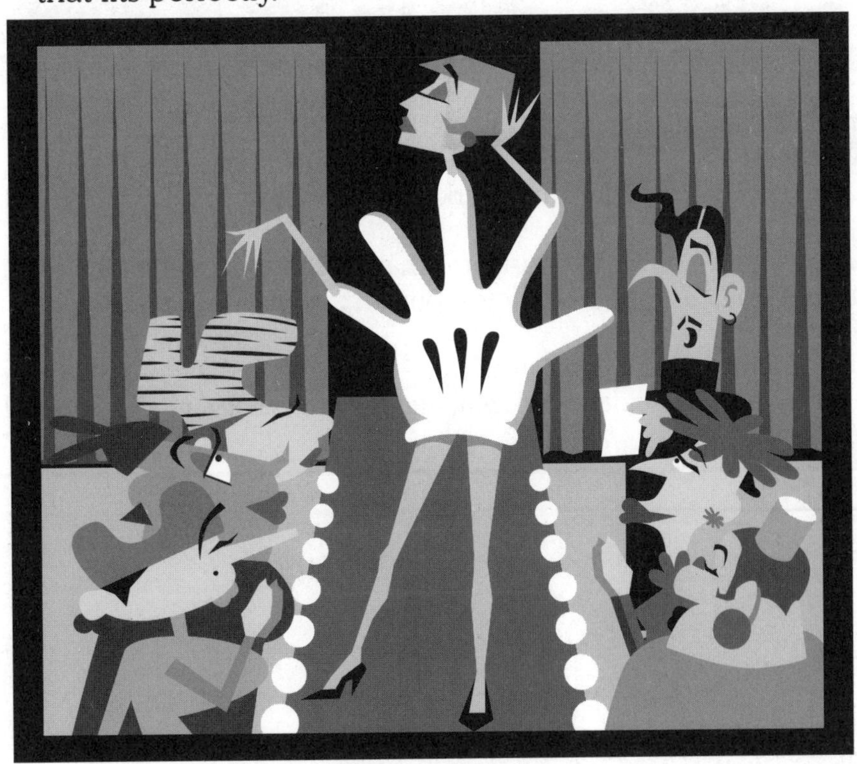

SLANGMAN DAVID BURKE

DEDICATION

This book is dedicated to Jason Reese and Jennifer Reese – my wonderful friends, confidants, and two of the most talented and creative people that I've ever had the pleasure to work with. Not a day goes by that I'm not grateful for their participation and spirit.

A SPECIAL THANKS

I'd like to give a very special thanks to Hemera Technologies, Inc. for their invaluable contribution to this book. The tailor-made clipart they created for us was no less than astounding. Their illustrations went far beyond my expectations of simply conveying the meaning of each slang term and idiom – each was wonderfully clever, creative, and most important, downright hilarious. I feel fortunate to have the opportunity of working with a group of people that is so professional, accommodating, and so very talented.

490 St-Joseph Boulevard, Suite 301 • Hall, Quebec • Canada J8Y 3Y7 • Contact: info@hemera.com • Tel: (819) 772-8200 • Fax: (819) 778-6252

For more information about Hemera™ and their products, including Hemera Photo-Objects 50,000 Volumes I & II and The Big Box of Art, please go to www.hemera.com

ACKNOWLEDGEMENTS

I'd like to give a special thanks to thank our talented "slang gang" of actors who are always at the ready when called in to record the audio portions of our SLANGMAN books. Their skill, support, and friendship mean the world to me: Grant Beehler, Nancy Burke, Noah Manne, and Debbie Wright.

Kathy Jones of United Audio is *da bomb!* I just can't thank her enough for her attention to the duplication phase of our audio CDs and cassettes. Her professionalism, service, wit, and kindness is always a treat.

There's no way I could give my publishing guru, Kim Hendrickson, the thanks she deserves. Throught the years, she's given me invaluable guidance, insight, and never-ending support. I thank her so much for her help and cherished friendship.

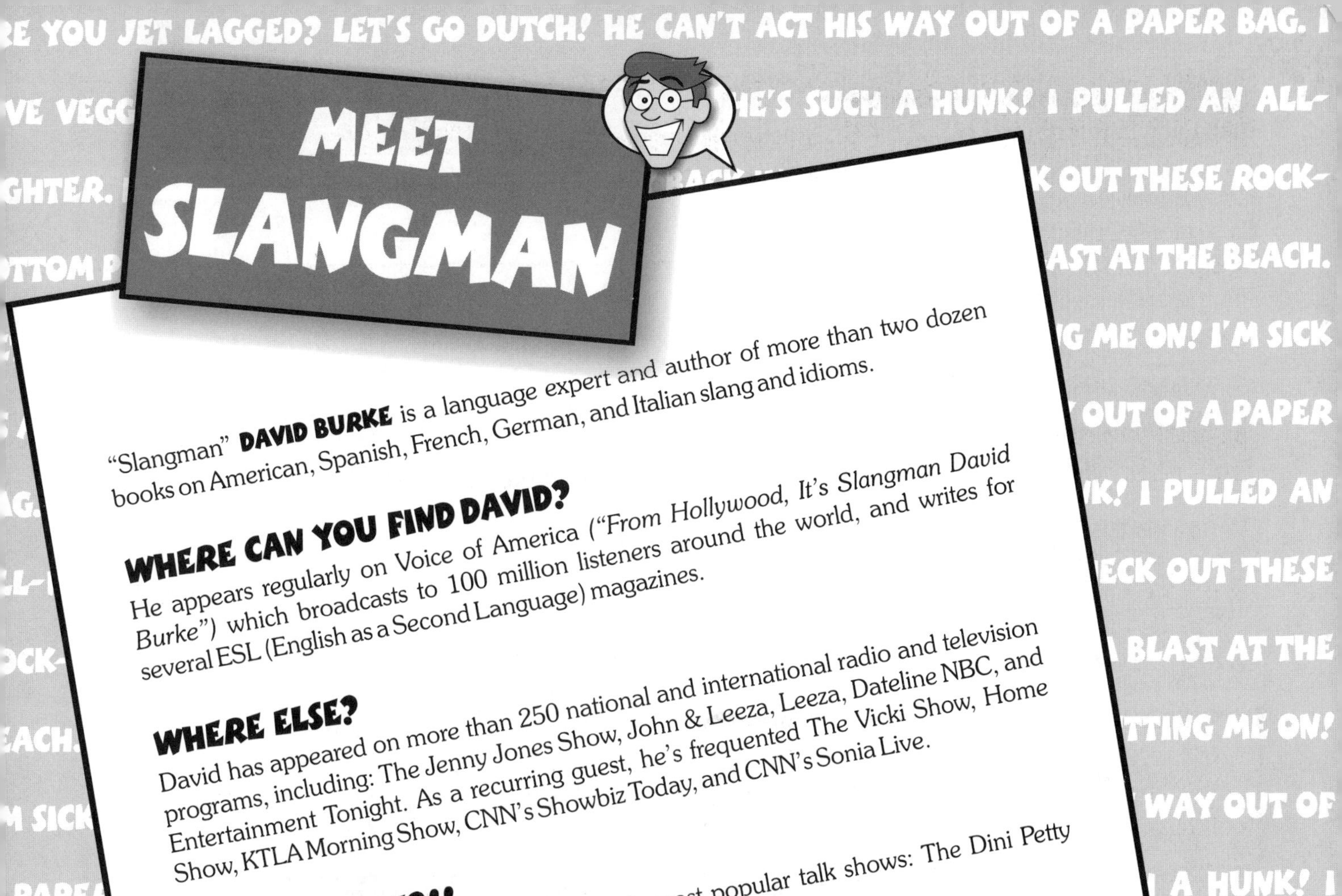

MEET SLANGMAN

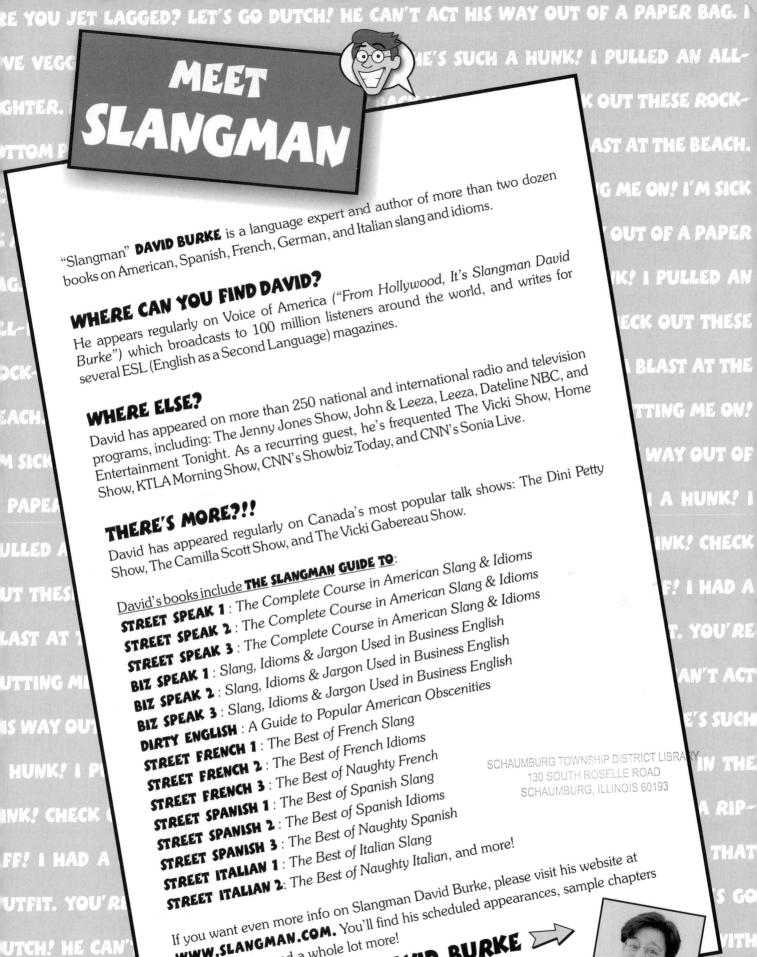

"Slangman" **DAVID BURKE** is a language expert and author of more than two dozen books on American, Spanish, French, German, and Italian slang and idioms.

WHERE CAN YOU FIND DAVID?

He appears regularly on Voice of America ("*From Hollywood, It's Slangman David Burke*") which broadcasts to 100 million listeners around the world, and writes for several ESL (English as a Second Language) magazines.

WHERE ELSE?

David has appeared on more than 250 national and international radio and television programs, including: The Jenny Jones Show, John & Leeza, Leeza, Dateline NBC, and Entertainment Tonight. As a recurring guest, he's frequented The Vicki Show, Home Show, KTLA Morning Show, CNN's Showbiz Today, and CNN's Sonia Live.

THERE'S MORE?!!

David has appeared regularly on Canada's most popular talk shows: The Dini Petty Show, The Camilla Scott Show, and The Vicki Gabereau Show.

David's books include **THE SLANGMAN GUIDE TO**:

STREET SPEAK 1 : *The Complete Course in American Slang & Idioms*
STREET SPEAK 2 : *The Complete Course in American Slang & Idioms*
STREET SPEAK 3 : *The Complete Course in American Slang & Idioms*
BIZ SPEAK 1 : *Slang, Idioms & Jargon Used in Business English*
BIZ SPEAK 2 : *Slang, Idioms & Jargon Used in Business English*
BIZ SPEAK 3 : *Slang, Idioms & Jargon Used in Business English*
DIRTY ENGLISH : *A Guide to Popular American Obscenities*
STREET FRENCH 1 : *The Best of French Slang*
STREET FRENCH 2 : *The Best of French Idioms*
STREET FRENCH 3 : *The Best of Naughty French*
STREET SPANISH 1 : *The Best of Spanish Slang*
STREET SPANISH 2 : *The Best of Spanish Idioms*
STREET SPANISH 3 : *The Best of Naughty Spanish*
STREET ITALIAN 1 : *The Best of Italian Slang*
STREET ITALIAN 2: *The Best of Naughty Italian*, and more!

If you want even more info on Slangman David Burke, please visit his website at **WWW.SLANGMAN.COM.** You'll find his scheduled appearances, sample chapters from his books, and a whole lot more!

SLANGMAN DAVID BURKE

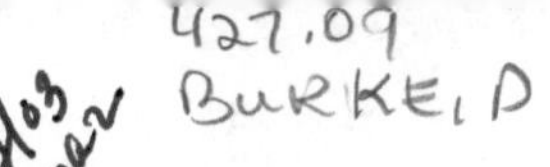

Book Design and Production: Slangman Publishing
Managing Partner/Brand & Marketing Director: Jason Reese
Design (Logo/Web): Jennifer Reese
Copy Editor: Nancy Burke
Illustrator – Outside cover: Ty Semaka
Illustrator – Main inside illustrations: Hemera Technologies
Photographer – Outside back cover: Rick Olson
Icon Design: Sharon Kim

Published by Slangman Publishing • 12206 Hillslope Street • Studio City, CA 91604-3603 • USA
Toll Free Telephone from the USA & Canada: 1-877-SLANGMAN (1-877-752-6462)
From outside North America: 1-818-769-1914
Worldwide Fax number: 1-413-647-1589
Email: editor@slangman.com
Website: http://www.slangman.com

ISBN 1-891888-226
Printed in the United States of America
10 9 8 7 6 5 4 3 2 1

LEGEND

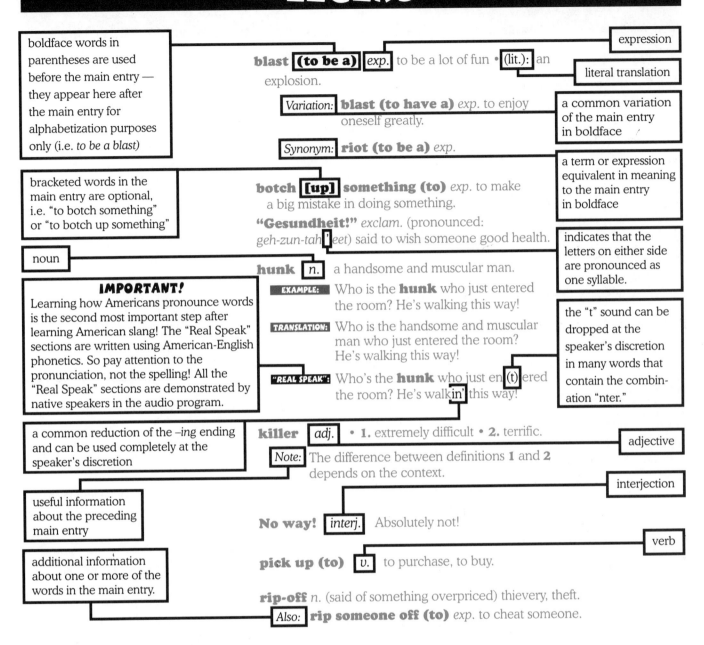

boldface words in parentheses are used before the main entry — they appear here after the main entry for alphabetization purposes only (i.e. *to be a blast*)

expression

blast (to be a) *exp.* to be a lot of fun • (lit.): an explosion.

literal translation

Variation: **blast (to have a)** *exp.* to enjoy oneself greatly.

a common variation of the main entry in boldface

Synonym: **riot (to be a)** *exp.*

a term or expression equivalent in meaning to the main entry in boldface

bracketed words in the main entry are optional, i.e. "to botch something" or "to botch up something"

botch [up] something (to) *exp.* to make a big mistake in doing something.

"Gesundheit!" *exclam.* (pronounced: *geh-zun-tah'eet*) said to wish someone good health.

indicates that the letters on either side are pronounced as one syllable.

noun

hunk *n.* a handsome and muscular man.

IMPORTANT!
Learning how Americans pronounce words is the second most important step after learning American slang! The "Real Speak" sections are written using American-English phonetics. So pay attention to the pronunciation, not the spelling! All the "Real Speak" sections are demonstrated by native speakers in the audio program.

EXAMPLE: Who is the **hunk** who just entered the room? He's walking this way!

TRANSLATION: Who is the handsome and muscular man who just entered the room? He's walking this way!

"REAL SPEAK": Who's the **hunk** who just en(t)ered the room? He's walkin' this way!

the "t" sound can be dropped at the speaker's discretion in many words that contain the combination "nter."

a common reduction of the –*ing* ending and can be used completely at the speaker's discretion

killer *adj.* • **1.** extremely difficult • **2.** terrific.

adjective

Note: The difference between definitions **1** and **2** depends on the context.

useful information about the preceding main entry

interjection

No way! *interj.* Absolutely not!

verb

pick up (to) *v.* to purchase, to buy.

additional information about one or more of the words in the main entry.

rip-off *n.* (said of something overpriced) thievery, theft.

Also: **rip someone off (to)** *exp.* to cheat someone.

EXPLANATION OF ICONS

These exercises reinforce visual recognition of the slang terms and idioms presented throughout this book.

These exercises include fill-ins, crossword puzzles, word matches and many other fun word games to help you use the new terms in context.

These exercises help you to understand not only *what* Americans speak, but *how* they speak! These exercises can all be found on the audio program. *(See back pages for details)*

These oral exercises are designed to help you to begin speaking and thinking like a native.

TABLE OF CONTENTS

LESSON TITLE | **WORDS PRESENTED**

ROGER STRIKES OUT WITH A PICK-UP LINE!

(Dating Slang – Phase 1: The Hunt for a Relationship)

PAGE 1

THIS LESSON FEATURES 10 NEW SLANG WORDS & IDIOMS

- blow someone off (to)
- check out someone or something (to)
- come on to someone (to)
- fix someone up (to)
- hit it off (to)
- let someone down easy (to)
- on the rebound (to be)
- pick-up line
- play hard to get (to)
- strike out (to)

KEN POPPED THE QUESTION!

(Dating Slang – Phase 2: The Thrill of the Relationship!)

PAGE 23

THIS LESSON FEATURES 10 NEW SLANG WORDS & IDIOMS

- crazy about/for someone (to be)
- "Get a room!"
- go together (to)
- hitched (to get)
- knocked up (to get)
- make out (to)
- pop the question (to)
- rob the cradle (to)
- shack up [together] (to)
- sugar daddy

JANE AND MIKE BROKE UP!

(Dating Slang – Phase 3: The End of the Relationship)

PAGE 41

THIS LESSON FEATURES 10 NEW SLANG WORDS & IDIOMS

- affair (to have an)
- break up (to)
- bust someone (to)
- drop someone like a hot potato (to)
- mistress
- on the rocks (to be)
- patch things up (to)
- pre-nup
- take someone to the cleaners (to)
- tramp

TOM IS WAY OFF BASE!

(Sports Terms Used in Slang)

PAGE 59

THIS LESSON FEATURES 12 NEW SLANG WORDS & IDIOMS

- ball in one's court (to have the)
- come out of left field (to)
- dirty pool
- off base (to be)
- play hardball (to)
- right off the bat
- settle the score (to)
- score (to)
- tackle (to)
- throw in the towel (to)
- throw someone a curve (to)
- touch base with someone (to)

5 MARGE IS THE BIGGEST KLUTZ!

(Foreign Words Used in Everyday Conversation)

PAGE 83

THIS LESSON FEATURES 12 FOREIGN WORDS COMMONLY USED IN ENGLISH

- angst
- blasé
- boutique
- camaraderie
- forte
- gung-ho
- kindergarten
- klutz
- kowtow [someone] (to)
- macho
- prima donna
- verbatim

ACTIVITIES		FROM THE SLANGMAN FILES
LET'S WARM UP! READING - *p. 1* **LET'S TALK!** SPEAKING/LISTENING A. Dialogue (Slang & Idioms) - *p. 3* B. Dialogue (Translated) - *p. 4* C. Dialogue (in "Real Speak") - *p. 5* **LET'S LEARN!** SPEAKING/LISTENING Vocabulary - *p. 5*	**LET'S PRACTICE!** READING A. Complete the Phrase - *p. 8* READING B. Context Exercise - *p. 9* SPEAKING C. Create Your Own Sentence - *p. 10* WRITING D. Create Your Own Newspaper Column - *p. 11*	More Dating Slang *Phase 1: The Hunt for a Relationship* *p. 12*
LET'S WARM UP! READING - *p. 23* **LET'S TALK!** SPEAKING/LISTENING A. Dialogue (Slang & Idioms) - *p. 25* B. Dialogue (Translated) - *p. 26* C. Dialogue (in "Real Speak") - *p. 27* **LET'S LEARN!** SPEAKING/LISTENING Vocabulary - *p. 27*	**LET'S PRACTICE!** WRITING A. True or False - *p. 31* SPEAKING B. Choose the Right Word - *p. 32* READING C. Match the Sentences - *p. 33*	More Dating Slang *Phase 2: The Thrill of the Relationship* *p. 35*
LET'S WARM UP! READING - *p. 41* **LET'S TALK!** SPEAKING/LISTENING A. Dialogue (Slang & Idioms) - *p. 43* B. Dialogue (Translated) - *p. 44* C. Dialogue (in "Real Speak") - *p. 45* **LET'S LEARN!** SPEAKING/LISTENING Vocabulary - *p. 45*	**LET'S PRACTICE!** READING A. What Does it Mean? - *p. 49* WRITING B. Complete the Fairy Tale - *p. 50* READING C. Context Exercise - *p. 51* WRITING D. Complete the Phrase - *p. 52*	More Dating Slang *Phase 3: The End of the Relationship* *p. 53*
LET'S WARM UP! READING - *p. 59* **LET'S TALK!** SPEAKING/LISTENING A. Dialogue (Slang & Idioms) - *p. 61* B. Dialogue (Translated) - *p. 62* C. Dialogue (in "Real Speak") - *p. 63* **LET'S LEARN!** SPEAKING/LISTENING Vocabulary - *p. 63*	**LET'S PRACTICE!** WRITING A. Choose the Right Word - *p. 68* WRITING B. Crossword Puzzle - *p. 69* READING C. Match the Column - *p. 71*	More Sports Terms Used in Slang *p. 72*
LET'S WARM UP! READING - *p. 83* **LET'S TALK!** SPEAKING/LISTENING A. Dialogue (Slang & Idioms) - *p. 85* B. Dialogue (Translated) - *p. 86* C. Dialogue (in "Real Speak") - *p. 87* **LET'S LEARN!** SPEAKING/LISTENING Vocabulary - *p. 87*	**LET'S PRACTICE!** WRITING A. I Know the Answer, But What's the Question? - *p. 91* READING B. Find Your Perfect Match - *p. 92* SPEAKING/WRITING C. You're the Author - *p. 93*	More Foreign Words Used in Everday Conversation *p. 94*

TABLE OF CONTENTS (CONTINUED)

LESSON TITLE	WORDS PRESENTED
6 KAREN WENT ON AND ON ABOUT HER KNICK-KNACKS! (*Alliterations and Repeating Words*) PAGE 113	THIS LESSON FEATURES 14 NEW SLANG WORDS & IDIOMS: chit-chat (to), criss-cross, face to face, flip-flop, froufrou, grin from ear to ear (to), junk food junkie, knick-knack, mishmash, on and on (to go), on the up and up, out and out, over and over, spic-and-span
7 JENNY BECOMES A FIREFIGHTER! (*How to be Politically Correct or "PC"*) PAGE 135	THIS LESSON FEATURES 14 NEW SLANG WORDS & IDIOMS: actor, anchor, comedian, firefighter, flight attendant, frosh, humankind, husband and wife, mail carrier, personnel, police officer, run something (to), self-made person, spokesperson
8 A BIG BREAK IN SHOW BIZ! (*Television & Entertainment Slang*) PAGE 157	THIS LESSON FEATURES 15 NEW SLANG WORDS & IDIOMS: big break, dog, ham, mug (to), one-liner, pilot, rerun, series, show biz, show-stopper, sitcom, slapstick, spin-off, spoof, walk-on
9 AL AND PEGGY ARE LIKE DATING! (*Teen/College Slang*) PAGE 185	THIS LESSON FEATURES 15 NEW SLANG WORDS & IDIOMS: all (to be), bail (to), diss someone (to), girlfriend, "Hello!", hottie, kick it (to), "Late!", like, so, tore up (to be), trip (to), "What up?", whatever, 24-7
10 FREEZE! THIS IS A STICK-UP! (*Emergency Slang & Expressions*) PAGE 205	THIS LESSON FEATURES 15 NEW SLANG WORDS & IDIOMS: "Can it!", "Chill out!", cuff someone (to), "Drop!", false move, "Freeze!", "Get your hands in the air!", "Give it a rest!", "Hand it over!", "I'll let you have it!", "Move it!", "No funny business!", "Spread 'em!", stick-up, "Watch out!"

ACTIVITIES		FROM THE SLANGMAN FILES
LET'S WARM UP! READING - *p. 113* **LET'S TALK!** SPEAKING/LISTENING A. Dialogue (Slang & Idioms) - *p. 115* B. Dialogue (Translated) - *p. 116* C. Dialogue (in "Real Speak") - *p. 117* **LET'S LEARN!** SPEAKING/LISTENING Vocabulary - *p. 117*	**LET'S PRACTICE!** WRITING A. The Unfinished Conversation - *p. 122* READING B. Choose the Right Word - *p. 123* WRITING C. Complete the Story - *p. 123* SPEAKING D. Create Your Own Sentence - *p. 125*	More Alliterations and Repeating Words *p. 126*
LET'S WARM UP! READING - *p. 135* **LET'S TALK!** SPEAKING/LISTENING A. Dialogue (Slang & Idioms) - *p. 137* B. Dialogue (Translated) - *p. 138* C. Dialogue (in "Real Speak") - *p. 139* **LET'S LEARN!** SPEAKING/LISTENING Vocabulary - *p. 139*	**LET'S PRACTICE!** WRITING A. "Across" Word Puzzle - *p. 144* WRITING B. Crossword Puzzle - *p. 145* READING C. You're the Author - *p. 147*	How to be Politically Correct or "P.C." *p. 148*
LET'S WARM UP! READING - *p. 157* **LET'S TALK!** SPEAKING/LISTENING A. Dialogue (Slang & Idioms) - *p. 159* B. Dialogue (Translated) - *p. 160* C. Dialogue (in "Real Speak") - *p. 161* **LET'S LEARN!** SPEAKING/LISTENING Vocabulary - *p. 161*	**LET'S PRACTICE!** WRITING A. Create Your Own Story *(Part 1)* - *p. 166* SPEAKING B. Create Your Own Story *(Part 2)* - *p. 167* READING C. What Would You Do If? - *p. 168* SPEAKING D. Create Your Own Sentences - *p. 169* READING E. True or False - *p. 169*	More Television and Entertainment Slang *p. 170*
LET'S WARM UP! READING - *p. 185* **LET'S TALK!** SPEAKING/LISTENING A. Dialogue (Slang & Idioms) - *p. 187* B. Dialogue (Translated) - *p. 188* C. Dialogue (in "Real Speak") - *p. 189* **LET'S LEARN!** SPEAKING/LISTENING Vocabulary - *p. 190*	**LET'S PRACTICE!** READING A. Truth or Lie - *p. 194* WRITING B. Find the Definition - *p. 195* WRITING C. Find-the-Word Grid - *p. 196*	More Teen/College Slang p. 197
LET'S WARM UP! READING - *p. 205* **LET'S TALK!** SPEAKING/LISTENING A. Dialogue (Slang & Idioms) - *p. 207* B. Dialogue (Translated) - *p. 208* C. Dialogue (in "Real Speak") - *p. 209* **LET'S LEARN!** SPEAKING/LISTENING Vocabulary - *p. 209*	**LET'S PRACTICE!** READING A. Correct or Incorrect? - *p. 213* WRITING/SPEAKING B. Create Your Own Story - *p. 214* READING C. True or False - *p. 215*	More Emergency Slang and Expressions *p. 216*

ROGER STRIKES OUT WITH A PICK-UP LINE!

Dating Slang
(Phase 1: The Hunt for a Relationship)

LET'S WARM UP!

MATCH THE PICTURES

As a fun way to get started, see if you can guess the meaning of the new slang words and expressions on the opposite page by using the pictures below and following the context of the sentences.

1. That girl over there kept smiling at me, so I walked over to say hello but she ignored me! Maybe she's just ***playing hard to get***.
   "*playing hard to get*" means: . ❑ pretending to be interested . . . ❑ pretending to be disinterested

2. That guy over there is ***checking you out***. I think he likes you!
   "*checking you out*" means: . . ❑ asking you on a date . . . . ❑ examining you

3. If you're going to tell Earl you don't want to see him anymore, try to ***let him down easy***.
   "*let him down easy*" means:. . ❑ reject him in a gentle way . . . . ❑ date him

4. I introduced myself to the new girl in our class and she ***blew me off***!
   "*blew me off*" means: . . . . . ❑ talked to me nonstop . . . . ❑ ignored me

5. Carol's husband was ***coming on to me***! She'd be so upset if she found out!
   "*coming on to me*" means: . . ❑ ignoring me . . . . ❑ flirting with me

6. My brother ***fixed me up*** with his best friend last night. It was the best date I ever had!
   "*fixed me up*" means: . . . . . ❑ arranged a date for me . . . . . . ❑ talked poorly about me

7. I can't believe you used such an old ***pick-up line*** on that girl. No wonder she rejected you!
   "*pick-up line*" means: . . . . . . ❑ phrase meant to reject . . . . . . ❑ phrase meant to entice

8. Every time I ask a girl on a date, I ***strike out***. Maybe I'm too aggressive.
   "*strike out*" means:. . . . . . . ❑ fail . . . . ❑ succeed

9. Bill and I ***hit it off*** the moment we met. We've been together ever since.
   "*hit it off*" means: . . . . ❑ liked each other immediately . . ❑ didn't like each other

10. Kim just ended a relationship and is ***on the rebound***. She wants a boyfriend desperately!
    "*on the rebound*" means: . . . ❑ goes to the gym . . . . ❑ eager to get back into a relationship

LET'S TALK!

A. DIALOGUE USING SLANG & IDIOMS

The words introduced on the first two pages are used in the dialogue below. See if you can understand the conversation. *Note:* The translation of the words in boldface is on the right-hand page.

CD-A: TRACK 2

Tony: Hey! That girl over there is **checking you out**! Why don't you go say hello?

Roger: The last time I said hello to a girl in a place like this, she thought I was **coming on to her** and **blew me off** before I even had a chance to introduce myself.

Tony: That doesn't surprise me. Usually you **strike out** after using one of your stupid **pick-up lines**!

Roger: I didn't get that far this time. Maybe she was just **playing hard to get**.

Tony: Oh, no! There's Bonnie Margolin. A year ago, some mutual friends of ours **fixed us up** because they thought we would **hit it off**. Unfortunately, she was **on the rebound**, so I didn't want to get involved. I tried to **let her down easy** but she got furious and started screaming at me. Oh, no! She's coming this way. Run!

B. DIALOGUE TRANSLATED INTO STANDARD ENGLISH

LET'S SEE HOW MUCH YOU REMEMBER!
Just for fun, move around in random order to the words and expressions in boldface below. See if you can remember their slang equivalents without looking at the left-hand page!

Tony: Hey! That girl over there is **examining you**! Why don't you go say hello?

Roger: The last time I said hello to a girl in a place like this, she thought I was **firting with her** and **rejected me** before I even had a chance to introduce myself.

Tony: That doesn't surprise me. Usually you **fail** after using one of your stupid **flirtatious opening statements**!

Roger: I didn't get that far this time. Maybe she was just **pretending not to be interested**.

Tony: Oh, no! There's Bonnie Margolin. A year ago, some mutual friends of ours **introduced us** because they thought we would **enjoy each other's company**. Unfortunately, she was **eager to get back into a relationship after recently ending one**, so I didn't want to get involved. I tried to **reject her gently** but she got furious and started screaming at me. Oh, no! She's coming this way. Run!

C. DIALOGUE USING "REAL SPEAK"

The dialogue below demonstrates how the slang conversation on the previous page would *really* be spoken by native speakers!

CD-A: TRACK 2

Tony: Hey! That girl over there's **checkin' ya out**! Why don'cha go say hello?

Roger: The las' time I said hello do a girl 'n a place like this, she thod I w'z **coming on to 'er** 'n **blew me off** b'fore I even had a chance ta intraduce myself.

Tony: That doesn' saprise me. Ujally ya **strike oud** after using one 'a yer stupid **pick-up lines**!

Roger: I didn' get that far this time. Maybe she w'z jus' **playing hard da get**.

Tony: Oh, no! There's Bonnie Margolin. A year ago, s'm mutual friends 'ev arz **fixed us up** b'cuz they thought we'd **hid id off**. Unfortunately, she w'z **on the reboun'**, so I didn' wanna ged involved. I tried da **led 'er down easy** b't she got furious 'n starded screaming 'it me. Oh, no! She's coming this way. Run!

LET'S LEARN!

VOCABULARY

The following words and expressions were used in the previous dialogues. Let's take a closer look at what they mean.

CD-A: TRACK 3

blow someone off (to) *v.* • **1.** to ignore • **2.** to reject • **3.** to keep someone waiting.

EXAMPLE 1: I walked up to that girl to say hello, but she **blew me off**!

TRANSLATION: I walked up to that girl to say hello, but she **ignored me**!

"REAL SPEAK": I walked up ta that girl da say hello, b't she **blew me off**!

EXAMPLE 2: I thought he loved me, but he **blew me off** for Barbara.

TRANSLATION: I thought he loved me, but he **rejected me** for Barbara.

"REAL SPEAK": I thod 'e loved me, b'd 'e **blew me off** fer Barb'ra.

EXAMPLE 3: I waited two hours at the café, but she just blew me off.

TRANSLATION: I waited two hours at the café, but she just **kept me** waiting.

"REAL SPEAK": I waided two hours 'it the café, b't she jus' **blew me off**.

Also: **blow something off (to)** *exp.* to make the decision not to do something • *I'm going to **blow off** my homework and go to the movies tonight instead;* I've decided ***not to do*** my homework and go to the movies tonight instead.

See: **blow off something (to) / to blow something off (to)**, *p. 197 (Lesson 9, Teen Slang).*

NOW YOU DO IT. COMPLETE THE PHRASE ALOUD:

I think [person's name] blew me off because...

check out someone or something (to) *exp.* to observe someone or something.

EXAMPLE: **Check out** that girl over there! She's beautiful! I've never seen her before.

TRANSLATION: **Observe** that girl over there! She's beautiful! I've never seen her before.

"REAL SPEAK": **Check out** that girl over there! She's beaudiful! I've never seen 'er b'fore.

Variation: **check someone or something out (to)** *exp.*

NOW YOU DO IT. COMPLETE THE PHRASE ALOUD:

Check out that...

come on to someone (to) *exp.* to flirt, to show sexual interest in someone.

EXAMPLE: Kim is so pretty that guys **come on to** her all the time. They don't really care whether or not she has a personality!

TRANSLATION: Kim is so pretty that guys **show sexual interest in** her all the time. They don't really care whether or not she has a personality!

"REAL SPEAK": Kim's so preddy th't guys **come on da** her all the time. They don't really care whether 'r not she has a personalidy!

NOW YOU DO IT. COMPLETE THE PHRASE ALOUD:

[Person's name] came on to me at the...

fix someone up (to) *exp.* to arrange a date for someone.

EXAMPLE: I haven't had a date for over a year. Do you think you can **fix me up** with Sheila?

TRANSLATION: I haven't had a date for over a year. Do you think you can **arrange a date for me** with Sheila?

"REAL SPEAK": I haven't had a date fer over a year. Ya think ya c'n **fix me up** with Sheila?

Variation: **set someone up (to)** *exp.*

NOW YOU DO IT. COMPLETE THE PHRASE ALOUD:

Last night, I was fixed up on a date with [person's name] and it was...

hit it ♥ off (to) *exp.* to like each other immediately.

EXAMPLE: Thank you so much for introducing me to Gary. We really **hit it off**!

TRANSLATION: Thank you so much for introducing me to Gary. We really **liked each other immediately**!

"REAL SPEAK": Thanks so much fer intraducing me da Gary. We really **hid id off**.

NOW YOU DO IT. COMPLETE THE PHRASE ALOUD:

[Person's name] and I didn't hit it off at first because...

let someone down easy (to) *exp.* to end a romantic relationship with someone in a gentle way.

EXAMPLE: When Donna broke up with me, she was very nice about it. She **let me down easy**.

TRANSLATION: When Donna broke up with me, she was very nice about it. She **ended our relationship in a gentle way.**

"REAL SPEAK": When Donna broke up w'th me, she w'z very nice aboud it. She **let me down easy**.

NOW YOU DO IT. COMPLETE THE PHRASE ALOUD:
I tried to let [person's name] down easy, but...

on the rebound (to be) *exp.* to be eager to get right back into a relationship after having recently ended one.

EXAMPLE: If you're going to go out with Tina, be careful. She's **on the rebound** and may want to get seriously involved too early.

TRANSLATION: If you're going to go out with Tina, be careful. She's **eager to get back into a relationship after having recently ended one** and may want to get seriously involved too early.

"REAL SPEAK": If y'r gonna go out with Tina, be careful. She's **on the rebound** 'n may wanna get seriously involve' too early.

NOW YOU DO IT. COMPLETE THE PHRASE ALOUD:
I think Bill is on the rebound because...

pick-up line *exp.* an overused, suggestive comment made typically to a stranger in the hope of having a sexual encounter such as, *"Where have you been all my life?"* or *"Haven't we met before?"*

EXAMPLE: The minute I heard his **pick-up line**, I knew immediately that he wasn't interested in my personality!

TRANSLATION: The minute I heard his **suggestive comment**, I knew immediately that he wasn't interested in my personality!

"REAL SPEAK": The minute I heard 'is **pick-up line**, I knew immediately thad 'e wasn' int'rested 'n my personalidy!

NOW YOU DO IT. COMPLETE THE PHRASE ALOUD:
That guy just walked up to me and said, "[use a pick-up line here]!" What a stupid pick-up line!

play hard to get (to) *exp.* to pretend to be disinterested in someone's romantic/sexual advances yet flattered by them.

EXAMPLE: I can't tell if she is **playing hard to get** or if she just doesn't like me.

TRANSLATION: I can't tell if she is **pretending to be disinterested in me** or if she just doesn't like me.

"REAL SPEAK": I can' tell if she's **playing hard da get** 'r if she jus' doesn' like me.

NOW YOU DO IT. COMPLETE THE PHRASE ALOUD:
[Person's name] plays hard to get because...

strike out (to) *v.* (from baseball – see Lesson 4, *Sports Terms Used in Slang, p. 59*) to fail.

EXAMPLE: – Did Nancy agree to go out with you?
– No. I totally **struck out**!

TRANSLATION: – Did Nancy agree to go out with you?
– No. I totally **failed**!

"REAL SPEAK": – Did Nancy agree da go out with you?
– No. I todally **struck out**!

NOW YOU DO IT. COMPLETE THE PHRASE ALOUD:
I struck out when I tried to...

LET'S PRACTICE!

A. COMPLETE THE PHRASE

CD-A: TRACK 4

Complete the phrase by choosing the appropriate words from the list below.

BLEW	EASY	HIT
CAME	FIX	REBOUND
CHECKING	HARD TO GET	STRIKE

1. Hey, that guy over there is ________________ you out. Why don't you go over and say hello?
2. How did it go when you introduced yourself to the new girl in class? You don't look very happy. Did you ____________ out?
3. Greg is a great guy, but I don't think we're a good match. I'm going to tell him that I just want to be friends. I'll try and let him down ____________ .
4. I thought I'd be nice and welcome the new neighbor to our street but when I introduced myself, he totally ____________ me off! He was so unfriendly!
5. Sally seems like she's interested in me but as soon as I approach her, she ignores me! I guess she's just playing ________________ .
6. Thank you for introducing me to your sister. She's great! We ________ it off right away. In fact, we're going to the movies together this weekend.
7. Mindy and John broke up this morning and tonight she's going on a date with Tim! I hope he understands that she's on the ________________ and may not have the best judgment.
8. I think you and my best friend would really like each other. Would you like me to __________ you up with him?
9. Tim's father ____________ on to me in the parking lot and he's married! In fact, they've been married for fifty years!

B. CONTEXT EXERCISE

Read the short conversations. Decide whether the slang used makes sense or doesn't make sense. Circle your answer.

CD-A: TRACK 5

– Bill is a great guy!
– That's why I blew him off.

MAKES SENSE DOESN'T MAKE SENSE

– Are you and Al getting married?
– Yes! I let him down easy.

MAKES SENSE DOESN'T MAKE SENSE

– Sue ignored me when I said hi.
– She's just playing hard to get.

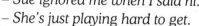

MAKES SENSE DOESN'T MAKE SENSE

– How was your date last night?
– Great! We really hit it off!

MAKES SENSE DOESN'T MAKE SENSE

– Did you ask Ann out on a date?
– Yes, but I struck out. She said no.

MAKES SENSE DOESN'T MAKE SENSE

Every time a guy approaches me, he uses the dumbest pick-up lines!

MAKES SENSE DOESN'T MAKE SENSE

– Check out the new student!
– Wow! She's beautiful!

MAKES SENSE DOESN'T MAKE SENSE

– Earl came on to me at the party!
– Why was he yelling at you?

MAKES SENSE DOESN'T MAKE SENSE

– Mel fixed me up with his brother.
– Did you have a good time?

MAKES SENSE DOESN'T MAKE SENSE

C. CREATE YOUR OWN SENTENCE

Read Person A's questions or statements aloud, then use the suggested words to create your response for Person B.

CD-A: TRACK 6

	PERSON A	PERSON B
1.	Why does that guy keep looking at me?	use: **checking you out**
2.	What happened when you said hi to Steve?	use: **blew me off**
3.	I want to introduce myself to that girl over there but I don't know what to say!	use: **pick-up line**
4.	I'd like to meet someone special.	use: **fix you up**
5.	Karen just ended her relationship with Eric. Do you think I should ask her on a date?	use: **on the rebound**
6.	I wonder why that girl keeps staring at me.	use: **coming on to you**
7.	How did it go when you asked Cecily out?	use: **struck out**
8.	Michelle acts as if she likes me but when I talk with her, she suddenly seems disinterested!	use: **playing hard to get**
9.	I heard you met Tom's sister last night. How did it go?	use: **hit it off**
10.	I've decided to end the relationship with Darlene tonight. It's just not working.	use: **let her down easy**

D. CREATE YOUR OWN NEWSPAPER COLUMN

Without looking at the newspaper column at the bottom of the page, fill in the blank lines of 1-10 directly below. Next, transfer your answers to the empty boxes in the newspaper column. Make sure to match the number of your answer with the numbered box. Next, read your column aloud. Remember: The funnier your answers, the funnier your column will be!

1. Write down a type of "insect" *(worm, cockroach, beetle, etc.)*: ____________________
2. Write down a "thing" *(pencil, potato, toothbrush, etc.)*: ____________________
3. Write down a "place" *(market, movie theater, hospital, etc.)*: ____________________
4. Write down an "adjective" *(strange, tall, fat, etc.)*: ____________________
5. Write down a "thing" in plural form *(pencils, potatoes, toothbrushes, etc.)*: ____________________
6. Write down a "body part" *(ear, liver, foot, etc.)*: ____________________
7. Write down an "adjective" *(strange, tall, fat, etc.)*: ____________________
8. Write down a "thing" *(pencil, potato, toothbrush, etc.)*: ____________________
9. Write down an "occupation" *(mechanic, doctor, janitor, etc.)*: ____________________
10. Write down an "adverb" *(strangely, quickly, sickeningly, etc.)*: ____________________

THE WEEKLY

BICHON-MOAN GAZETTE

THE WEEKLY NEWSPAPER THAT LETS YOU LET IT ALL OUT

"Dear Blabby..."

by Blabby Bichon-Moan
Advice Columnist

Dear Blabby...

There is a [1.] in my [2.] class who **checks me out** all the time. I'd like to invite her to the [3.] but I'm afraid she'll think it's a **pick-up line** and that I'm **coming on to her** and she'll **blow me off**. That would make me very [4.]. I know a lot of [5.] **play hard to get**, but I always seem to **strike out** with them. Some day I'd like to meet one and if we **hit it off**, I'd like to ask for her [6.] in marriage. The big question now is, where can I go to get **fixed up** with a [7.] [8.]? I just don't want to date a [9.] who's on the rebound that I may have to **let down easy** later. I need your help [10.]!

Signed,
Desperate for love

MORE DATING SLANG

(Phase 1: The Hunt for a Relationship)

Since the beginning of time, there have been three phases of a relationship — **Phase 1**: The Hunt for a Relationship; **Phase 2**: The Thrill of the Relationship!; and **Phase 3**: The End of the Relationship.

Since dating and relationships are such a big part of our daily lives, it's no wonder there are so many slang terms and idioms dedicated to love! The following terms and expressions are extremely popular and used by just about anyone entering that first unpredictable phase of a relationship— The Hunt.

Welcome to Slangman's world of romance!

airhead *n.* a stupid and forgetful person.

EXAMPLE: Why would Gina ever date a guy like Bill. He's such an **airhead**! He locked his keys in his car for the fourth time this week!

TRANSLATION: Why would Gina ever date a guy like Bill. He's such a **stupid and forgetful person**! He locked his keys in his car for the fourth time this week!

"REAL SPEAK": Why would Gina ever dade a guy like Bill. He's such 'n **airhead**! He locked 'is keys 'n 'is car fer the fourth time this week!

Synonym 1: **all four oars in the water (not to have)** *exp.* to be stupid.

Synonym 2: **all one's marbles (not to have)** *exp.* to be stupid.

Synonym 3: **bonehead** *n.* idiot.

Synonym 4: **cooking on all four burners (not to be)** *exp.* to be stupid.

Synonym 5: **ditz** *n.* (usually applied only to a woman).

Variation: **ditzy (to be)** *adj.* to be forgetful.

ask someone out (to) *exp.* to invite someone on a date.

EXAMPLE: I want **to ask Sybil out** but I'm afraid she'll say no.

TRANSLATION: I want **to invite Sybil on a date** but I'm afraid she'll say no.

"REAL SPEAK": I wanna **ask Sybil out** b'd I'm afraid she'll say no.

be easy (to) *exp.* to be readily available for sex.

EXAMPLE: I was surprised when Jill wouldn't sleep with me because everyone said she **was easy**.

TRANSLATION: I was surprised when Jill wouldn't sleep with me because everyone said she **was readily available for sex**.

"REAL SPEAK": I w'z saprised when Jill wouldn' sleep with me b'cuz ev'ryone said she **w'z easy**.

blind date *exp.* a date with someone you have not seen before (usually arranged by a friend).

EXAMPLE: I hate **blind dates**. The last one was with a woman three times my age!

TRANSLATION: I hate **arranged dates with people I don't know**. The last one was with a woman three times my age!

"REAL SPEAK": I hate **blin' dates**. The las' one w'z w'th a woman three times my age!

brush off (to give someone the) *exp.* to show complete disinterest in someone.

EXAMPLE: When Ted finally got the courage to introduce himself to Carol, she **gave him the brush off**!

TRANSLATION: When Ted finally got the courage to introduce himself to Carol, she **showed complete disinterest in him**!

"REAL SPEAK": When Ted fin'lly got the courage ta intraduce 'imself ta Carol, she **gave 'im the brush off**!

Variation: **brush someone off (to)** *exp.*

Synonym 1: **"Burr!"** *interj.* the sound of shivering due to extreme cold — in this case, indicating that the other person is being emotionally cold.

Synonym 2: **diss someone (to)** *v.* short for "to have disrespect for someone"– probably the newest slang word for the verb "to snub," used primarily by the younger generations.

Synonym 3: **freeze someone out (to)** *exp.*

Synonym 4: **give someone the cold shoulder (to)** *exp.*

Synonym 5: **give someone the time of day (not to)** *exp.*

Synonym 6: **look right through someone (to)** *exp.*

buzz (to give someone a) *exp.* to telephone someone.

EXAMPLE: It was really nice meeting you. Can I **give you a buzz** some time?

TRANSLATION: It was really nice meeting you. Can I **telephone you** some time?

"REAL SPEAK": It w'z really nice meeding you. C'n I **give ya a buzz** some time?

Note: Did you notice the grammatical mistake made in the example sentence? *It was made on purpose!* You'll notice that the verb "Can" was used in the question, *Can I give you a buzz some time?* To the frustration of English teachers everywhere, this is an extremely common mistake made even by native-born Americans. In proper English, "May I" should be used since it means, *Do I have permission to...* "Can I" means, *Am I able to...* However, although it is incorrect, "Can I" is most commonly used in everyday, casual conversation.

Synonym 1: **holler (to give someone a)** *exp.*

Synonym 2: **jingle (to give someone a)** *exp.*

Synonym 3: **phone someone (to)** *v.* short for "to telephone someone."

Synonym 4: **ring (to give someone a)** *exp.*

Synonym 5: **shout (to give someone a)** *exp.*

Synonym 6: **touch base with someone (to)** *exp.* (from baseball).

butt-ugly (to be) *exp.* to be extremely ugly.

EXAMPLE: Dan's girlfriend is **butt-ugly** and he is so handsome. What a pair!

TRANSLATION: Dan's girlfriend is **extremely ugly** and he is so handsome. What a pair!

"REAL SPEAK": Dan's girlfriend's **budd-ugly** 'n he's so han'some. Whad a pair!

Synonym 1: **beaten with an ugly stick (to be)** *exp.*

Synonym 2: **death warmed over (to look like)** *exp.* also applied to someone who looks very sick.

Synonym 3: **dog (to be a)** *n.*
Note: This can also be replaced by "Bow wow!" which is the barking sound of a dog. Oddly enough, if you say "Woof!" (also a sound made by a dog), it indicates beauty and sex appeal!

Synonym 4: **face that only a mother could love (to have a)** *exp.*

Synonym 5: **face that could stop a clock (to have a)** *exp.*

Synonym 6: **fall off the ugly tree and hit every branch on the way down (to)** *exp.*

Synonym 7: **gross (to be)** *adj.*

Synonym 8: **nice personality (to have a)** *exp.* said when there is nothing nice to say about the person's looks.

Synonym 9: **short on looks (to be)** *exp.*

Synonym 10: **ugly as sin (to be as)** *exp.*

chick *n.* girl.

EXAMPLE: That **chick** over there is our new math professor. She's so pretty!

TRANSLATION: That **girl** over there is our new math professor. She's so pretty!

"REAL SPEAK": That **chick** over there's 'ar new math prafesser. She's so preddy!

creep *n.* a very undesirable person.

EXAMPLE: You're going out with Rob? He's such a **creep**!

TRANSLATION: You're going out with Rob? He's such an **undesirable person**!

"REAL SPEAK": Y'r going out w'th Rob? He's such a **creep**!

cruise (to) *v.* to flirt.

EXAMPLE: For the last hour, that guy has been **cruising you**. Why don't you just go say hello?

TRANSLATION: For the last hour, that guy has been **flirting with you**. Why don't you just go say hello?

"REAL SPEAK": Fer the last hour, that guy's been **cruising you**. Why don'cha jus' go say hello?

Also: **cruisy** *adj.* said of a flirtatious person or an establishment where a lot of flirting takes place.

dirty old man *n.* an older man who is obsessed with sex.

EXAMPLE: Did you see the way Anne's father hugged me? I think he's a **dirty old man**.

TRANSLATION: Did you see the way Anne's father hugged me? I think he's an **older man who is obsessed with sex**.

"REAL SPEAK": Did'ja see the way Anne's father hugged me? I think 'e a **dirdy ol' man**.

dreamy *adj.* attractive and sexy.

EXAMPLE: My heart pounds every time I see Mark. He's so **dreamy**.

TRANSLATION: My heart pounds every time I see Mark. He's so **attractive and sexy**.

"REAL SPEAK": My heart poun's ev'ry time I see Mark. He's so **dreamy**.

eye on someone (to have one's) *exp.* to be interested in someone.

EXAMPLE: I've **had my eye on** Diane ever since I met her at Rick's party. She's so beautiful!

TRANSLATION: I've **been interested in** Diane ever since I met her at Rick's party. She's so beautiful!

"REAL SPEAK": I've **had my eye on** Diane ever since I med 'er 'it Rick's pardy. She's so beautiful!

fling *n.* brief sexual encounter.

EXAMPLE: Gary thinks his wife is faithful, but she has had three **flings** that I know of.

TRANSLATION: Gary thinks his wife is faithful, but she has had three **brief sexual encounters** that I know of.

"REAL SPEAK": Gary thinks 'is wife 'ez faithful, b't she's had three **flings** th'd I know of.

get turned down (to) *exp.* to be rejected.

EXAMPLE: I asked Sue to go to the prom with me, but I **got turned down**.

TRANSLATION: I asked Sue to go to the prom with me, but she **rejected me**.

"REAL SPEAK": I ast Sue da go da the prom w'th me, b'd I **got turn' down**.

Variation: **turn someone down (to)** *exp.* to reject someone.

go Dutch (to) *exp.* to pay only for oneself on a date.

EXAMPLE: I'm an independent woman. I will only go out with someone if we **go Dutch**.

TRANSLATION: I'm an independent woman. I will only go out with someone if we **pay individually**.

"REAL SPEAK": I'm 'n independent woman. A'll only go out w'th someone if we **go Dutch**.

go out (to) *v.* to leave one's house in order to go do something entertaining.

EXAMPLE: I'm **going out** with Ron tonight. We're going to a movie.

TRANSLATION: I'm **leaving my house to go do something entertaining** with Ron tonight. We're going to a movie.

"REAL SPEAK": I'm **going out** w'th Ron tanight. W'r going to a movie.

gold digger *n.* a person who looks for someone with a lot of money to date or to marry • (lit.): one who digs for gold.

EXAMPLE: Pam isn't interested in your personality. She's only interested in your money. She's a **gold digger**!

TRANSLATION: Pam isn't interested in your personality. She's only interested in your money. She's a **person who looks for someone with a lot of money for a relationship**!

"REAL SPEAK": Pam isn' int'rested 'n yer personalidy. She's only int'rested 'n yer money. She's a **gol' digger**!

guy *n.* a very common slang term for "man."

EXAMPLE: Did you see the **guy** Mindy is going out with? He's really handsome!

TRANSLATION: Did you see the **man** Mindy is going out with? He's really handsome!

"REAL SPEAK": Did'ja see the **guy** Mindy's going out with? He's really han'some!

Note: In the plural form, *guys* is used in American slang to mean "friends" and is commonly used when greeting a group of men or women! For example: *Hi, **guys**! What's up?*; Hi, ***friends***! How are you?

Synonym 1: **dude** *n.* • see *p. 199*.

Synonym 2: **fellow** *n.* used primarily by the older generations and often pronounced "*fella.*"

heavy date *exp.* an important date.

EXAMPLE: I just had a really **heavy date** with John. He asked me to marry him!

TRANSLATION: I just had a really **important date** with John. He asked me to marry him!

"REAL SPEAK": I jus' had a really **heavy date** with John. He ast me da marry 'im!

hit on someone (to) *exp.* to make sexual advances toward someone.

EXAMPLE: Every time I go to Debbie's house, her boyfriend **hits on me**!

TRANSLATION: Every time I go to Debbie's house, her boyfriend **makes sexual advances toward me**!

"REAL SPEAK": Ev'ry time I go da Debbie's house, 'er boyfrien' **hits on me**!

Synonym 1: **come on to someone (to)** *exp.* • see *p.* 6.

Synonym 2: **give someone the eye (to)** *exp.*

Synonym 3: **make a pass at someone (to)** *exp.*

Synonym 4: **make a play for someone (to)** exp.

Synonym 5: **make eyes at someone (to)** *exp.* to flirt with someone by giving meaningful glances.

Synonym 6: **make goo-goo eyes at someone (to)** *exp.*

Synonym 7: **move in on someone (to)** *exp.* to approach someone with the intention of flirting.

hook up (to) *exp.* to get together (with someone).

EXAMPLE: I really enjoyed meeting you. Would you like to **hook up** this weekend?

TRANSLATION: I really enjoyed meeting you. Would you like to **get together** this weekend?

"REAL SPEAK": I really enjoyed meeding you. Would'ja like ta **hook up** this weekend?

Note: In teen slang, this expression also means "to have sex."

hottie *n.* (from the adjective *hot* meaning "sexy") a sexy man or woman.

EXAMPLE: Wow! I'd love to go out with Lee. She's such a **hottie**!

TRANSLATION: Wow! I'd love to go out with Lee. She's such a **sexy woman**!

"REAL SPEAK": Wow! I'd love da go out with Lee. She's such a **hoddie**!

Synonym 1: **babe (to be a)** *n.* used to refer to a sexy man or woman.

Synonym 2: **beaut (to be a)** *adj.* • **1.** used to refer to a beautiful woman • **2.** used to refer to something or someone in an impressive yet negative way • *That black eye is a real beaut!* • *Gerry lied to get his job. He's a real beaut!*

Synonym 3: **bombshell** *n.* only applied to a beautiful woman.

Synonym 4: **built (to be)** *adj.* to have a great body.

Synonym 5: **cutie** *n.*

Synonym 6: **drop-dead gorgeous (to be)** *adj.*

Synonym 7: **easy on the eyes (to be)** *exp.*

Synonym 8: **fox** *n.* someone good-looking and sexy.

Synonym 9: **foxy (to be)** *adj.* to be good-looking and sexy.

Synonym 10: **hard to look at (not to be)** *exp.*

Synonym 11: **hot (to be)** *adj.* to be very sexy.

Synonym 12: **hunk** *n.* a muscular and sexy man.

Synonym 13: **jock** *n.* an athletic-looking man but can be applied to a woman when used in jest.

Synonym 14: **killer looks (to have)** *exp.* to be exceptionally attractive.

Synonym 15: **knockout** *adj.* an extremely good-looking woman.

Synonym 16: **long on looks (to be)** *exp.*
Also: **long on looks, short on brains (to be)** *exp.* to be extremely good-looking but not very intelligent.

Synonym 17: **looker** *n.* an extremely good-looking man or woman.

Synonym 18: **out of my league (to be)** *exp.* said of someone who is too pretty to approach.

Synonym 19: **pretty as a picture (to be as)** *exp.*

Synonym 20: **raving beauty (to be a)** *n.* an extremely gorgeous woman or girl.

Synonym 21: **stud** *n.* a sexy-looking man.

Synonym 22: **stunner** *n.* an extremely good-looking man or woman.

Synonym 23: **stunning (to be)** *adj.* to be extremely good looking.

Synonym 24: **tall, dark and handsome (to be)** *adj.* (said of a man).

Synonym 25: **ten (to be a)** *exp.* meaning "to be a ten on a scale from 1 to 10."

Synonym 26: **traffic-stopper (to be a)** *n.* someone whose good looks causes drivers to brake and stare.

hunk *n.* a muscular and virile man.

EXAMPLE: That's Jeff Leshay? He used to be so thin and weak. He's really turned into a **hunk**! I guess he's been working out.

TRANSLATION: That's Jeff Leshay? He used to be so thin and weak. He's really turned into a **muscular and virile man**! I guess he's been working out.

"REAL SPEAK": That's Jeff Leshay? He usta be so thin 'n weak. He's really turned into a **hunk**! I guess 'e's been working out.

Synonym 1: **he-man** *n.*

Synonym 2: **jock** *n.*

Synonym 3: **macho** *adj.*

Synonym 4: **stallion** *n.* • (lit.): male horse.

Synonym 5: **stud** *n.* • (lit.): male horse.

ladies' man *n.* a man who is very attractive to women.

EXAMPLE: Rick is a real **ladies' man**. The moment he walks into a room, women come running up to him.

TRANSLATION: Rick is a really **attractive to women**. The moment he walks into a room, women come running up to him.

"REAL SPEAK": Rick's a real **ladies' man**. The moment 'e walks into a room, women come running up to 'im.

lech *n.* (short for *lecher*) one who flirts constantly in hope of finding sex.

EXAMPLE: Did you see the way Stan behaved when that beautiful model walked into the room? He didn't leave her alone for a second. He's such a **lech**!

TRANSLATION: Did you see the way Stan behaved when that beautiful model walked into the room? He didn't leave her alone for a second. He's such a **constant flirt**!

"REAL SPEAK": Did'ja see the way Stan behaved wh'n that beaudiful model walked inda the room? He didn' leave 'er alone fer a second. He's such a **lech**!

Synonym 1: **looking to get lucky (to be)** *exp.* to be looking for sex.

Synonym 2: **operator** *n.* one who knows exactly what to say in order to attract someone sexually.
Variation: **smooth operator** *n.*

Synonym 3: **playboy** *n.* a man who is devoted to having fun with few or no responsibilities.

Synonym 4: **player** *n.* one who enjoys the game of flirting.

Synonym 5: **tease** *n.*

Synonym 6: **woman chaser** *n.*

Synonym 7: **womanizer** *n.* a man who engages many women romantically and/or sexually knowing that he will never have a serious relationship with them.

love at first sight *exp.* immediate attraction for another person.

EXAMPLE: The moment I met your mother, I knew I wanted to marry her. It was **love at first sight**.

IT'S ALL ABOUT
♥ CHEMISTRY ♥

TRANSLATION: The moment I met your mother, I knew I wanted to marry her. It was **immediate attraction**.

"REAL SPEAK": The momen' I met 'cher mother, I knew I wan'ed da marry 'er. It w'z **love 'it firs' sight**.

LTR *n.* an abbreviation of "long-term relationship" which is commonly seen in the personals sections of the Internet and newspapers.

EXAMPLE: Did you see this ad in the personals? "Romantic and handsome man looking for an **LTR**." I think I'll answer his ad.

TRANSLATION: Did you see this ad in the personals? "Romantic and handsome man looking for a **long-term relationship**." I think I'll answer his ad.

"REAL SPEAK": Did'ja see this ad 'n the personals? "Romantic 'n han'some man looking fer 'n **LTR**." I think a'll answer 'is ad.

Note: There are several other common initials used in the personals that may look like some kind of secret code. For example: *A* ***BBW ISO*** *an* ***LTR*** *with a romantic* ***SWM***. ***N/D*** *and* ***N/S*** *a must!;* A ***big beautiful woman in search of*** a ***long-term relationship*** with a romantic ***single (or straight) white male***. ***Non-drinker*** and ***non-smoker*** a must! • Here are some other common initials:

A = Asian
B = Black
BB = Bodybuilder
BBW = Big Beautiful Woman
BI = Bisexual
F = Female
G = Gay
H = Hispanic
ISO = In search of
J = Jewish
M = Male
N/D = Non-Drinker or Non-Drug User
N/S = Non-smoker
S = Single or *Straight* which is slang for "heterosexual."
W = White

make the first move (to) *exp.* to initiate something.

EXAMPLE: I want to date her, but I'm too shy to **make the first move**.

TRANSLATION: I want to date her, but I'm too shy to **initiate it**.

"REAL SPEAK": I wanna date 'er, b'd I'm too shy da **make the firs' move**.

Variation: **make a move (to)** *exp.*

meat market *exp.* any place where people go to look for sexual encounters, such as a bar, a party, the gym, etc. • (lit.): a market where people shop for meat.

EXAMPLE: I hate going to my gym. It's turned into a **meat market**! The guys won't leave me alone!

TRANSLATION: I hate going to my gym. It's turned into a **place where people go to look for sexual encounters**! The guys won't leave me alone!

"REAL SPEAK": I hate going da my gym. It's turned into a **meat market**! The guys won't leeme alone!

nerd *n.* a person who has an unsophisticated appearance and personality.

EXAMPLE: Did you see the guy Beth is going out with? He's the biggest **nerd** and she's very sophisticated.

TRANSLATION: Did you see the guy Beth is going out with? He's the most **unsophisticated person** and she's very sophisticated.

"REAL SPEAK": Did'ja see the guy Beth 'ez going out with? He's the bigges' **nerd** 'n she's very safisticaded.

Variation: **nerdy** *adj.* said of someone with an unsophisticated appearance and personality.

Synonym 1: **dork** *n.* a weak and unsophisticated-looking person.
Variation: **dorky** *adj.* said of someone with an unsophisticated appearance and personality.

Synonym 2: **geek** *n.* a strange or eccentric person.
Variation: **geeky** *adj.* said of someone with an unsophisticated appearance and personality.

nooner *n.* a brief sexual encounter that occurs during the lunch hour.

EXAMPLE: When Mitch came back from lunch today, his hair was all messed up. I wonder if he had a **nooner**!

TRANSLATION: When Mitch came back from lunch today, his hair was all messed up. I wonder if he had a **brief sexual encounter during lunch**!

"REAL SPEAK": When Mitch came back fr'm lunch taday, his hair w'z all messed up. I wonder if 'e had a **nooner**!

Also: **afternoon delight** *exp.*

nympho *n.* (short for *nymphomaniac*) a woman with an abnormally excessive and uncontrollable sexual desire.

EXAMPLE: Michelle told me she has sex with a different guy every night! I didn't know she was such a **nympho**!

TRANSLATION: Michelle told me she has sex with a different guy every night! I didn't know she had such an **abnormally excessive and uncontrollable sexual desire**!

"REAL SPEAK": Michelle tol' me she has sex w'th a diff'rent guy ev'ry night! I didn' know she w'z such a **nympho**!

old maid (to be an) *n.* said of an old, unmarried woman.

EXAMPLE: Jody is fifty years old and still not married. I think she's destined to be an **old maid**.

TRANSLATION: Jody is fifty years old and still not married. I think she's destined to be an **old, unmarried woman**.

"REAL SPEAK": Jody's fifdy years old 'n still not married. I think she's destin' ta be 'n **ol' maid**.

Synonym 1: **single** *adj.* said of an unmarried man or woman.

Synonym 2: **spinster (old)** *n.* an old, unmarried woman.

on the prowl (to be) *exp.* to be looking for someone for an intimate relationship or sexual encounter • (lit.): said of an animal that is looking for food.

EXAMPLE: Every time I go out with Steve, he flirts with all the women. That guy is aways **on the prowl**.

TRANSLATION: Every time I go out with Steve, he flirts with all the women. That guy is aways **looking for someone for an intimate relationship or sexual encounter**.

"REAL SPEAK": Ev'ry time I go out w'th Steve, he flirts w'th all the women. That guy's ahways **on the prowl**.

Synonym: **on the make (to be)** *exp.*

one-night stand *n.* recreational sex that lasts for one night only.

EXAMPLE: I don't like **one-night stands**. I'm looking for a long-term relationship.

TRANSLATION: I don't like **recreational sex that lasts for just one night**. I'm looking for a long-term relationship.

"REAL SPEAK": I don't like **one-night stan'z**. I'm looking fer a long-term relationship.

pick someone up (to) *exp.* to approach someone for a sexual encounter.

EXAMPLE: Kim is so pretty that guys try to **pick her up** all the time. She can't even go shopping in peace!

TRANSLATION: Kim is so pretty that guys try to **approach her for sex** all the time. She can't even go shopping in peace!

"REAL SPEAK": Kim's so preddy th't guys try da **pick 'er up** all the time. She can' even go shopping 'n peace!

put out (to) *exp.* (usually said of a woman) to engage in sex willingly.

EXAMPLE: Tony will only take a woman out to dinner if he knows she is going **to put out**.

TRANSLATION: Tony will only take a woman out to dinner if he knows she is going **to engage in sex willingly**.

"REAL SPEAK": Tony'll only take a woman out ta dinner if 'e knows she's gonna **pud out**.

quickie *n.* a quick sexual encounter.

EXAMPLE: Now I know why the boss hired his girlfriend to work here. He calls her into his office for a **quickie** several times a day!

TRANSLATION: Now I know why the boss hired his girlfriend to work here. He calls her into his office for a **quick sexual encounter** several times a day!

"REAL SPEAK": Now I know why the boss hired 'is girlfrien' da work here. He calls 'er into 'is office fer a **quickie** sev'ral times a day!

runt *n.* a derogatory term for a short person.

EXAMPLE: I have no luck meeting men. The only guy who approached me was some **runt** named Marvin.

TRANSLATION: I have no luck meeting men. The only guy who approached me was some **short person** named Marvin.

"REAL SPEAK": I have no luck meeding men. The only guy who approached me w'z some **runt** named Marvin.

Synonym 1: **half-pint** *n.*

Synonym 2: **short stuff** *n.*

Synonym 3: **shorty** *n.*

Synonym 4: **shrimp** *n.*

Synonym 5: **small fry** *n.*

Synonym 6: **squirt** *n.*

Variation: **little squirt** *n.*

scope out (to) *exp.* to observe carefully.

EXAMPLE: Saturday nights I like to go to the mall **to scope out** the girls.

TRANSLATION: Saturday nights I like to go to the mall **to observe** the girls.

"REAL SPEAK": Saturday nights I like ta go da the mall **da scope out** the girls.

Synonym: **check out (to)** *exp.*

set someone up with (to) *exp.* to arrange for someone to go out on a date (with another).

EXAMPLE: I **set Al up** with my sister last night. He said he had the best time!

TRANSLATION: I **arranged for Al to go out on a date** with my sister. He said he had the best time!

"REAL SPEAK": I **sed Al up** w'th my sister las' night. He said 'e 'ad the bes' time!

shake someone (to) *v.* to get rid of someone.

EXAMPLE: No matter how many times I tell Caroline I'm not interested in going out with her, I can't **shake her**.

TRANSLATION: No matter how many times I tell Caroline I'm not interested in going out with her, I can't **get rid of her**.

"REAL SPEAK": No madder how many times I tell Caroline I'm nod int'rested 'n going out with 'er, I can't **shake 'er**.

sleep around (to) *exp.* to travel around having sex with several different people (at different times).

EXAMPLE: Candy told you she's a virgin?! Everyone knows she **sleeps around**.

TRANSLATION: Candy told you she's a virgin?! Everyone knows she **travels around having sex with several different people**.

"REAL SPEAK": Candy tol'ju she's a virgin?! Ev'ryone knows she **sleeps around**.

small talk (to make) *exp.* to engage in light, casual conversation.

EXAMPLE: Take your mother's advice. On your first date, just make **small talk** and don't kiss him!

TRANSLATION: Take your mother's advice. On your first date, just make **light, casual conversation** and don't kiss him!

"REAL SPEAK": Take yer mother's advice. On yer firs' date, jus' make **small talk** 'n don't kiss 'im!

smooth *adj.* said of someone who pretends to be sincere by making sure to say exactly what the other person wants to hear (in order to gain that other person's trust).

EXAMPLE: Terry sure is **smooth**, but I didn't believe he was sincere for a moment.

TRANSLATION: Terry sure **says everything I want to hear**, but I didn't believe he was sincere for a moment.

"REAL SPEAK": Terry sher is **smooth**, b'd I didn' believe 'e w'z sincere fer a moment.

Variation: **smooth operator** *n.*

spaz *n.* short for "spastic" idiot, fool.

EXAMPLE: You know that guy I went out with last night? He acted like the biggest **spaz** at the restaurant. I was so embarrassed!

TRANSLATION: You know that guy I went out with last night? He acted like the biggest **idiot** at the restaurant. I was so embarrassed!

"REAL SPEAK": Ya know that guy I wen' out with las' night? He acted like the bigges' **spaz** 'it the resterant. I w'z so embarrassed!

Note: This comes from the adjective "spastic," literally meaning "someone affected by involuntary muscular contractions."

Synonym 1: **all there (not to be)** *exp.* not to be functioning completely rationally.

Synonym 2: **lame-o** *n.* idiot.

Synonym 3: **lamebrain** *n.* idiot.

Synonym 4: **nitwit** *n.* idiot.

Synonym 5: **out of it (to be)** *exp.* not to be functioning completely rationally.

Synonym 6: **playing with a full deck (not to be)** *exp.* not to be functioning completely rationally.

Synonym 7: **slow on the draw (to be a little)** *exp.* • (lit.): (from Westerns) said of a cowboy who is slow at shooting his gun during a duel.

Synonym 8: **"The elevator doesn't go up to the top"** *exp.* said of someone stupid.

Synonym 9: **"The lights are on but nobody's home"** *exp.* said of someone stupid.

Synonym 10: **twit** *n.* idiot.

Synonym 11: **winner** *n.* (used sarcastically).

Variation: **a real winner (to be)** *exp.* to be a total loser in every way.

Note: The term *winner* meaning "one who is very successful," is commonly used to mean the opposite when used sarcastically. Being sarcastic is very American!! This is why it's so important to listen not only to what Americans say, but how they say it, especially since sarcasm is so commonly used. For example, upon seeing a woman walk into the room wearing an ugly dress, it would be common to hear someone whisper sarcastically, "Nice dress!" meaning "What a horrible dress!"

stand someone up (to) *exp.* to fail to keep an appointment or date with someone.

EXAMPLE: If Tim **stands me up** tonight, I'll never agree to go out with him again.

TRANSLATION: If Tim **doesn't show up for our date** tonight, I'll never agree to go out with him again.

"REAL SPEAK": If Tim **stanz me up** tanight, a'll never agree da go out w'th 'im again.

Variation: **be/get stood up (to)** *exp.* to be left waiting (for a date or appointment) for someone who never arrives as planned.

sweep someone off his/her feet (to) *exp.* said of a man who charms a woman.

EXAMPLE: Bill came into my life and **swept me off my feet**. We're going to be married next month!

TRANSLATION: Bill came into my life and **completely charmed me**. We're going to be married next month!

"REAL SPEAK": Bill came inta my life 'n **swep' me off my feet**. W'r gonna be married nex' month!

swoon (to) *v.* to faint due to overwhelming joy.

EXAMPLE: I'll never forget the day I saw Harrison Ford on Fifth Avenue in New York. I **swooned**!

TRANSLATION: I'll never forget the day I saw Harrison Ford on Fifth Avenue in New York. I **fainted due to overwhelming joy**!

"REAL SPEAK": A'll never ferget the day I saw Harrison Ford on Fifth Avenue 'n New York. I **swooned**!

troll *n.* a really ugly person • (lit.): a supernatural creature (either a dwarf or a giant) that is said to live in caves or in the mountains.

EXAMPLE: Nancy is a model but she's dating Melvin who's a **troll**!

TRANSLATION: Nancy is a model but she's dating Melvin who's a **really ugly person**!

"REAL SPEAK": Nancy is a model b't she's dading Melvin who's a **troll**!

KEN POPPED THE QUESTION!

Dating Slang
(Phase 2: The Thrill of the Relationship!)

THIS LESSON FEATURES 10 NEW SLANG WORDS & IDIOMS

LET'S WARM UP!

MATCH THE PICTURES

As a fun way to get started, see if you can guess the meaning of the new slang words and expressions on the opposite page by using the pictures below and following the context of the sentences.

1. Is that a ring on your finger?! Did David finally ***pop the question***?
   - ❑ ask you to marry him
   - ❑ answer your question

2. Brenda is dating a guy who's twenty years younger than she is. She's really ***robbing the cradle***!
   - ❑ stealing babies
   - ❑ dating someone much younger than she is

3. I think Monica has a ***sugar daddy***. She doesn't have a job but she wears new expensive clothes and jewelry every day!
   - ❑ rich father
   - ❑ rich older man she is dating

4. Look at them kissing and touching like that in public. ***Get a room***!
   - ❑ They should make room for others to join in
   - ❑ They should take it to a private place

5. Nancy and Dominic just got ***hitched***. They're spending their honeymoon in Hawaii!
   - ❑ arrested
   - ❑ married

6. Fran is ***crazy about*** Dan. She thinks about him all the time.
   - ❑ mentally insane around
   - ❑ very much in love with

7. You and Mitch have been seeing each other for years. When are you finally going to ***shack up***?
   - ❑ live together
   - ❑ build a house

8. I heard that Kim had a baby! Who ***knocked her up***?
   - ❑ got her pregnant
   - ❑ paid her a visit at her house

9. I just saw your brother and Jenny ***making out***! I didn't know they were dating!
   - ❑ arguing
   - ❑ kissing

10. Tom and Patty are so different! How long have they been ***going together***.
    - ❑ working together
    - ❑ dating each other

LET'S TALK!

A. DIALOGUE USING SLANG & IDIOMS

The words introduced on the first two pages are used in the dialogue below. See if you can understand the conversation. *Note:* The translation of the words in boldface is on the right-hand page.

CD-A: TRACK 7

Lee: You're not going to believe this. Debbie and Ken are getting **hitched** next month! He finally **popped the question** last night.

Nancy: You've got to be kidding. Ken is so much older than she is. He's **robbing the cradle**. Well, Debbie has always wanted a **sugar daddy** and now she's going to have one. I have to admit, they do seem **crazy about each other**. I mean, they're always **making out** in public.

Lee: I know. I hate that. **Get a room**!

Nancy: Well, they have been **going together** for three years and have been **shacked up** for one year. I guess they wanted to make it official.

Lee: Either that or Ken **knocked her up** and now they want to get married before the parents find out. But you didn't hear it from me!

B. DIALOGUE TRANSLATED INTO STANDARD ENGLISH

LET'S SEE HOW MUCH YOU REMEMBER!
Just for fun, move around in random order to the words and expressions in boldface below. See if you can remember their slang equivalents without looking at the left-hand page!

Lee: You're not going to believe this. Debbie and Ken are getting **married** next month! He finally **proposed** last night.

Nancy: You've got to be kidding. Ken is so much older than she is. He's **dating someone so much younger than he is**. Well, Debbie has always wanted a **rich husband** and now she's going to have one. I have to admit, they do seem **very much in love**. I mean, they're always **kissing** in public.

Lee: I know. I hate that. **Get a hotel room and do it in private**!

Nancy: Well, they have been **dating** for three years and have been **living together** for one year. I guess they wanted to make it official.

Lee: Either that or Ken **got her pregnant** and now they want to get married before the parents find out. But you didn't hear it from me!

C. DIALOGUE USING "REAL SPEAK"

The dialogue below demonstrates how the slang conversation on the previous page would *really* be spoken by native speakers!

CD-A: TRACK 7

Lee: Y'r not gonna believe this. Debbie 'n Ken'er gedding **hitched** nex' month! He fin'lly **popped the question** las' night.

Nancy: You've godda be kidding. Ken's so much older th'n she is. He's **robbing the cradle**. Well, Debbie's ahways wan'ed a **sugar daddy** 'n now she's gonna have one. I hafta admit, they do seem **crazy aboud each other**. I mean, they're ahweez **making oud** 'n public.

Lee: I know. I hate that. **Ged a room**!

Nancy: Well, they've been **going dagether** fer three years 'n 'ev been **shacked up** fer one year. I guess they wan'ed ta make id afficial.

Lee: Either thad 'r Ken **knocked 'er up** 'n now they wanna get married b'fore the parents find out. But'cha didn' hear it fr'm me!

LET'S LEARN!

VOCABULARY

The following words and expressions were used in the previous dialogues. Let's take a closer look at what they mean.

CD-A: TRACK 8

crazy about someone (to be) *exp.* to love someone very much.

EXAMPLE: I'm **crazy about** Albert. He's wonderful!

TRANSLATION: I **love** Albert **very much**. He's wonderful!

"REAL SPEAK": I'm **crazy aboud** Albert. He's wonderful!

Synonym 1: **crush on someone (to have a)** *exp.*

Synonym 2: **fall for someone (to)** *exp.*

Synonym 3: **have it bad for someone (to)** *exp.*

Synonym 4: **head over heels for someone (to be)** *exp.*
Variation: **head over heels in love with someone (to be)** *exp.*

Synonym 5: **hots for someone (to have the)** *exp.*

Synonym 6: **lovesick (to be)** *adj.* to be deeply in love.

Synonym 7: **mad about someone (to be)** *exp.*

Synonym 8: **nuts about someone (to be)** *exp.*

Synonym 9: **stuck on someone (to be)** *exp.*

Synonym 10: **wild about someone (to be)** *exp.*

NOW YOU DO IT. COMPLETE THE PHRASE ALOUD:
I'm crazy about Leslie because...

"Get a room!" *exp.* (said to two people who are excessively physically affectionate in public) "Take your lovemaking to a private place!"

EXAMPLE: Look how they're kissing each other in public! Hey! **Get a room**!

TRANSLATION: Look how they're kissing each other in public! Hey! **Take it to a private place**!

"REAL SPEAK": Look how they're kissing each other 'n public! Hey! **Gedda room**!

NOW YOU DO IT. COMPLETE THE PHRASE ALOUD:
...Get a room!

go together (to) *exp.* to date on a regular basis.

EXAMPLE: I didn't know David and Margaret were **going together**. They're as different as night and day!

TRANSLATION: I didn't know David and Margaret were **dating on a regular basis**. They're as different as night and day!

"REAL SPEAK": I didn' know David 'n Marg'ret were **going tagether**. They're 'ez diff'rend 'ez night 'n day!

Synonym 1: **go steady (to)** *exp.*

Synonym 2: **go with someone (to)** *exp.*

NOW YOU DO IT. COMPLETE THE PHRASE ALOUD:
I just found out that ... and ... are going together!

hitched (to get) *exp.* to get married • (lit.): to get connected.

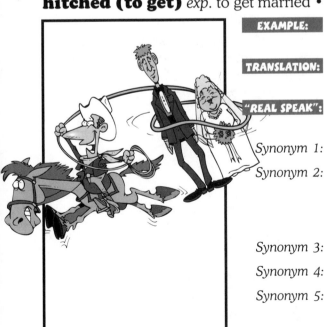

EXAMPLE: After dating for fourteen years, Jim and Cecily are finally going **to get hitched**.

TRANSLATION: After dating for fourteen years, Jim and Cecily are finally going **to get married**.

"REAL SPEAK": After dading fer fourteen years, Jim 'n Cecily 'er fin'lly gonna **get hitched**.

Synonym 1: **settle down (to)** *exp.*

Synonym 2: **snap on the ol' ball and chain (to)** *exp.* (humorous).
Note: The adjective "old" is commonly reduced to *ol'* as seen in this expression.

Synonym 3: **take the plunge (to)** *exp.*

Synonym 4: **tie the knot (to)** *exp.*

Synonym 5: **walk down the aisle (to)** *exp.*

NOW YOU DO IT. COMPLETE THE PHRASE ALOUD:
...got hitched last week!

knocked up (to get) *exp.* (somewhat vulgar) to get pregnant.

EXAMPLE: I just heard that Lisa **got knocked up** by Barry! Is that true?

TRANSLATION: I just heard that Lisa **got pregnant** by Barry! Is that true?

"REAL SPEAK": I jus' heard th't Lisa **got knocked up** by Barry! Izat true?

Variation: **knock someone up (to)** *exp.* to impregnate someone.

Synonym 1: **bun in the oven (to have a)** *exp.* (humorous).

Synonym 2: **expecting (to be)** *adj.* (very popular)

Note: In England, the expression *to knock someone up* means "to knock on someone's door when going for a visit" rather than the American definition of "to impregnant someone."

NOW YOU DO IT. COMPLETE THE PHRASE ALOUD:
... got knocked up when she was only...

make out (to) *exp.* to kiss.

EXAMPLE: After **making out** with Alice for an hour, Bill had more of her lipstick on him than she did!

TRANSLATION: After **kissing** Alice for 'n hour, Bill had more of her lipstick on him than she did!

"REAL SPEAK": After **making out** with Alice fer an hour, Bill had more 'ev 'er lipstick on 'im th'n she did!

Synonym 1: **French kiss (to)** *exp.* to kiss with the tongue.
Variation: **give a French kiss (to)** *exp.*

Synonym 2: **hickey (to give someone a)** *exp.* to leave a mark on someone's skin by kissing and sucking.

Synonym 3: **neck (to)** *v.* to kiss (old fashioned).

Synonym 4: **play tonsil hockey (to)** *exp.* (humorous and popular among the younger generations) to kiss with the tongue.

Synonym 5: **suck face (to)** *exp.* (crude yet humorous).

Synonym 6: **tongue tonsillectomy (to give someone a)** *exp.* (humorous and popular among the younger generations) to kiss deeply with the tongue.

NOW YOU DO IT. COMPLETE THE PHRASE ALOUD:
Last night, I saw Larry and Susan making out in/at...

pop the question (to) *exp.* to propose marriage.

EXAMPLE: Greg **popped the question** tonight! He said he's in love with Lisa and wants her to be his wife.

TRANSLATION: Greg **proposed marriage** tonight! He said he's in love with Lisa and wants her to be his wife.

"REAL SPEAK": Greg **popped the question** tanight! He said 'e's 'n love with Lisa 'n wants 'er da be 'is wife.

NOW YOU DO IT. COMPLETE THE PHRASE ALOUD:
I popped the question to Jane in/at...

rob the cradle (to) *exp.* to date or marry someone much younger than oneself.

EXAMPLE: Joanne is 53 and Tony is 22. I know she likes younger men, but that's really **robbing the cradle**!

TRANSLATION: Joanne is 53 and Tony is 22. I know she likes younger men, but that's really **dating someone much younger than herself**!

"REAL SPEAK": Joanne's fifdy-three 'n Tony's twen'y-two. I know she likes younger men, b't that's really **robbing the cradle**!

NOW YOU DO IT. COMPLETE THE PHRASE ALOUD:
I think Brad is robbing the cradle because...

shack up [together] (to) *exp.* to move in together.

EXAMPLE: We've been dating for over a year. Don't you think it's time we **shacked up**?

TRANSLATION: We've been dating for over a year. Don't you think it's time we **moved in together**?

"REAL SPEAK": We've been dading fer over a year. Doncha think it's time we **shacked up**?

Variation: **be shacked up [together] (to)** *exp.* to be living together.

NOW YOU DO IT. COMPLETE THE PHRASE ALOUD:
I told Gary I wasn't ready to shack up because...

sugar daddy *exp.* a wealthy older man who gives money and presents to a younger woman in exchange for her intimate companionship.

EXAMPLE:
– Every time I see Trish, she is with a much older man. Is that her father?
– No, that's her **sugar daddy**. That's why she is always wearing new jewelry and clothing.

TRANSLATION:
– Every time I see Trish, she is with a much older man. Is that her father?
– No, that's her **wealthy older man who gives her money and presents in exchange for her intimate companionship**. That's why she is always wearing new jewelry and clothing.

"REAL SPEAK":
– Ev'ry time I see Trish, she's with a much older man. Izat 'er father?
– No, that's 'er **suger daddy**. That's why she's ahweez wearing new jewelry 'n clothing.

NOW YOU DO IT. COMPLETE THE PHRASE ALOUD:
I think that's Susan's sugar daddy because...

LET'S PRACTICE!

A. TRUE OR FALSE

Decide if the definition is true or false.

CD-A: TRACK 9

1. 

make out (to) *exp.* to argue.

❑ True ❑ False

2. 

crazy about someone (to be) *exp.* to love someone very much.

❑ True ❑ False

3. 

pop the question (to) *exp.* to propose marriage.

❑ True ❑ False

4. 

sugar daddy *exp.* a wealthy older man who is known for being miserly.

❑ True ❑ False

5. 

rob the cradle (to) *exp.* said of a babysitter who keeps the baby up late.

❑ True ❑ False

6. 

"Get a room!" *exp.* (said to two people who are excessively physically affectionate in public) "Take your lovemaking to a private place!"

❑ True ❑ False

7. 

shack up [together] (to) *exp.* to move in together.

❑ True ❑ False

8. 

knocked up (to get) *exp.* (somewhat vulgar) to have a great time.

❑ True ❑ False

9. **go together (to)** *exp.* to date on a regular basis.

❑ True ❑ False

10. 

hitched (to get) *exp.* to get divorced

❑ True ❑ False

B. CHOOSE THE RIGHT WORD

CD-A: TRACK 10

Underline the words that best complete the phrase.

1. Congratulations! I heard your boyfriend popped the (**statement**, **interjection**, **question**) last night!

2. Can you believe how physical Jennifer and Kenny were with each other in the restaurant? They never stopped making (**in**, **out**, **up**)!

3. Did you see Jody? She's pregnant! Who knocked her (**up**, **down**, **out**)?

4. See that man standing next to Kim? That's her (**pepper**, **salt**, **sugar**) daddy. That explains why she's always wearing expensive jewelry and clothing every time we see her.

5. Look at those two kissing like that in public! (**Get a room**, **Rob the cradle**, **Pop the question**)!

6. I just heard that Marge and Homer are getting (**itched**, **hitched**, **switched**) next month. They want to have a family right away.

7. Did you see the guy Gail is dating? He must be fifteen years younger than she is. She's really robbing the (**ladle**, **bagel**, **cradle**)!

8. My mother and father have been married fifty years and they're still (**crazy**, **hazy**, **lazy**) about each other!

9. Isn't that Jill and Steve holding hands over there? When did they start (**going**, **coming**, **arriving**) together?

10. After dating each other for only a month, Lisa and Bill decided to shack (**in**, **out**, **up**). I think that's a little too early!

C. MATCH THE SENTENCES

Match the numbered sentences below with the lettered sentences on the opposite page. Write your answers in the boxes at the bottom of the pages.

READING
CD-A: TRACK 11
1 Are you going to Bill and Sue's wedding?
2 Steve is dating a twenty-year-old girl!
3 Todd asked me to marry him!
4 I'd like you to meet my new boyfriend.
5 Betty is pregnant for the sixth time!
6 I didn't know Carol and Tim were living together.
7 Look at those two hugging and kissing in the middle of the bank!
8 Have you ever kissed your girlfriend in the market?
9 Your parents look like they really love each other.
10 Ann doesn't have a job but she has very expensive clothes.

NUMBERS	1	2	3	4	5
LETTERS					

C. MATCH THE SENTENCES - *(continued)*

NUMBERS	6	7	8	9	10
LETTERS					

DATING SLANG

(Phase 2: The Thrill of the Relationship!)

A romantic relationship certainly has many levels such as initial attraction, love, marriage, family, etc. The following list offers a large assortment of slang terms and idioms you're sure to hear in reference to any type of relationship.

all over each other (to be) *exp.* said of two people who are excessively physically affectionate with each other.

EXAMPLE: Ron and Emily were **all over each other** during today's church service!

TRANSLATION: Ron and Emily were **excessively physically affectionate** during today's church service!

"REAL SPEAK": Ron 'n Emily were **all over each other** during taday's church service!

Synonym: **paw each other (to)** *exp.*

B.F. *n.* an abbreviation of "boyfriend."

EXAMPLE: Jill and Steve do everything together. Is Steve her new **B.F.**?

TRANSLATION: Jill and Steve do everything together. Is Steve her new **boyfriend**?

"REAL SPEAK": Jill 'n Steve do ev'rything tagether. Is Steve 'er new **B.F.**?

Synonym 1: **honey man** *n.* an affectionate abbreviation of "boyfriend" or "husband."

Synonym 2: **life-mate** *n.* boyfriend or girlfriend in a homosexual relationship.

Synonym 3: **lover** *n.* boyfriend or girlfriend, and used typically to refer to one's partner in a homosexual relationship.

Synonym 4: **main man** *n.*

Synonym 5: **main squeeze** *n.* (gangster lingo, used in jest).

Synonym 6: **man (my)** *n.* "my boyfriend" or "my husband."

Synonym 7: **partner** *n.* boyfriend or girlfriend in a homosexual relationship.

Synonym 8: **significant other** *n.* (also known as one's **S.O.**) boyfriend or girlfriend, and used typically to refer to one's partner in a homosexual relationship.

Note 1: Any term of affection can be used as a synonym for either "boyfriend" or "girlfriend." See – **sweetie**, *p. 40.*

Note 2: Many of the same terms here can be used as synonyms for "husband." See – **hubby**, *p. 37.*

See: **G.F.** *f.* girlfriend, *p. 36.*

breadwinner *n.* the person in the family who earns a living and supports the family by working at a job.

EXAMPLE: Susie is an attorney and Tom is a janitor. It's obvious which one is the **breadwinner** in that family!

TRANSLATION: Susie is an attorney and Tom is a janitor. It's obvious which one is the **person who earns a living** in that family!

"REAL SPEAK": Susie's 'n atterney 'n Tom's a janider. It's obvious which one's the **breadwinner** 'n that fam'ly!

Note: The term *bread* is an outdated term for "money." However, it's interesting to note that the term *breadwinner* is popular!

Also: **bring home the bacon (to)** *exp.* to earn a living and support the family by working at a job.

bro *n.* an abbreviation of "brother."

EXAMPLE: Hey, **bro**. Do you need some help with your homework?

TRANSLATION: Hey, **brother**. Do you need some help with your homework?

"REAL SPEAK": Hey, **bro**. Ya need s'm help with yer homework?

Note 1: The noun *bro* is commony used by the younger generations to mean "male friend" • *Hey, **bro**! I haven't seen you in a long time;* Hey, ***friend***! I haven't seen you in a long time.

Note 2: When used to mean "male friend," *bro* may be pronounced *brah* (from surfer lingo).

cuddle (to) *exp.* said of two lovers who hold each other very closely for an extended and affectionate embrace.

EXAMPLE: Sally and I woke up at seven o'clock, but we stayed in bed **cuddling** until noon.

TRANSLATION: Sally and I woke up at seven o'clock, but we stayed in bed **holding each other affectionately** until noon.

"REAL SPEAK": Sally 'n I woke up 'it seven a'clock, b't we stayed 'n bed **cuddling** 'til noon.

Synonym: **snuggle (to)** *v.*

get along (to) *exp.* said of two people who enjoy each other's company.

EXAMPLE: We didn't like each other at first, but now we really **get along**.

TRANSLATION: We didn't like each other at first, but now we really **enjoy each other's company**.

"REAL SPEAK": We didn' like each other 'it first, b't now we really **ged along**.

G.F. *n.* an abbreviation of "girlfriend."

EXAMPLE: Carl thinks his new **G.F.** is the most beautiful girl in the world.

TRANSLATION: Carl thinks his new **girlfriend** is the most beautiful girl in the world.

"REAL SPEAK": Carl thinks 'is new **G.F.** is the most beaudiful girl 'n the world.

Synonyms: See – **my woman**, *p. 38*.

go all the way (to) *exp.* to have sex (an adolescent usage).

EXAMPLE: Have you ever **gone all the way** in the back seat of a car?

TRANSLATION: Have you ever **had sex** in the back seat of a car?

"REAL SPEAK": Have ya ever **gone all the way** 'n the back sead 'ev a car?

go out with someone (to) *exp.* to date someone.

EXAMPLE: Have you started **going out with** Stan on a regular basis?

TRANSLATION: Have you started **dating** Stan on a regular basis?

"REAL SPEAK": Have you starded **going out with** Stan on a regular basis?

Synonym: **go with someone (to)** *exp.*

heavy petting *adj.* extreme physical affection.

EXAMPLE: Al and Sue got into some **heavy petting** last night!

TRANSLATION: Al and Sue enjoyed some **very physical affection** last night!

"REAL SPEAK": Al 'n Sue god inta s'm **heavy pedding** las' night!

Note: In the example, the expression *to get into* was used, which is popular slang for "to enjoy."

horny (to be) *adj.* to be sexually stimulated (like an adolescent deer who grows horns).

EXAMPLE: Jim is constantly **horny**. All he ever does is talk about sex!

TRANSLATION: Jim is constantly **sexually stimulated**. All he ever does is talk about sex!

"REAL SPEAK": Jim's constantly **horny**. All 'e ever does 'ez talk about sex!

Synonym: **horn dog** *n.* said of someone who is constantly sexually stimulated.

hubby *n.* an affectionate abbreviation of "husband."

EXAMPLE: That guy over there is Jan's **hubby**. Isn't he cute?

TRANSLATION: That guy over there is Jan's **husband**. Isn't he cute?

"REAL SPEAK": That guy over there's Jan's **hubby**. Isn' 'e cute?

Synonym 1: **honey man** *n.* an affectionate abbreviation of "husband" or "boyfriend."

Synonym 2: **main man** *n.*

Synonym 3: **main squeeze** *n.* (gangster lingo, used in jest).

Synonym 4: **man (my)** *n.* "my husband" or "my boyfriend."

Synonym 5: **old man** *n.* can be used to mean husband, boyfriend, or father, depending on the context.

Note: Any term of affection can be used as a synonym for "husband." See – **sweetie**, *p. 40*.

into someone (to be) *exp.* to be interested in someone romantically.

EXAMPLE: John is really **into you**. I hear he calls you several times a day!

TRANSLATION: John is really **interested in you romantically**. I hear he calls you several times a day!

"REAL SPEAK": John's really **inta ya**. I hear 'e calls ya sev'ral times a day!

item (an) *n.* said of two people who are romantically involved.

EXAMPLE: Every time I see you, you're with Andy. Are you two **an item**?

TRANSLATION: Every time I see you, you're with Andy. Are you two **romantically involved**?

"REAL SPEAK": Ev'ry time I see you, y'r w'th Andy. Are you two **'n idem**?

kid *n.* child, baby • (lit.): baby goat.

EXAMPLE: Congratulations! I heard you and Eric just had a **kid**!

TRANSLATION: Congratulations! I heard you and Eric just had a **child**!

"REAL SPEAK": C'ngradjalations! I heard'ju 'n Eric jus' had a **kid**!

Synonym 1: **little bundle of joy** *exp.*

Synonym 2: **preemie** *n.* a baby that is born prematurely. • See *p. 39*.

Synonym 3: **punk** *n.* a youth who acts tough.

Synonym 4: **rug rat** *n.*

Synonym 5: **small fry** *n.*

Synonym 6: **squirt** *n.* a small child (also used as an insult for a short man).

Variation: **little squirt** *n.*

Synonym 7: **toddler** *n.* refers to a very young child who hasn't been walking for a long time.

lovebirds *exp.* two people in love • (lit.): small African parrots known for showing great affection toward their mates.

EXAMPLE: Look at those two **lovebirds**. It's obvious they're in love.

TRANSLATION: Look at those two **people in love**. It's obvious they're in love.

"REAL SPEAK": Look 'it those two **lovebirds**. It's obvious they're 'n love.

lovey-dovey (to be) *adj.* to be extremely affectionate.

EXAMPLE: Jack and Irene have been married for thirty years and they're still **lovey-dovey**.

TRANSLATION: Jack and Irene have been married for thirty years and they're still **extremely affectionate**.

"REAL SPEAK": Jack 'n Irene 'ev been married fer thirdy years 'n they're still **lovey-dovey**.

meal ticket *n.* a person who is being taken advantage of by someone pretending to be in love in order to get financial support.

EXAMPLE: The only reason Ann is staying with Tim is because he's her **meal ticket**. She doesn't have any emotional feelings for him.

TRANSLATION: The only reason Ann is staying with Tim is because he's her **means of financial support**. She doesn't have any emotional feelings for him.

"REAL SPEAK": The only reason Ann's staying w'th Tim 'ez b'cuz 'e's 'er **meal ticket**. She doesn' have any emotional feelings for 'im.

Note: When used in jest, this term is a humorous synonym for "husband" or "boyfriend" as well as wealthy "wife" or "girlfriend."

my woman *n.* "my wife" or "my girlfrend" (depending on the context).

EXAMPLE: This is **my woman**. We've been dating for a year.

TRANSLATION: This is **my girlfriend**. We've been dating for a year.

"REAL SPEAK": This 'ez **my woman**. We've b'n dading fer a year.

Synonym 1: **baby/babe** *n.*

Synonym 2: **chick** *n.* also a slang term for "girl" in general.

Synonym 3: **G.F.** *n.* an abbreviation of "girlfriend."

Synonym 4: **life-mate** *n.* boyfriend or girlfriend typically in a homosexual relationship.

Synonym 5: **lover** *n.* boyfriend or girlfriend used typically in a homosexual relationship.

Synonym 6: **old lady** *n.* can be used to mean wife, girlfriend, or mother, depending on the context.

Synonym 7: **partner** *n.* boyfriend or girlfriend in a homosexual relationship.

Synonym 8: **significant other** (also known as one's **S.O.**) *n.* boyfriend or girlfriend typically in a homosexual relationship.

Note: Any term of affection can be used as a synonym for "wife" or "girlfriend."
See – **sweetie**, *p. 40*.

old lady *n.* wife or mother (depending on the context).

EXAMPLE: I promised my **old lady** I'd take her out for our anniversary.

TRANSLATION: I promised my **wife** I'd take her out for our anniversary.

"REAL SPEAK": I promised my **ol' lady** I'd take 'er out fer 'ar anniversery.

Synonym 1: **ma** *n.* mother.

Synonym 2: **mom** *n.* mother.

Synonym 3: **mommy** *n.* (child language). mother.

See: **my woman**, *p. 38*.

old man *n.* husband or father (depending on the context).

EXAMPLE: That's your **old man**? He's so young and muscular!

TRANSLATION: That's your **father**? He's so young and muscular!

"REAL SPEAK": That's yer **ol' man**? He's so young 'n musculer!

Synonym 1: **dad** *n.* father.

Synonym 2: **daddy** *n.* (child language) father.

Synonym 3: **papa** *n.* father.

Synonym 4: **pop** or **pops** *n.* father.

See: **hubby**, *p. 37.*

play footsie (to) *exp.* to flirt with someone by secretly touching feet.

EXAMPLE: My sister's husband was **playing footsie with me** under the table during dinner!

TRANSLATION: My sister's husband was **flirting with me by secretly touching my foot with his** under the table during dinner!

"REAL SPEAK": My sister's husban' w'z **playing footsie** w'th me under the table during dinner!

preemie *n.* a premature baby.

EXAMPLE: I was a **preemie**. I was born six weeks early.

TRANSLATION: I was a **premature baby**. I was born six weeks early.

"REAL SPEAK": I w'z a **preemie**. I w'z born six weeks early.

puppy love *exp.* temporary infatuation (usually said of a young boy or girl).

EXAMPLE: Those two teens are crazy about each other. It's probably just **puppy love**.

TRANSLATION: Those two teens are crazy about each to her. It's probably just **temporary infatuation**.

"REAL SPEAK": Those two teens 'er crazy aboud each other. It's prob'ly jus' **puppy love**.

see each other (to) *v.* to date.

EXAMPLE: Craig and I have been **seeing each other** for nearly a year.

TRANSLATION: Craig and I have been **dating** for nearly a year.

"REAL SPEAK": Craig 'n I 'ev been **seeing each other** fer nearly a year.

sis *n.* an abbreviation of "sister."

EXAMPLE: Hey, **sis**! Mom wants you to drive her to the market.

TRANSLATION: Hey, **sister**! Mom wants you to drive her to the market.

"REAL SPEAK": Hey, **sis**! Mom wants ya da drive 'er da the market.

Note: The noun *sister* is also commonly used to mean "female friend" • *Hey,* ***sis****! What's up?;* Hey, ***friend***! How are you?

soul mate *n.* a person with whom you feel a deep understanding and connection.

EXAMPLE: Tessa and I are **soul mates**. We'll be together forever.

TRANSLATION: Tessa and I **have a deep connection**. We'll be together forever.

"REAL SPEAK": Tessa 'n I 'er **soul mates**. We'll be dagether ferever.

spoon (to) *v.* to be in a position where both partners are lying on their sides, pressed up against each other (facing the same direction) with legs bent, fiting together like two spoons.

EXAMPLE: I love being the one in front when we **spoon**. I love being held all night!

TRANSLATION: I love being the one in front when we **lie on our sides, pressed up against each other, facing the same direction, with our legs bent**. I love being held all night!

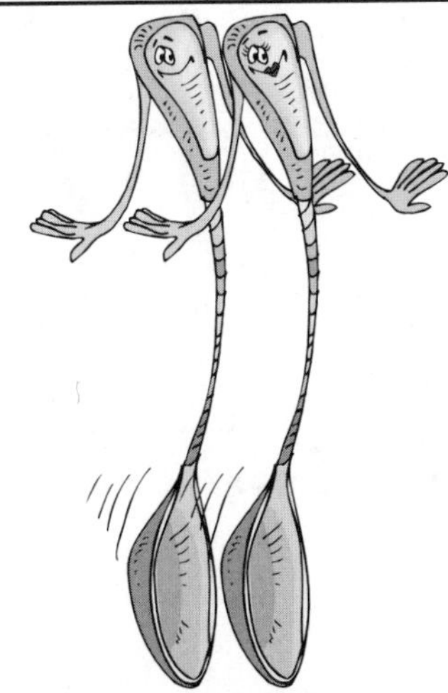

"REAL SPEAK": I love being the one 'n front when we **spoon**. I love being held all night!

Note: Many years ago, the verb *to spoon* meant "to kiss." Over the years, it has taken on a new meaning.

sweetie *n.* (very popular) a term of endearment.

EXAMPLE: **Sweetie**, could you pick up some groceries for me at the market on your way home tonight?

TRANSLATION: **My dear one**, could you pick up some groceries for me at the market on your way home tonight?

"REAL SPEAK": **Sweetie**, could'ja pick up s'm groc'ries fer me 'it the marked on yer way home tanight?

Synonym 1: **honey** *n.* (very popular).

Synonym 2: **lambchop** *n.* used primarily in jest (see note below).

Synonym 3: **snookums** *n.* used primarily in jest (see note below).

Synonym 4: **sugar** *n.* used primarily in the south.

Synonym 5: **sugar pie** *n.* used primarily in jest (see note below).

Synonym 6: **sweetie pie** *n.*

Note: It's important to note that some terms of endearment are used in jest because they are overly sweet and affectionate to the point of being sickening!

trophy wife *exp.* an older, prestigious man's beautiful and stylish wife that he shows off as a symbol of his social and economic status with little or no affection between them.

EXAMPLE: Ann is just a **trophy wife**. It's a loveless marriage. He gets the beautiful woman and she gets the rich husband.

TRANSLATION: Ann is just a **wife to show off to others**. It's a loveless marriage. He gets the beautiful woman and she gets the rich husband.

"REAL SPEAK": Ann's just a **trophy wife**. It's a loveless marr'age. He gets the beaudiful woman 'n she gets the rich husband.

turn someone on (to) *exp.* to stimulate someone sexually.

EXAMPLE: Look at those biceps! Big muscles really **turn me on**!

TRANSLATION: Look at those biceps! Big muscles really **stimulate me sexually**!

"REAL SPEAK": Look 'it those biceps! Big muscles really **turn me on**!

ups and downs (to have) *exp.* to have good moments and bad moments.

EXAMPLE: Our relationship has its **ups and downs** but Ted and I are basically very happy.

TRANSLATION: Our relationship has its **good moments and bad moments** but Ted and I are basically very happy.

"REAL SPEAK": 'Ar relationship has its **ups 'n downs** b't Ted 'n I 'er basic'lly very happy.

wear the pants in the family (to) *exp.* to be in charge of the family.

EXAMPLE: I let Bill make all the decisions in our house. He **wears the pants in the family**.

TRANSLATION: I let Bill make all the decisions in our house. He **is in charge of the family**.

"REAL SPEAK": I let Bill make all the decisions 'n 'ar house. He **wears the pants 'n the fam'ly**.

Synonym: **call the shots (to)** *exp.* to be in charge.

JANE AND MIKE BROKE UP!

Dating Slang

(Phase 3: The End of the Relationship)

THIS LESSON FEATURES 10 NEW SLANG WORDS & IDIOMS

LET'S WARM UP!

MATCH THE PICTURES

As a fun way to get started, see if you can guess the meaning of the new slang words and expressions on the opposite page by using the pictures below and following the context of the sentences. Each answer can only be used once!

☐ 1. When Ann found out that her boyfriend cheated on her, she ***dropped him like a hot potato***.

☐ 2. When Pam divorced Doug, she ***took Doug to the cleaners***!

☐ 3. John and Anne had a big fight, but I'm sure they'll be able to ***patch things up***.

☐ 4. It's a good idea to sign a ***pre-nup*** before getting married. It can make things a lot easier if the marriage doesn't work out.

☐ 5. Ted's father has a ***mistress***?! Does his mother know!? Doesn't she mind sharing her husband?!

☐ 6. Ginger goes to bed with a different guy every night. She's such a ***tramp***!

☐ 7. After ten years of marriage, Vivian and Al ***broke up***!

☐ 8. Did you know Greg had an ***affair*** behind Cathy's back?! I wonder who the other woman is!

☐ 9. I'm not surprised Jim and Peg ended their relationship. Their marriage has ***been on the rocks*** for a long time.

☐ 10. Scott was in bed with another woman when his wife came in and ***busted*** him!

A. woman who enjoys having a continuing sexual relationship with a married man

B. left him abruptly and finally

C. not been going well

D. ended their relationship

E. contract specifying what each person gets in the event of a divorce

F. romantic relationship with someone other than one's spouse

G. caught him doing something inappropriate

H. was awarded all his possessions

I. sexually promiscuous woman

J. reconcile

LET'S TALK!

A. DIALOGUE USING SLANG & IDIOMS

The words introduced on the first two pages are used in the dialogue below. See if you can understand the conversation. *Note:* The translation of the words in boldface is on the right-hand page.

Jennifer: I just heard that Jane and Mike **broke up** because Mike was having an **affair** for the past year! She **busted him** when she walked into their bedroom and found him with some **tramp**.

Kenny: How horrible! Jane must have been so upset!

Jennifer: She sure was. She **dropped him like a hot potato** the next day! I don't think they'll ever be able to **patch things up**, either. With Jane, there are no second chances.

Kenny: Well, it doesn't surprise me one bit that he had a **mistress**. Their marriage has been **on the rocks** for a long time. I just hope they both signed a **pre-nup** or she'll end up **taking him to the cleaners**!

B. DIALOGUE TRANSLATED INTO STANDARD ENGLISH

LET'S SEE HOW MUCH YOU REMEMBER!
Just for fun, move around in random order to the words and expressions in boldface below. See if you can remember their slang equivalents without looking at the left-hand page!

Jennifer: I just heard that Jane and Mike **ended their relationship** because Mike was having a **secretive romantic relationship** for the past year! She **caught him doing something inappropriate** when she walked into their bedroom and found him with some **sexually promiscuous woman**.

Kenny: How horrible! Jane must have been so upset!

Jennifer: She sure was. She **left him** the next day! I don't think they'll ever be able to **reconcile**, either. With Jane, there are no second chances.

Kenny: Well, it doesn't surprise me one bit that he found a **woman who enjoys having a continuing sexual relationship with a married man**. Their marriage has been **unsteady** for a long time. I just hope they both signed a **pre-nuptial agreement** or she'll end up **being awarded everything he owns**!

C. DIALOGUE USING "REAL SPEAK"

The dialogue below demonstrates how the slang conversation on the previous page would *really* be spoken by native speakers!

CD-A: TRACK 12

Jennifer: I just heard th't Jane 'n Mike **broke up** b'cuz Mike w'z having 'n **affair** fer the past year! She **busded 'im** when she walked inda their bedroom 'n found 'im with some **tramp**.

Kenny: How horr'ble! Jane must 'a been so upset!

Jennifer: She sher was. She **dumped 'im** the nex' day! I don't think they'll ever be able da **patch things up**, either. With Jane, there 'er no secon' chances.

Kenny: Well, it doesn' serprise me one bit th'd 'e had a **mistress**. Their marr'age 'ez been **on the rocks** fer a long time. I just hope they both signed a **pre-nup** 'r she'll end up **taking 'im ta the cleaners**!

LET'S LEARN!

VOCABULARY

The following words and expressions were used in the previous dialogues. Let's take a closer look at what they mean.

CD-A: TRACK 13

affair (to have an) *n.* to have a secret romantic relationship (often with someone other than one's spouse or boyfriend/girlfriend).

EXAMPLE: I just saw Scott leave that hotel with some woman and it wasn't his wife. I wonder if he's **having an affair**.

TRANSLATION: I just saw Scott leave that hotel with some woman and it wasn't his wife. I wonder if he's **having a secret romantic relationship with someone else**.

"REAL SPEAK": I jus' saw Scott leave that hotel w'th some woman an' it wasn' 'is wife. I wonder if 'e's **having 'n affair**.

Synonym 1: **bed-hop (to)** *v.*

Synonym 2: **fling (to have a)** *n.*

Synonym 3: **get some on the side (to)** *exp.*

Variation: **get a little something on the side (to)** *exp.*

Synonym 4: **mess around (to)** *exp.*

Synonym 5: **play around (to)** *exp.*

Synonym 6: **play musical beds (to)** *exp.*

Synonym 7: **some extracurricular activity (to do)** *exp.*

Also: **hanky-panky** *n.* secretive sexual relations.

NOW YOU DO IT. COMPLETE THE PHRASE ALOUD:
I think Ron is having an affair because...

break up (to) *v.* to end a relationship.

EXAMPLE: Melissa and Tom haven't been happy together for years. So yesterday, they finally **broke up**.

TRANSLATION: Melissa and Tom haven't been happy together for years. So yesterday, they finally **ended their relationship**.

"REAL SPEAK": Melissa 'n Tom haven't been happy dagether fer years. So yesterday, they fin'lly **broke up**.

Synonym 1: **break it off (to)** *exp.*

Synonym 2: **come to a parting of the ways (to)** *exp.*

Synonym 3: **split up (to)** *v.*

NOW YOU DO IT. COMPLETE THE PHRASE ALOUD:

Tina and Bill broke up because...

bust someone (to) *v.* to discover someone doing something improper • (lit.): to arrest someone.

EXAMPLE: Last night, Carol **busted** Henry. She caught him kissing another woman!

TRANSLATION: Last night, Carol **discovered** Henry **doing something improper**. She caught him kissing another woman!

"REAL SPEAK": Las' night, Carol **busded** Henry. She caught 'im kissing another woman!

Also 1: **"Busted!"** *exclam.* an exclamation used to indicate that someone was caught doing something inappropriate.

Also 2: **busted (to get)** *adj.* to get caught doing something inappropriate • *Bill got **busted** for lying to his wife;* Bill got ***caught*** lying to his wife.

NOW YOU DO IT. COMPLETE THE PHRASE ALOUD:

Janice busted me because...

drop someone like a hot potato (to) *exp.* to end a romantic relationship with someone abruptly.

EXAMPLE: When Debbie discovered that her boyfriend was married, she **dropped him like a hot potato**.

TRANSLATION: When Debbie discovered that her boyfriend was married, she **ended their romantic relationship abruptly**.

"REAL SPEAK": When Debbie discovered thad 'er boyfrien' w'z married, she **dropped 'im like a hot patado**.

Synonym 1: **bail on someone (to)** *v.*

Synonym 2: **dump someone (to)** *exp.*

Synonym 3: **jilt (to)** *v.*

Synonym 4: **leave someone high and dry (to)** *exp.*

Synonym 5: **run out on someone (to)** *exp.*

Synonym 6: **walk out on someone (to)** *exp.*

NOW YOU DO IT. COMPLETE THE PHRASE ALOUD:

Laura dropped Cliff like a hot potato because...

mistress *n.* a woman who has a continuing sexual relationship with a married man.

EXAMPLE: I always thought that Mr. Henderson and his wife had the perfect marriage. But I just found out that he has had a **mistress** for years.

TRANSLATION: I always thought that Mr. Henderson and his wife had the perfect marriage. But I just found out that he has had a **continuing relationship with another woman** for years.

"REAL SPEAK": I ahweez thought th't Mr. Henderson an' 'is wife had the perfect marr'age. B'd I jus' found out th'd 'e's had a **mistress** fer years.

NOW YOU DO IT. COMPLETE THE PHRASE ALOUD:
I think Ron may have a mistress because...

on the rocks *exp.* said of a marriage that is not going well.

EXAMPLE: Laura and Don's marriage has been **on the rocks** for such a long time. I hope they will be able to solve their problems soon.

TRANSLATION: Laura and Don's marriage has **not been going well** for such a long time. I hope they will be able to solve their problems soon.

"REAL SPEAK": Laura 'n Don's marr'age 'ez been **on the rocks** fer such a long time. I hope they'll be able da solve their problems soon.

Synonym: **shaky ground (to be on)** *exp.*

Variation: **shaky (to be)** adj.

NOW YOU DO IT. COMPLETE THE PHRASE ALOUD:
I think Liz and Mark's marriage is on the rocks because every time I see them together...

patch things up (to) *exp.* to reconcile one's differences.

EXAMPLE: Peter and Marsha used to be in love but then they had a big fight and haven't spoken in months. Well today, they finally **patched things up**!

TRANSLATION: Peter and Marsha used to be in love but then they had a big fight and haven't spoken in months. Well today, they finally **reconciled their differences**!

"REAL SPEAK": Peter 'n Marsha usta be 'n love b't then they had a big fight 'n haven't spoken 'n munts. Well taday, they fin'lly **patched things up**!

Synonym 1: **bury the hatchet (to)** *exp.*

Synonym 2: **kiss and make up (to)** *exp.* used in reference to two people in a romantic relationship.

Synonym 3: **talk it out (to)** *exp.*

NOW YOU DO IT. COMPLETE THE PHRASE ALOUD:
Frank and Margaret patched things up after...

pre-nup *n.* an abbreviation of "pre-nuptial agreement" which is a contract between two people who are soon to be married — this contract specifies what each person gets in the event of a divorce.

EXAMPLE: After years of marriage, Angela and Tony are getting a divorce. Luckily they had a **pre-nup**, so the entire process should be very easy.

TRANSLATION: After years of marriage, Angela and Tony are getting a divorce. Luckily they had a **pre-nuptial agreement**, so the entire process should be very easy.

"REAL SPEAK": After years 'ev marr'age, Angela 'n Tony 'er gedding a divorce. Luckily they had a **pre-nup**, so the entire process should be very easy.

NOW YOU DO IT. COMPLETE THE PHRASE ALOUD:
It's important to have a pre-nup because...

take someone to the cleaners (to) *exp.* to acquire all of someone's possessions (or money) either dishonestly or in a court battle.

EXAMPLE: When Caroline discovered that her husband was dating another woman, she divorced him and **took him to the cleaners**.

TRANSLATION: When Caroline discovered that her husband was dating another woman, she divorced him and **acquired all his possessions**.

"REAL SPEAK": When Caroline discovered thad 'er husban' w'z dading another woman, she divorced 'im 'n **took 'im da the cleaners**.

NOW YOU DO IT. COMPLETE THE PHRASE ALOUD:
Brenda took her husband to the cleaners when...

tramp *n.* a sexually promiscuous woman • (lit.): a homeless person who sleeps in a different place every night.

EXAMPLE: Don't let your husband get near that woman. Everyone in the neighborhood knows she's nothing but a **tramp**!

TRANSLATION: Don't let your husband get near that woman. Everyone in the neighborhood knows she's nothing but a **sexually promiscuous woman**!

"REAL SPEAK": Don't let cher husban' get near that wom'n. Ev'ryone 'n the neighborhood knows she's nothing b'd a **tramp**!

Synonym 1: **slut** *n.*

Synonym 2: **whore** *n.*

Note: The younger generations commonly pronounce this word using a southern, African-American urban accent, where the "R" sound is typically omitted. Therefore, it is extremely common today to hear the word *whore* pronounced "ho." • See: **tore up (to be)**, *p. 195.*

NOW YOU DO IT. COMPLETE THE PHRASE ALOUD:
I think... is a tramp because...

LET'S PRACTICE!

A. WHAT DOES IT MEAN?

Choose the correct definition of the words in boldface.

1. **to have an affair:**
   - ❑ to have a romantic relationship with someone other than one's spouse or boyfriend/girlfriend
   - ❑ to have an anniversary party

2. **to break up**:
   - ❑ to begin a new relationship
   - ❑ to end a relationship

3. **to bust someone**:
   - ❑ to hit someone
   - ❑ to discover someone doing something inappropriate

4. **to drop someone like a hot potato**:
   - ❑ to end a romantic relationship with someone abruptly
   - ❑ to drop someone off at his/her house quickly

5. **mistress:**
   - ❑ a woman who enjoys having a continuing sexual relationship with a married man
   - ❑ a young bride

6. **on the rocks**:
   - ❑ said of a marriage that is going very well
   - ❑ said of a marriage that is not going well

7. **to patch things up**:
   - ❑ to argue
   - ❑ to reconcile one's differences

8. **pre-nup**:
   - ❑ an abbreviation of "pre-nuptial agreement," which is a contract specifying what each person gets in the event of a divorce
   - ❑ an abbreviation of "pre-nuptial agreement," which is a contract specifying what each person will get as soon as they are married

9. **to take someone to the cleaners**:
   - ❑ to empty or "clean out" someone of all his/her possessions either dishonestly or in a court battle
   - ❑ to clean someone's house from top to bottom

10. **tramp**:
    - ❑ a woman who is not promiscuous
    - ❑ a sexually promiscuous woman

B. COMPLETE THE FAIRY TALE

Fill in the blanks by choosing the correct words from the list at the bottom of the page.

CD-A: TRACK 15

Once upon a time, there was a girl named Cinderella who lived in a little cottage with her stepmother and two stepsisters who were very mean to Cinderella. They made her clean the house all day long. Cinderella was especially sad today because the prince was having a big ball that evening and she couldn't go because she had nothing to wear. And this was a special ball because this is where the prince would find his princess! The prince was actually supposed to get married the previous year, but his relationship had been on the ______________ for quite some time and it just didn't work out.

The special evening finally came and everyone, except Cinderella, went to the prince's ball. She was so sad that she didn't have a beautiful dress she could wear and through her tears she cried out, "Oh, Fairy Godmother, please help me!" Suddenly she heard a voice from behind her say, "Hello, Sweetie! I'm here to help you." Cinderella could hardly believe her eyes and said, "But...you're the tooth fairy. You don't know anything about clothes!" "True," she said. "But I can give you a lovely set of teeth made of high quality porcelain laminate veneer!" With that, she waved her magic wand over Cinderella who was now wearing the most beautiful smile in the land. And Cinderella ran off to the prince's ball.

When she arrived ,the prince couldn't believe his eyes. He'd never seen such a bright smile! He was so entranced by her grin that he insisted that they get married right away! "This is the happiest day of my life!" said Cinderella. "First, I just need you to sign this pre-____________ stating that in the event of a divorce I get the items listed below. Just sign here..and here. Great! Now let's get married!" And they did.

They were so happy until one day, Cinderella found the prince in bed with some ______________! She ______________ him! It was actually his ______________ that he had been having an ______________ with for months! Cinderella was so angry that she dropped him like a ______________ then and there. "I'm sure we can ______________ things up, Sweetie, Darling" said the prince. "Don't you Sweetie, Darling me!" said Cinderella. "You can do whatever you want now because we have officially ______________! I'm calling my attorney at Dewey Screwum and Howe and I'm taking you to the ______________!"

AFFAIR	**BUSTED**	**HOT POTATO**	**NUP**	**ROCKS**
BROKEN UP	**CLEANERS**	**MISTRESS**	**PATCH**	**TRAMP**

C. CONTEXT EXERCISE

Look at the phrase in the left column, then find the best response in the right column. Write the appropriate letter in the box.

CD-A: TRACK 16

☐ 1. I don't think Ken and Jill are seeing each other anymore.

☐ 2. Poor Alice. Her husband just told her that he has been seeing another woman.

☐ 3. I know that's Mel's wife standing next to him. But who's the other woman that he has his arm around?

☐ 4. Wendy came home early from work and found Ron in bed with another woman! Can you believe it?

☐ 5. Connie sleeps with a different guy every night!

☐ 6. What did you do when you discovered that you weren't the only woman Pete was dating?

☐ 7. I heard you and George had a big fight!

☐ 8. Did you know that Bonnie and Anthony have been seeing a marriage counselor?

☐ 9. Our divorce went very smoothly.

☐ 10. By the end of your divorce, what are you hoping to get from Bob?

A. I **dropped him like a hot potato**.

B. Everything! I'm **taking him to the cleaners**!

C. Why? Did you both sign a **pre-nup**?

D. Of course! I knew he'd get **busted** one of these days.

E. It didn't last long. We already **patched things up**.

F. No, but I'm not surprised. Their marriage has **been on the rocks** for a long time.

G. What a **tramp**!

H. Really? When did they **break up**?

I. That's his **mistress**. It seems pretty strange but they all live together!

J. How long has this **affair** been going on?

D. COMPLETE THE PHRASE

Complete the opening dialogue using the list below. Try not to look at the dialogue at the beginning of the lesson until you're done!

AFFAIR	NUP
BROKE	PATCH
BUSTED	POTATO
CLEANERS	ROCKS
MISTRESS	TRAMP

Jennifer: I just heard that Jane and Mike ________________ **up** because Mike was having an ________________ for the past year! She ______________ **him** when she walked into their bedroom and found him with some ________________.

Kenny: How horrible! Jane must have been so upset!

Jennifer: She sure was. She **dropped him like a hot** ________________ the next day! I don't think they'll ever be able to ________________ **things up**, either. With Jane, there are no second chances.

Kenny: Well, it doesn't surprise me one bit that he had a ________________. Their marriage has been **on the** ________________ for a long time. I just hope they both signed a **pre-**____________ or she'll end up **taking him to the** ____________________!

DATING SLANG

(Phase 3: The End of the Relationship)

The slang terms and expressions that are associated with the end of a relationship are just as colorful and expressive as the emotions behind them. The following list demonstrates popular slang relating to everything from arguments to divorce.

blow one's top (to) *exp.* to become furious.

EXAMPLE: Earl **blew his top** when he found out his wife gave away his favorite sweater.

TRANSLATION: Earl **became furious** when he found out his wife gave away his favorite sweater.

"REAL SPEAK": Earl **blew 'is top** when 'e found oud 'is wife gave away 'is fav'rit sweader.

Synonym 1: **blow up (to)** *v.*

Synonym 2: **flip one's lid (to)** *exp.*

Synonym 3: **flip [out] (to)** *v.*

Synonym 4: **fly off the handle (to)** *exp.*

Synonym 5: **freak [out] (to)** *v.*

Synonym 6: **hit the ceiling (to)** *exp.*

Synonym 7: **pissed off (to get)** *adj.*

Synonym 7: **ticked off (to get)** *adj.*

break someone's heart (to) *exp.* to hurt someone very deeply.

EXAMPLE: John was the love of Marsha's life. When he left her, it **broke her heart**.

TRANSLATION: John was the love of Marsha's life. When he left her, it **hurt her very deeply**.

"REAL SPEAK": John w'z the love 'ev Marsha's life. When 'e left 'er, it **broke 'er heart**.

Variation 1: **break a lot of hearts (to)** *exp.* said of someone who moves from one relationship to another.

Variation 2: **brokenhearted (to be)** *adj.* to be extremely sad because of the end of a romantic relationship.

See: **heartbreaker**, *p. 56.*

call it quits (to) *exp.* to abandon something.

EXAMPLE: Karen and I decided to **call it quits**. All we ever do is argue!

TRANSLATION: Karen and I decided to **end our relationship**. All we ever do is argue!

"REAL SPEAK": Karen 'n I decided ta **call it quits**. All we ever do 'ez argue!

cheat on someone (to) *exp.* to be unfaithful to someone.

EXAMPLE: After seventeen years of marriage, my husband **cheated on me**.

TRANSLATION: After seventeen years of marriage, my husband **was unfaithful to me**.

"REAL SPEAK": After seventeen years 'a marr'age, my husban' **cheeded on me**.

custody *n.* legal responsibility for one's children.

EXAMPLE: After Carol and Eric's divorce, the court gave **custody** of the children to Carol. Eric will be allowed to visit them on weekends.

TRANSLATION: After Carol and Eric's divorce, the court gave **legal responsibility** of the children to Carol. Eric will be allowed to visit them on weekends.

"REAL SPEAK": After Carol 'n Eric's divorce, the court gave **cusdady** 'a the children ta Carol. Eric'll be allowed ta visit th'm on weekends.

deadbeat dad *n.* a father who neglects to pay child support to his ex-wife.

EXAMPLE: Did you hear the news? Rob was arrested last night for being a **deadbeat dad**. He owes his ex-wife ten thousand dollars!

TRANSLATION: Did you hear the news? Rob was arrested last night for **neglecting to pay child support**. He owes his ex-wife ten thousand dollars!

"REAL SPEAK": Did'ja hear the news? Rob w'z arrested las' night fer being a **deadbeat dad**. He owes 'is ex-wife ten thousan' dollers!

drag someone into court (to) *exp.* to sue someone.

EXAMPLE: I just discovered that Carl has been dating another woman for years! I'm going to **drag him into court** and get a divorce!

TRANSLATION: I just discovered that Carl has been dating another woman for years! I'm going to **sue him** for divorce!

"REAL SPEAK": I jus' discovered th't Carl's been dading another woman fer years! I'm gonna **drag 'im inta court** 'n ged a divorce!

Synonym 1: **battle it out in court (to)** *exp.*

Synonym 2: **haul someone into court (to)** *exp.*

ex *n.* a person with whom you formerly had a romantic relationship (such as a boyfriend, girlfriend, husband, wife, etc.).

EXAMPLE: Anthony is my **ex**, but we get along better now than when we were married.

TRANSLATION: Anthony is my **former husband,** but we get along better now than when we were married.

"REAL SPEAK": Anthony's my **ex**, b't we ged along bedder now th'n when we were married.

falling-out *n.* a quarrel (usually leading to the end of a relationship).

EXAMPLE: Greg and I had a **falling out** two years ago and haven't spoken since.

TRANSLATION: Greg and I had a **quarrel** two years ago and haven't spoken since.

"REAL SPEAK": Greg 'n I had a **falling out** two years ago 'n haven't spoken since.

fizzle [out] (to) *v.* to end slowly.

EXAMPLE: After only a few years of marriage, Gina and Tony's relationship **fizzled [out]**.

TRANSLATION: After only a few years of marriage, Gina and Tony's relationship **ended slowly**.

"REAL SPEAK": After only a few years 'ev marr'age, Gina 'n Tony's relationship **fizzled [out]**.

Synonym: **peter out (to)** *v.*

Note: The main entry can be either *to fizzle* or *to fizzle out*. However, its synonym, *to peter out*, must retain the preposition *out*.

forgive and forget (to) *exp.* to forgive someone and leave the past behind.

EXAMPLE: You have been angry with Al for over a year. You need to **forgive and forget**.

TRANSLATION: You have been angry with Al for over a year. You need to **forgive him and leave the past behind**.

"REAL SPEAK": You've been angry with Al fer over a year. Ya need da **fergive 'n ferget**.

Synonym 1: **get over it (to)** *exp.*

Synonym 2: **let bygones be bygones (to)** *exp.*

Synonym 3: **let it go (to)** *exp.*

give it another shot (to) *exp.* to try again.

EXAMPLE: After being divorced for a year, Betty and Victor decided to **give it another shot**. They just started dating again yesterday!

TRANSLATION: After being divorced for a year, Betty and Victor decided to **try again**. They just started dating again yesterday!

"REAL SPEAK": After being divorced fer a year, Betty 'n Victor decided da **give id another shot**. They jus' starded dading again yesterday!

Synonym 1: **give it another go (to)** *exp.*

Synonym 2: **take another crack at it (to)** *exp.*

Synonym 3: **take another stab at it (to)** *exp.*

give someone the cold shoulder (to) *exp.* to refuse to speak to someone.

EXAMPLE: Darin is **giving me the cold shoulder** because I forgot his birthday.

TRANSLATION: Darin is **refusing to speak to me** because I forgot his birthday.

"REAL SPEAK": Darin's **giving me the cold shoulder** b'cuz I fergod 'is birthday.

Variation: **give someone the cold-shoulder treatment (to)** *exp.*

go down the tubes (to) *exp.* to end quickly.

EXAMPLE: Monica and Jeff's relationship **went down the tubes** after he discovered she was also dating his best friend behind his back.

TRANSLATION: Monica and Jeff's relationship **ended quickly** after he discovered she was also dating his best friend behind his back.

"REAL SPEAK": Monica 'n Jeff's relationship **went down the tubes** after 'e discovered she w'z dading 'is bes' friend b'hind 'is back.

Synonym: **go down the drain (to)** *exp.*

have it out (to) *exp.* to have big, verbal fight.

EXAMPLE: Rachel and Ross **had it out** at the restaurant last night. It was so embarrassing!

TRANSLATION: Rachel and Ross **had a big verbal fight** at the restaurant last night. It was so embarrassing!

"REAL SPEAK": Rachel 'n Ross **had id out** 'it the resterant las' night. It w'z so embarrassing!

Synonym 1: **blow up at each other (to)** *exp.*
Variation: **blow up (to have a)** *exp.*

Synonym 2: **go at each other (to)** *exp.*

Synonym 3: **have words (to)** *exp.*

Synonym 4: **knockdown drag out (to have a)** *exp.*

Synonym 5: **make a scene (to)** *exp.*

Synonym 6: **lay into each other (to)** *exp.*

Synonym 7: **let each other have it (to)** *exp.*

Synonym 8: **lock horns (to)** *exp.*

Synonym 9: **rip into each other (to)** *exp.*

Synonym 10: **screaming match (to have a)** *exp.*

heartbreaker *n.* someone who hurts another person deeply by rejecting that person for someone else, consequently "breaking his/her heart" – See: **break someone's heart (to)**, *p. 53*.

EXAMPLE: Be careful not to get too emotionally close to Erica. She's a **heartbreaker**.

TRANSLATION: Be careful not to get too emotionally close to Erica. She's a **person who hurts people deeply by rejecting them for others**.

"REAL SPEAK": Be careful not ta get too emotionally close ta Erica. She's a **heartbreaker**.

jerk *n.* a person who behaves in an obnoxious manner.

EXAMPLE: Kevin is such a **jerk**. He played jokes on everyone all night!

TRANSLATION: Kevin is such an **obnoxious person**. He played jokes on everyone all night!

"REAL SPEAK": Kevin's such a **jerk**. He played jokes on ev'ryone all night!

Variation: **jerky** *adj.* said of someone who behaves in an obnoxious manner.

kick someone to the curb (to) *exp.* to rid oneself of someone (as you would put the trash at the curb to be picked up and disposed of).

EXAMPLE: Kirk cheated on you again?! **Kick him to the curb**!

TRANSLATION: Kirk cheated on you again?! **Get rid of him**!

"REAL SPEAK": Kirk cheaded on ya again?! **Kick 'im da the curb**!

leave someone standing at the altar (to) *exp.* to desert one's mate at his/her own wedding.

EXAMPLE: Poor Dennis. His bride **left him standing at the altar**. Maybe she ran away with another man.

TRANSLATION: Poor Dennis. His bride **deserted him at their wedding**. Maybe she ran away with another man.

"REAL SPEAK": Poor Dennis. His bride **left 'im standing 'it the altar**. Maybe she ran away w'th another man.

loser *n.* a person who has no positive qualities.

EXAMPLE: Bob is a terrible husband and father. He's a total **loser**.

TRANSLATION: Bob is a terrible husband and father. He's a **person with no positive qualities**.

"REAL SPEAK": Bob's a terr'ble husband 'n father. He's a todal **loser**.

meet halfway (to) *exp.* to compromise.

EXAMPLE: You and Brian have been arguing about this for an hour! Can't you just **meet halfway**?

TRANSLATION: You and Brian have been arguing about this for an hour! Can't you just **compromise**?

"REAL SPEAK": You 'n Brian 'ev been arguing about this fer 'n hour! Can'cha jus' **meet halfway**?

Synonym: **strike a happy medium (to)** *exp.*

messy *adj.* said of a divorce that is complicated and emotional • (lit.): disorderly.

EXAMPLE: Lee and Marvin's divorce got really **messy**. Neither one of them was willing to compromise.

TRANSLATION: Lee and Marvin's divorce got really **complicated and emotional**. Neither one of them was willing to compromise.

"REAL SPEAK": Lee 'n Marvin's divorce got really **messy**. Neither one 'a th'm w'z willing da compramise.

on bad terms with someone (to be) *exp.* to have an unfriendly relationship with someone.

EXAMPLE: William and I used to be great friends, but now **we're on bad terms**.

TRANSLATION: William and I used to be great friends, but now **we're no longer friendly with one another**.

"REAL SPEAK": William 'n I usta be great frenz, b't now **w'r on bad terms**.

palimony *n.* (from *pal* meaning "friend") monetary support paid by one half of an unmarried partnership after the relationship ends.

EXAMPLE: Pat received $100,000 in **palimony** from Fred because they had a relationship for twenty years.

TRANSLATION: Pat received $100,000 in **monetary support** from Fred because they had a relationship for twenty years.

"REAL SPEAK": Pat received a hundred thousan' dollers 'n **palimony** fr'm Fred b'cuz they had a relationship fer twen'y years.

point the finger at someone (to) *exp.* to blame someone.

EXAMPLE: All you ever do is **point the finger at me** for everything. You never assume any responsibility!

TRANSLATION: All you ever do is **blame me** for everything. You never assume any responsibility!

"REAL SPEAK": All ya ever do 'ez **point the finger 'it me** fer ev'rything. Ya never assume any responsibilidy!

Also: **finger-pointing** *n.* blaming • *During their argument, there was a lot of **finger-pointing**;* During their argument, there was a lot of ***blaming***.

Synonym 1: **pass the buck (to)** *exp.* to blame someone other than oneself.

Synonym 2: **pin something on someone (to)** *exp.* to blame something on someone.

read someone the riot act (to) *exp.* to reprimand someone severely.

EXAMPLE: Larry **read Tony the riot act** for forgetting to pick him up at the airport.

TRANSLATION: Larry **reprimanded Tony severely** for forgetting to pick him up at the airport.

"REAL SPEAK": Larry **read Tony the riod act** fer fergedding da pick 'im up 'it the airport.

Synonym 1: **all over someone (to be)** *exp.*

Synonym 2: **bawl someone out (to)** *exp.*

Synonym 3: **call someone on the carpet (to)** *exp.*

Synonym 4: **chew someone out (to)** *exp.*

Synonym 5: **come down hard on someone (to)** *exp.*

Synonym 6: **give someone a piece of one's mind (to)** *exp.*

Synonym 7: **give someone hell (to)** *exp.*

Synonym 8: **give someone what for (to)** *exp.*

Synonym 10: **jump all over someone (to)** *exp.*

Synonym 11: **light into someone (to)** *exp.*

Synonym 12: **let someone have it (to)** *exp.*

Synonym 13: **lower the boom (to)** *exp.*

Synonym 14: **mop up the floor with someone (to)** *exp.*

Synonym 15: **rake someone over the coals (to)** *exp.*

Synonym 16: **ream someone out (to)** *exp.*

Synonym 17: **settle the score with someone (to)** *exp.*

Synonym 18: **tell someone a thing or two (to)** *exp.*

Synonym 19: **tell someone off (to)** *exp.*

separate (to) *v.* to end a relationship temporarily while both people decide whether or not they want to end it permanently in divorce.

EXAMPLE: Sue and Jim are going to **separate**. They have been having marital trouble for years and need some time apart before making any serious decisions.

TRANSLATION: Sue and Jim are going to **end their relationship temporarily**. They have been having marital trouble for years and need some time apart before making any serious decisions.

"REAL SPEAK": Sue 'n Jim'er gonna **seperate**. They've been having marid'l trouble fer years 'n need s'm time apart b'fore making any serious decisions.

two-time someone (to) *v.* to be unfaithful to someone.

EXAMPLE: I found out my wife was **two-timing** me with my best friend the whole time we were engaged.

TRANSLATION: I found out my wife was **being unfaithful to** me with my best friend the whole time we were engaged.

"REAL SPEAK": I found out my wife w'z **two-timing** me with my best friend the whole time we were engaged.

Variation: **two-timing** *adj. Jeff is a* ***two-timing*** *jerk! He's been seeing another woman behind my back!;* Jeff is an ***unfaithful*** jerk! He's been seeing another woman behind my back!

TOM IS WAY OFF BASE!

Sports Terms Used in Slang

THIS LESSON FEATURES 12 NEW SLANG WORDS & IDIOMS

LET'S WARM UP!

MATCH THE PICTURES

As a fun way to get started, see if you can guess the meaning of the new slang words and expressions on the opposite page by using the pictures below and following the context of the sentences.

1. I was having the nicest dinner with Jason when suddenly he made a comment that ***came out of left field***!
   ❑ was completely unexpected
   ❑ was the same thing I was thinking

2. We need to ***tackle*** this problem before our next meeting.
   ❑ ignore
   ❑ try hard to solve

3. Bob told the boss that I come to work late every day just so that he would get the promotion instead of me. That's ***dirty pool***!
   ❑ unethical behavior
   ❑ fair behavior

4. If you think I'd go on a date with you again after the way you behaved last time, you're ***off base***!
   ❑ absolutely correct
   ❑ badly mistaken

5. I just can't seem to find a job anywhere. I'm ready to ***throw in the towl***.
   ❑ give up
   ❑ take a shower

6. Dan tries to ***score with*** all the new girls in our class. He's such an animal!
   ❑ seduce
   ❑ study with

7. Al went shopping for a new home and bought the first one he saw ***right off the bat***!
   ❑ and played baseball together
   ❑ instantly

8. I have to leave but I'll ***touch base with*** you tonight. Talk to you later!
   ❑ play some sports with
   ❑ contact

9. Gilbert refuses to pay me the money he owes me. Well, I'm ready to ***play hardball***. I'm going to contact an attorney to help me!
   ❑ behave aggressively
   ❑ cooperate

10. I apologized to Steve three times and he still won't talk to me. I'm finished trying. ***The ball's in his court now***.
    ❑ He's always been terrible at sports
    ❑ It's up to him to respond to the situation

11. I thought Ted was going to give me good news. Instead, he told me he got fired. He really ***threw me a curve***!
    ❑ likes to tease
    ❑ surprised me

12. Chris cheated me! He'll be sorry. I'm going to ***settle the score*** if it's the last thing I do!
    ❑ get revenge
    ❑ have a long talk with him

LET'S TALK!

A. DIALOGUE USING SLANG & IDIOMS

The words introduced on the first two pages are used in the dialogue below. See if you can understand the conversation. *Note:* The translation of the words in boldface is on the right-hand page.

CD-A: TRACK 18

Tom: I know I may be **way off base** here, but did you and Judy break up?

Bill: Well, that sure **came out of left field**!

Tom: It's just that I heard Bob ask her out today and wondered if you guys decided to **throw in the towel**.

Bill: Of course not! I told him that we had a disagreement, but nothing serious. I can't believe he would try to **score** with my girlfriend at a time when she's feeling vulnerable. That's such **dirty pool**. He sure did **throw me a curve**. I thought we were friends!

Tom: I disliked the guy **right off the bat**. I never trusted him.

Bill: Well, if he wants to **play hardball**, I'm ready to **settle the score**! **The ball is in my court now**.

Tom: Hey, I agree you need to **tackle** the problem, but don't sink down to his level.

Bill: You're right. Okay. I'm going to give him a call right now. I'll **touch base with you** later tonight.

B. DIALOGUE TRANSLATED INTO STANDARD ENGLISH

LET'S SEE HOW MUCH YOU REMEMBER!
Just for fun, move around in random order to the words and expressions in boldface below. See if you can remember their slang equivalents without looking at the left-hand page!

Tom: I know I may be very **totally wrong** here, but did you and Judy break up?

Bill: Well, that sure **was completely unexpected**!

Tom: It's just that I heard Bob ask her out today and wondered if you guys decided to **give up**.

Bill: Of course not! I told him that we had a disagreement, but nothing serious. I can't believe he would try to **succeed** with my girlfriend at a time when she's feeling vulnerable. That's such **an unethical thing to do**. He sure did **surprise me in a negative way**. I thought we were friends!

Tom: I disliked the guy **instantly**. I never trusted him.

Bill: Well, if he wants to **compete aggressively**, I'm ready to **retaliate**! **It's my turn to respond to the situation**.

Tom: Hey, I agree you need to **attack** the problem, but don't sink down to his level.

Bill: You're right. Okay. I'm going to give him a call right now. I'll **contact you** later tonight.

C. DIALOGUE USING "REAL SPEAK"

The dialogue below demonstrates how the slang conversation on the previous page would *really* be spoken by native speakers!

CD-A: TRACK 18

Tom: I know I may be way **off base** here, b't did'ju 'n Judy break up?

Bill: Well, that sher **came oudda lef' field**!

Tom: It's just th'd I heard Bob ask 'er out taday 'n wondered if you guys decided da **throw 'n the towel**.

Bill: Of course not! I told 'im th't we had a disagreement, b't nothing serious. I can't believe he'd try da **score** with my girlfriend ad a time when she's feeling vulnerable. That's such **dirdy pool**. He sher did **throw me a curve**. I thought we were frienz!

Tom: I disliked the guy **ride off the bat**. I never trusded 'im.

Bill: Well, if 'e wants ta **play hardball**, I'm ready da **seddle the score**! **The ball's 'n my court now**.

Tom: Hey, I agree ya need da **tackle** the problem, b't don't sink down ta his level.

Bill: Y'r right. Okay. I'm gonna give 'im a call right now. A'll **touch base with ya** lader tanight.

LET'S LEARN!

VOCABULARY

The following words and expressions were used in the previous dialogues. Let's take a closer look at what they mean.

CD-A: TRACK 19

ball in one's court (to have the) *exp.* (tennis) to be responsible for taking the next action.

EXAMPLE: I've apologized to Mark two times and he still won't talk to me. Now, **the ball is in his court**.

TRANSLATION: I've apologized to Mark two times and he still won't talk to me. Now, **it's his turn to take the next action**.

"REAL SPEAK": I've apalagize' ta Mark two times 'n 'e still won't talk ta me. Now, **the ball's 'n his court**.

Origin: In tennis, players take their turn when the ball is in their court (on their side of the net).

NOW YOU DO IT. COMPLETE THE PHRASE ALOUD:

... The ball's in your/his/her/their court now.

come out of left field (to) *exp.* (baseball) to be completely unexpected.

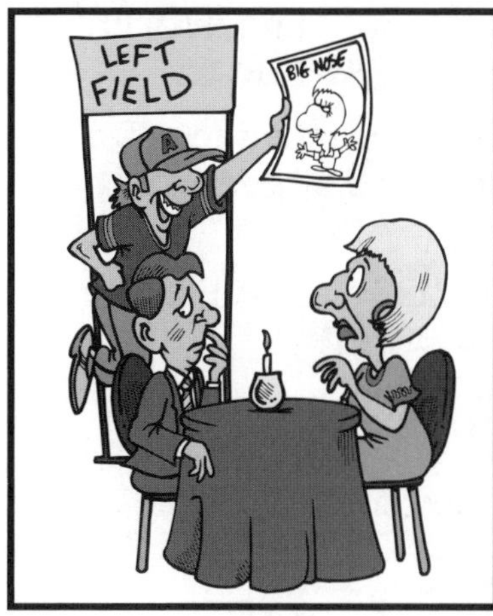

EXAMPLE: Gary and I were having a romantic dinner together when all of a sudden, he made a comment about my nose being too big. His comment **came out of left field**!

TRANSLATION: Gary and I were having a romantic dinner together when all of a sudden, he made a comment about my nose being too big. His comment **was completely unexpected**!

"REAL SPEAK": Gary 'n I were having a roman(t)ic dinner dagether when all 'ev a sudden, he made a comment about my nose being too big. His comment **came oudda lef' field!**

NOW YOU DO IT. COMPLETE THE PHRASE ALOUD:
...That sure came out of left field!

dirty pool *exp.* (billiards or pool) unfair or unethical behavior.

EXAMPLE: William hid my car keys so that I wouldn't be able to get to the chess tournament and compete against him. That's **dirty pool**!

TRANSLATION: William hid my car keys so that I wouldn't be able to get to the chess tournament and compete against him. That's **unfair, and unethical behavior**!

"REAL SPEAK": William hid my car keys so th't I wouldn' be able da get ta the chess tournament 'n compede against 'im. That's **dirdy pool**!

Origin: Originally used in reference to someone cheating at a game of pool and now used to refer to any unfair or dishonest behavior.

NOW YOU DO IT. COMPLETE THE PHRASE ALOUD:
... That's dirty pool!

off-base (to be [way]) *adj.* (baseball) to be badly mistaken, to be totally wrong.

EXAMPLE: I'm sorry if Anthony thought I was interested in him, but he was **[way] off-base** when he thought he could kiss me.

TRANSLATION: I'm sorry if Anthony thought I was interested in him, but he was **totally wrong** when he thought the could kiss me.

"REAL SPEAK": I'm sorry if Anthony thod I w'z int'rested 'n 'im, b'd 'e w'z **[way] off-base** when 'e thod 'e could kiss me.

Origin: In baseball, a player who is not touching a base (*off-base*) is vulnerable to being tagged out.

NOW YOU DO IT. COMPLETE THE PHRASE ALOUD:
Karen was off-base when she said...

play hardball (to) *exp.* (baseball) to behave or compete aggressively or ruthlessly.

EXAMPLE: Be careful when you negotiate your contract with Mr. Grant. He has a tendency to **play hardball**.

TRANSLATION: Be careful when you negotiate your contract with Mr. Grant. He has a tendency to **behave aggressively or ruthlessly.**

"REAL SPEAK": Be careful when ya negotiate yer contract with Mr. Grant. He has a tendency da **play hardball**.

Origin: Baseball is played with a small, hardball (as opposed to a bigger, softer ball used in the game of softball) whose speed and impact are extreme and, for that reason, can be dangerous.

NOW YOU DO IT. COMPLETE THE PHRASE ALOUD:

John played hardball with me when we...

right off the bat *exp.* (baseball) instantly.

EXAMPLE: I fell in love with the house **right off the bat** and bought it that very day.

TRANSLATION: I fell in love with the house **instantly** and bought it that very day.

"REAL SPEAK": I fell 'n love w'th the house **ride off the bat** 'n bod it that very day.

Origin: In baseball, when the ball comes in direct contact with the bat, it is sent forward in an instant.

NOW YOU DO IT. COMPLETE THE PHRASE ALOUD:

When I asked my boss for a raise, he said... right off the bat!

settle the score (to) *exp.* (general sports) to get revenge.

EXAMPLE: Grant got me fired from my job, but I **settled the score** by telling his wife that he was seeing another woman!

TRANSLATION: Grant got me fired from my job, but I **got revenge** by telling his wife that he was seeing another woman!

"REAL SPEAK": Grant got me fired fr'm my job, b'd I **seddled the score** by telling 'is wife th'd 'e w'z seeing another woman!

Origin: Keeping the score even maintains equality between two players or teams and prevents one from defeating the other.

Also: **score to settle with someone (to have a)** *exp.* to want revenge against someone.

NOW YOU DO IT. COMPLETE THE PHRASE ALOUD:

I'm going to settle the score with Robert because he...

score (to) *v.* to succeed in seducing someone, to succeed (in general).

EXAMPLE:
– Did you **score** last night?
– Are you kidding? She didn't even invite me up to her apartment.

TRANSLATION:
– Did you **succeed in seducing her** last night?
– Are you kidding? She didn't even invite me up to her apartment.

"REAL SPEAK":
– Did'ja **score** las' night?
– Are you kidding? She didn' even invite me up to 'er apartment.

Variation 1: **score big (to)** *exp.*

Variation 2: **score points (to)** *exp.*

NOW YOU DO IT. COMPLETE THE PHRASE ALOUD:
Last night Tim scored with...at...

tackle (to) *v.* (football) to try to solve a problem aggressively.

EXAMPLE: This is a huge problem, but I have to **tackle** it if I want to finish my work before leaving on vacation.

TRANSLATION: This is a huge problem, but I have to **try to solve it aggressively** if I want to finish my work before leaving on vacation.

"REAL SPEAK": This 'ez a huge problem, b'd I hafta **tackle** id if I wanna finish my work b'fore leaving on vacation.

Origin: In football, a player who tackles a member of the opposing team, removes that person (who could be a problem) from the action.

NOW YOU DO IT. COMPLETE THE PHRASE ALOUD:
Our problem is ... We need to tackle this problem as soon as possible.

throw in the towel (to) *exp.* (boxing) to admit defeat by quitting, to quit.

EXAMPLE: No matter how hard the job is or how many obstacles I have to overcome, I'll never **throw in the towel**.

TRANSLATION: No matter how hard the job is or how many obstacles I have to overcome, I'll never **admit defeat by quitting**.

"REAL SPEAK": No madder how hard the job is 'r how many obstacles I hafta overcome, a'll never **throw 'n the towel**.

Origin: In boxing, the manager of the losing boxer throws a towel into the ring to signify defeat and stop the fight.

NOW YOU DO IT. COMPLETE THE PHRASE ALOUD:
After being unsuccesful at... I finally decided to throw in the towel.

throw someone a curve (to) *exp.* (baseball – short for "to throw someone a curve ball") to surprise someone, usually in a negative way.

EXAMPLE: When the boss called me into his office, I was sure he was going to offer me a promotion. Instead, he told me that if I didn't start working harder, he'd fire me! He really **threw me a curve**!

TRANSLATION: When the boss called me into his office, I was sure he was going to offer me a promotion. Instead, he told me that if I didn't start working harder, he'd fire me! He really **surprised me**!

"REAL SPEAK": When the boss called me into 'is office, I w'z sher 'e w'z gonna offer me a pramotion. Instead, 'e told me th'd if I didn' start working harder, he'd fire me! He really **threw me a curve**!

Origin: In baseball, when the pitcher throws a ball that curves unexpectedly, it makes the ball harder to hit.

NOW YOU DO IT. COMPLETE THE PHRASE ALOUD:
Mary really threw me a curve when she...

touch base with someone (to) *exp.* (baseball) to make contact with someone.

EXAMPLE: I'll **touch base with you** tomorrow while I'm on vacation. I want to make sure everything is going well while I'm gone.

TRANSLATION: I'll **contact you** tomorrow while I'm on vacation. I want to make sure everything is going well while I'm gone.

"REAL SPEAK": A'll **touch base with ya** damorrow wall I'm on vacation. I wanna make sher ev'rything's going well wall I'm gone.

Origin: In baseball, the runner must make contact with each base in order to score a point.

NOW YOU DO IT. COMPLETE THE PHRASE ALOUD:
I'll touch base with you as soon as I...

LET'S PRACTICE!

A. CHOOSE THE RIGHT WORDS

Underline the words that best complete the sentences.

CD-A: TRACK 20

1. The boss refused to give the employees a raise. I think it's time to play (**hard**, **soft**, **rigid**) ball and threaten to quit!
2. I exercise every day and eat all the right things, but I just can't seem to lose weight. I'm ready to throw in the (**scarf**, **sheet**, **towel**).
3. I was having a nice conversation with Julie and then suddenly she started yelling at me for something I did ten years ago. That certainly came out of (**right**, **left**, **center**) field!
4. Robert let all the air out of my tires so that I would be late for my job interview. Then he went to the interview himself and got hired! That was dirty (**bowling**, **pool**, **tennis**)!
5. We need to bring in more money for the company. If we (**tackle**, **tangle**, **table**) this together, I know we can find a solution to this problem.
6. I need to leave for the airport right away. Let's talk later. I'll (**fondle**, **caress**, **touch**) base with you tonight.
7. Can you believe what Ernie did? He tried to (**snore**, **score**, **tackle**) with my mother!
8. I know I may be way (**off**, **on**, **up**) base, but is Jerry dating our math teacher? I saw them go into the movie theater last night!
9. Janet really (**tossed**, **hit**, **threw**) me a curve when she said she was moving out of the city. We've been best friends for ten years.
10. When David came into my office five years ago to ask for a job, I hired him right off the (**golf club**, **tennis racket**, **bat**)! I knew he'd be a valuable employee.
11. I'm tired of Michael spreading rumors about me. I'm ready to (**settle**, **relax**, **calm**) the score!
12. I wrote Ed a long letter apologizing for my behavior. The (**puck**, **ball**, **basketball**) is in his court now. If he wants to see me again, he'll have to call me.

B. CROSSWORD PUZZLE

Fill in the crossword puzzle by choosing the correct word from the list below.

AGGRESSIVELY	REVENGE
CONTACT	SEDUCING
INSTANTLY	SOLVE
MISTAKEN	SURPRISE
NEXT	UNETHICAL
QUITTING	UNEXPECTED

ACROSS

2. **throw someone a curve (to)** *exp.* to _____ someone, usually in a negative way.

14. **right off the bat** *exp.* _____.

19. **settle the score (to)** *exp.* to get _____.

25. **come out of left field (to)** *exp.* to be completely _____.

30. **dirty pool** *exp.* unfair or _____ behavior.

36. **score (to)** *v.* to succeed in _____ someone.

DOWN

7. **tackle (to)** *v.* to try to _____ a problem aggressively.

9. **off-base (to be)** adj. to be badly _____.

15. **play hardball (to)** *exp.* to behave or compete _____ or ruthlessly.

28. **throw in the towel (to)** *exp.* to admit defeat by _____.

29. **ball in one's court (to have the)** *exp.* to be responsible for taking the _____ action.

31. **touch base with someone (to)** *exp.* to make _____ with someone.

CROSSWORD PUZZLE

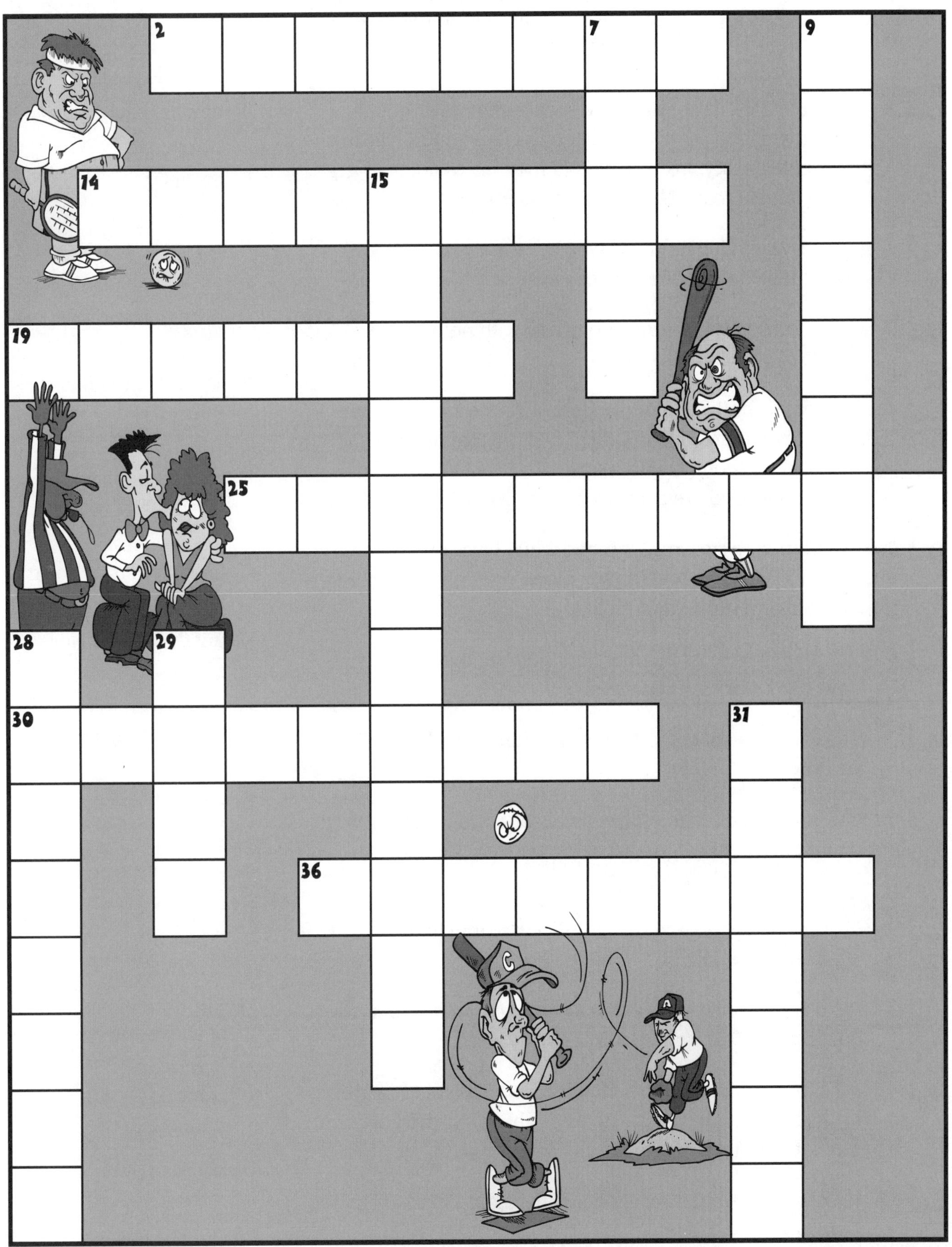

C. MATCH THE COLUMN

Match the words in boldface with their meaning in the right-hand column. Write the letter of the definition in the box. *Note:* Not all the answers will be used.

CD-A: TRACK 21

☐ 1. When Mark said he wanted to speak with me, I thought he was going to ask my advice on what to get his wife for their anniversary. Instead, he told me they're going to get divorced! He really ***threw me a curve***.

☐ 2. Anne's comment about my weight ***came out of left field***! It was so inappropriate!

☐ 3. If you think you can start a company with no money, you're ***off base***!

☐ 4. I know you and Ron are competing for the same job, but I think he has an advantage. He told me that he gave the owner of the company four tickets to Paris! I think if you want this job, you're going to need to ***play hardball***.

☐ 5. Oliver tried to steal my girlfriend while I was on vacation. Well, I'm going to ***settle the score*** right now. I'm going to tell his girlfriend what he did.

☐ 6. We need to discuss this more but I don't have time right now. Let's ***touch base*** tomorrow.

☐ 7. I heard you went out last night with Kim! So tell me, did you ***score***?

☐ 8. Our products used to sell very well, but as of this year, no one is purchasing them! What happened? We need to ***tackle*** this problem right away.

☐ 9. My new neighbor is a great guy. We became friends ***right off the bat***!

☐ 10. I told Greg exactly how much it would cost if he wants to buy my car. ***The ball's in his court now***.

☐ 11. I just found out that Bob lied to the boss and told him that I was arrested last year for stealing. That's why he got promoted instead of me! That's ***dirty pool***.

☐ 12. My new job is much harder than I thought! I'm ready to ***throw in the towel***.

A. contact each other

B. instantly

C. compete aggressively

D. get revenge

E. succeed in seducing her

F. was completely unexpected

G. try very hard to solve

H. unethical behavior

I. It's his turn to respond to the situation

J. admit defeat by quitting

K. badly mistaken

L. argue

M. surprised me in a negative way

N. ended the relationship

O. kissed in public

P. ignored me

FROM THE SLANGMAN FILES

More Sports Terms Used in Slang

There's no doubt about it. Sports have always been the most popular American pastime. American schoolchildren are introduced to the world of sports at an early age and are expected to participate in some type of sport activity in a class called *Physical Education* or, commonly, *Phys Ed*. Since Americans tend to live and breathe sports, it's no wonder that so many sports expressions have become part of our everyday usage, as the following list clearly demonstrates.

GENERAL SPORTS TERMS

choke (to) *v.* to be suddenly unable to do something due to stress and pressure • (lit.): to play suddenly poorly due to stress and pressure.

EXAMPLE: Mark spent hours preparing his presentation but when he got up in front of the executives, he **choked**.

TRANSLATION: Mark spent hours preparing his presentation but when he got up in front of the executives, he **was suddenly unable to present it well due to stress and pressure**.

"REAL SPEAK": Mark spen' hours preparing 'is presentation b't when 'e god up 'n fronnna the execudives, he **choked**.

Note: This term has been called the most popular slang term of this century and refers to any sport!

drop the ball (to) *exp.* to fail to complete one's responsibilities.

EXAMPLE: You promised you'd water my plants while I was on vacation. I can't believe you forgot. You really **dropped the ball**.

TRANSLATION: You promised you'd water my plants while I was on vacation. I can't believe you forgot. You really **failed to complete your responsibility**.

"REAL SPEAK": Ya promised ya'd wader my plants wall I w'z on vacation. I can't believe ya fergot. Ya really **dropped the ball**.

Origin: If the player carrying the ball drops it during a game, the game must stop until the ball is once again put into play.

even up the score (to) *exp.* to retaliate by doing something equal to what was done to you.

EXAMPLE: Shirley went out last week with my ex-boyfriend, but I **evened up the score** by going out with her ex-husband.

TRANSLATION: Shirley went out last week with my ex-boyfriend, but I **retaliated by doing something equal to what was done to me** by going out with her ex-husband.

"REAL SPEAK": Shirley wen' out las' week w'th my ex-boyfrien', b'd I **evened up the score** by going out with 'er ex-husband.

good sport *n.* an accommodating and agreeable person.

EXAMPLE: Every time Ernie asks his grandmother to play games with him, she always says yes. She's such a **good sport**.

TRANSLATION: Every time Ernie asks his grandmother to play games with him, she always says yes. She's such an **accommodating and agreeable person**.

"REAL SPEAK": Ev'ry time Ernie asks 'is gran'mother da play games w'th 'im, she ahweez says yes. She's such a **good sport**.

Variation: **real sport** *exp.*

Antonym 1: **bad sport** *exp.*

Antonym 2: **spoilsport** *exp.*

play by the rules (to) *exp.* to conduct oneself without breaking the rules, either legally or ethically.

EXAMPLE: Jim is taking the boss' daughter to dinner in order to get the promotion. He's not **playing by the rules**!

TRANSLATION: Jim is taking the boss' daughter to dinner in order to get the promotion. He's not **conducting himself ethically**!

"REAL SPEAK": Jim's taking the boss' dawder da dinner 'n order da get the pramotion. He's not **playing by the rules**!

start the ball rolling (to) *exp.* to begin something.

EXAMPLE: We have a lot of work to finish by next week. We'd better **start the ball rolling**.

TRANSLATION: We have a lot of work to finish by next week. We'd better **begin**.

"REAL SPEAK": We have a lod 'a work ta finish by nex' week. We' bedder **start the ball rolling**.

team player *exp.* a person who works well with others.

EXAMPLE: In order to be successful in this company, you have to forget about being uncooperative and learn to be a **team player**.

TRANSLATION: In order to be successful in this company, you have to forget about being uncooperative and learn to be a **person who works well with others**.

"REAL SPEAK": In order da be successful 'n this comp'ny, ya hafta ferged about being uncooperadive 'n learn da be a **team player**.

BASEBALL

ballpark *adj.* approximate.

EXAMPLE: Can you give me a **ballpark** price on what a new compact car costs?

TRANSLATION: Can you give me an **approximate** price on what a new compact car costs?

"REAL SPEAK": C'n ya gimme a **ballpark** price on whad a new compac' car costs?

batting a thousand (to be) *exp*. to be extremely successful.

EXAMPLE: Fred could never get a date but now that he's been exercising, he's been **batting a thousand**.

TRANSLATION: Fred could never get a date but now that he's been exercising, he's been **extremely successful**.

"REAL SPEAK": Fred could never ged a date b't now th'd 'e's been exercising, he's been **badding a thousan'**.

Origin: One thousand is a perfect batting percentage, an ideal that is impossible to achieve.

go to bat for someone (to) *exp*. to defend someone.

EXAMPLE: When I was about to get fired, my manager **went to bat for me** and convinced the boss to keep me employed.

TRANSLATION: When I was about to get fired, my manager **defended me** and convinced the boss to keep me employed.

"REAL SPEAK": When I w'z about ta get fired, my manager **went ta bat fer me** 'n convinced the boss ta keep me employed.

Origin: Said of a baseball player who bats in another player's place.

in the ballpark *exp*. within acceptable limits.

EXAMPLE: You won't believe the salary the boss offered me. It wasn't even **in the ballpark**! I deserve twice as much!

TRANSLATION: You won't believe the salary the boss offered me. It wasn't even **within acceptable limits**! I deserve twice as much!

"REAL SPEAK": You won't believe the salary the boss offered me. It wasn' even **in the ballpark**! I deserve twice 'ez much!

Origin: The ballpark is the stadium in which a baseball game is played.

out in left field (to be) *exp*. to be completely mistaken.

EXAMPLE: Jeff actually thought I was interested in his girlfriend. I told him he was **out in left field**!

TRANSLATION: Jeff actually thought I was interested in his girlfriend. I told him he was **completely mistaken**!

"REAL SPEAK": Jeff akshelly thod I w'z int'rested 'n 'is girlfriend. I told 'im 'e w'z **out 'n lef' field**!

Variation: **way out in left field (to be)** *exp*. to be totally and completely mistaken.

Origin: Beyond the baseball diamond (which is where most of the activity takes place during a game) is a large area which is divided into three fields: right field, center field, and left field.

out of one's league (to be) *exp*. • **1.** to be in a situation where everyone is more experienced than you • **2**. said of someone who is unattainable.

EXAMPLE 1: I just got a job working with some of the smartest scientists in the country. I think I'm **out of my league**. I just graduated college last week!

TRANSLATION: I just got a job working with some of the smartest scientists in the country. I think I'm **in a situation where everyone is more experienced than I am**. I just graduated college last week!

"REAL SPEAK": I jus' god a job working w'th some 'a the smardes' scientis' 'n the country. I think I'm **oudda my league**. I jus' gradjuaded college las' week!

EXAMPLE 2: I'd love to go out with Linda but she's **out of my league**. She's so beautiful! She probably only likes guys as gorgeous as she is.

TRANSLATION: I'd love to go out with Linda but she's **unattainable for someone like me**. She's so beautiful! She probably only likes guys as gorgeous as she is.

"REAL SPEAK": I'd love da go out w'th Linda b't she's **oudda my league**. She's so beaudiful! She prob'ly only likes guys 'ez gorgeous 'ez she is.

Origin: Said of a baseball player who is promoted to the major leagues before he has the needed experience.

pinch-hit (to) *exp.* to substitute for someone, usually in an emergency.

EXAMPLE: I have to leave the office because of an emergency at home. Can you **pinch-hit** for me at the meeting today?

TRANSLATION: I have to leave the office because of an emergency at home. Can you **substitute** for me at the meeting today?

"REAL SPEAK": I hafta leave the office b'cuz 'ev 'n emergency 'it home. C'n ya **pinch-hit** fer me 'it the meeding taday?

Origin: When a coach feels another batter will do better than the one currently at bat, he will substitute one batter for another.

Also: **pinch hitter** *exp.* substitute, usually in an emergency.

play ball (to) *exp.* to cooperate.

EXAMPLE: If we don't **play ball** with the board of education, we'll never get the money we need for the after-school programs.

TRANSLATION: If we don't **cooperate** with the board of education, we'll never get the money we need for the after-school programs.

"REAL SPEAK": If we don't **play ball** w'th the board 'ev edjacation, we'll never get the money we need fer the after-school programs.

Origin: The umpire of a baseball game calls out, "Play ball!" to start the game.

strike out (to) *v.* to fail.

EXAMPLE: Lance tried to get the boss to give him a raise but he **struck out**.

TRANSLATION: Lance tried to get the boss to give him a raise but he **failed**.

"REAL SPEAK": Lance tried da get the boss ta give 'im a raise b'd 'e **struck out**.

Origin: A batter is given three tries to hit a properly thrown (or *pitched*) ball. After he has missed the ball three times, he *strikes out* and loses his turn.

two strikes against someone *exp.* two negative traits associated with a person.

EXAMPLE: I know that Pete wants to be a model but he's overweight and has bad skin. That's **two strikes against him**.

TRANSLATION: I know that Pete wants to be a model but he's overweight and has bad skin. That's **two negative traits against him**.

"REAL SPEAK": I know th't Pete wansta be a model b'd 'e's overweight 'n has bad skin. That's **two strikes against 'im**.

Origin: In baseball, when a batter misses the ball, that's called a *strike*. After three strikes, the player loses his turn.

BASKETBALL

give something one's best shot (to) *exp.* to try one's best to accomplish a goal.

EXAMPLE: I'm nervous about my audition, but I'm going to **give it my best shot**. Maybe I'll actually get the role!

TRANSLATION: I'm nervous about my audition, but I'm going to **try my best**. Maybe I'll actually get the role!

"REAL SPEAK": I'm nervous about my audition, b'd I'm gonna **give it my bes' shot**. Maybe a'll akshelly get the role!

Origin: A *shot* is a basketball player's attempt to throw the ball into the hoop.

"He shoots, he scores!" *exp.* "He attempts something and is successful!"

EXAMPLE: You got the job?! That's great! **He shoots, he scores!**

TRANSLATION: You got the job?! That's great! **You were successful!**

"REAL SPEAK": Ya got the job?! That's great! **He shoots, 'e scores!**

Origin: During a basketball game, if a player makes the shoot (an attempt at throwing the ball into the hoop), the TV or radio announcer describes the action as: *"He shoots, he scores!"* literally meaning, "He is successful at making the shot and earns points for his team!"

BOXING

hit someone below the belt (to) *exp.* to do or say something shameful or despicable to someone that attacks him/her in a vulnerable area.

EXAMPLE: Bob told the boss that I have a drinking problem so that he could get the promotion instead of me. He certainly **hit me below the belt**.

TRANSLATION: Bob told the boss that I have a drinking problem so that he could get the promotion instead of me. He certainly **did something shameful to me**.

"REAL SPEAK": Bob told the boss th'd I have a drinking problem so th'd 'e could get the pramotion instead 'a me. He certainly **hit me b'low the belt**.

Variation: **hitting below the belt** *exp.* • *That sure is* ***hitting below the belt****!; That sure is* ***despicable****!*

Origin: In boxing, it is considered unethical to disable one's opponent by hitting him below the belt where he is more sensitive.

heavyweight *n.* an influential and powerful person.

EXAMPLE: Beth started as secretary at Paramount Studios, but she has worked her way to the top. Now she's a **heavyweight** in the movie business.

TRANSLATION: Beth started as a secretary at Paramount Studios but she has worked her way to the top. Now she's an **influential and powerful person** in the movie business.

"REAL SPEAK": Beth starded 'ez a secretary 'it Paramount Studios, b't she's worked 'er way da the top. Now she's a **heavywade** 'n the movie bizness.

Origin: Boxers only fight opponents in their same weight class (such as bantamweight, featherweight, lightweight, middleweight, light heavyweight, heavyweight).

Also: **lightweight** *n.* a person with little influence or importance.

pull any punches (not to) *exp.* not to hold back in one's criticism.

EXAMPLE: Karen told Mark exactly what she thought of him. You should have heard the terrible things she said. She **doesn't pull any punches**.

TRANSLATION: Karen told Mark exactly what she thought of him. You should have heard the terrible things she said. She **doesn't hold back in her criticisms**.

"REAL SPEAK": Karen told Mark exac'ly what she thod of 'im. Ya should 'ev heard the terr'ble things she said. She **doesn' pull any punches**.

Origin: Said of a boxer who holds back from punching his opponent hard, usually when the fight has been staged.

roll with the punches (to) *exp.* to accept something unpleasant without fighting back.

EXAMPLE: I know the boss is always mean to you, but just try to **roll with the punches**. He's retiring in just one more week.

TRANSLATION: I know the boss is always mean to you, but just try to **accept it without fighting back**. He's retiring in just one more week.

"REAL SPEAK": I know the boss 'ez ahweez mean da you, b't jus' try da **roll w'th the punches**. He's retiring 'n jus' one more week.

Origin: If a boxer *rolls with the punches* (literally, "to allow one's body to move in the direction of the punches without resisting"), he is less likely to get hurt.

saved by the bell (to be) *exp.* to get out of a bad situation due to luck.

EXAMPLE:
– Oh, no. There's Pam and she's coming this way! If she sees us, she'll talk to us for hours.
– Look! She got stopped by some guy. **Saved by the bell**!

TRANSLATION:
– Oh, no. There's Pam and she's coming this way! If she sees us, she'll talk to us for hours.
– Look! She got stopped by some guy. **We got out of that bad situation by luck**!

"REAL SPEAK":
– Oh, no. There's Pam 'n she's coming this way! If she sees us, she'll talk ta us fer hours.
– Look! She got stop' by s'm guy. **Saved by the bell**!

Origin: The moment the bell rings, the boxers must stop fighting. For the losing boxer, he is often saved from getting more injuries thanks to the bell.

teach someone the ropes (to) *exp.* to teach someone the basics of a new job.

EXAMPLE: Since you're new here, let me **teach you the ropes**.

TRANSLATION: Since you're new here, let me **teach the basics of the job**.

"REAL SPEAK": Since y'r new here, lemme **teach ya the ropes**.

Origin: *Ropes* refer to the boxing ring, since it is enclosed by ropes. Therefore, in boxing slang, *to teach someone the ropes* means "to teach someone how to box within the ropes (or ring)."

Variation: **show someone the ropes (to)** *exp.*

FOOTBALL

kick off (to) *v.* to start something.

EXAMPLE: We're going to **kick off** the party by having a comedian perform. Then we're going to have a live band play the entire night!

TRANSLATION: We're going to **start** the party by having a comedian perform. Then we're going to have a live band play the entire night!

"REAL SPEAK": We're gonna **kick off** the pardy by having a comedian perform. Then w'r gonna have a live ban' play the entire night!

Origin: In football, the ball is "kicked off" to start the game or a play.

take the ball and run with it (to) *exp.* to accept an opportunity and make the most of it.

EXAMPLE: – My boss offered me a promotion to vice president of the company. The only problem is that I would have to move to a different city.
– This is an amazing opportunity for you. If I were you, I'd **take the ball and run with it**.

TRANSLATION: – My boss offered me a promotion to vice president of the company. The only problem is that I would have to move to a different city.
– This is an amazing opportunity for you. If I were you, I'd **accept the opportunity and make the most of it**.

"REAL SPEAK": – My boss offered me a pramotion da vice president 'a the comp'ny. The only problem is th'd I'd hafta move to a diff'rent cidy.
– This 'ez 'n amazing oppertunidy fer you. If I were you, I'd **take the ball 'n run w'th it**.

Origin: Once the ball is passed to the player known as the *receiver*, he must take the ball and run with it to the goal in order to score points for the team.

HORSE RACING

first out of the gate (to be) *exp.* to be the first to go toward a common goal.

EXAMPLE: Your idea for the new product is great! Let's start working on it right away. We need to be **first out of the gate**.

TRANSLATION: Your idea for the new product is great! Let's start working on it right away. We need to be **the first company to produce it**.

"REAL SPEAK": Yer idea fer the new produc's great! Let's start working on it ride away. We need da be **first outta the gate**.

Origin: The horse that is *first out of the gate* (which is lifted when the starting bell sounds at the beginning of a race) has an advantage over the other horses.

free rein (to have) *exp.* to be allowed to do anything one wants without having to get permission.

EXAMPLE: In my new job, I **have free rein** to hire any assistant I want.

TRANSLATION: In my new job, I am **allowed** to hire any assistant I want **without having to get permission**.

"REAL SPEAK": In my new job, I have **free rein** da hire any assistant I want.

Origin: When a horse's reins are pulled back, the horse slows down. But when the reins are completely loose, the horse is free to move as quickly as it can.

in the home stretch (to be) *exp.* to be close to completion.

EXAMPLE: Okay, everybody. Don't stop working now. We're **in the home stretch**!

TRANSLATION: Okay, everybody. Don't stop working now. We're **close to completion**!

"REAL SPEAK": Okay, ev'rybody. Don't working now. W'r **'n the home stretch**!

Origin: The *home stretch* is the last length of straight track before the finish line.

in the running (to be) *exp.* to be in consideration for something.

EXAMPLE: I know **I'm in the running** for the job at the advertising agency but I think someone with more experience will get it.

TRANSLATION: I know **I'm being considered** for the job at the advertising agency but I think someone with more experience will get it.

"REAL SPEAK": I know **I'm 'n the running** fer the job 'it the advertising agency b'd I think someone w'th more experience'll ged it.

Origin: The horses who perform well enough during the course of the race are considered to be *in the running* as potential winners.

long shot *n.* said of something that is not likely to happen.

EXAMPLE: You're going to ask Tom Cruise to donate money to your charity? Well, it's a **long shot** but maybe it's a cause that's important to him.

TRANSLATION: You're going to ask Tom Cruise to donate money to your charity? Well, it's **not likey to happen** but maybe it's a cause that's important to him.

"REAL SPEAK": Y'r gonna ask Tom Cruise ta donate money ta yer charidy? Well, it's a **long shot** b't maybe it's a cause th't's important to 'im.

Origin: A racehorse is called a *long shot* if the horse isn't likey to win but pays off greatly if it does.

neck and neck *exp.* even or very close (as in a competition).

EXAMPLE: We were **neck and neck** the whole race but I managed to beat Hilary by a tenth of a second.

TRANSLATION: We were **even** the whole race but I managed to beat Hilary by a tenth of a second.

"REAL SPEAK": We were **neck 'n neck** the whole race b'd I manage' ta beat Hilary by a tenth 'ev a second.

Origin: When two or more horses are running next to each other at exactly the same speed, they are considered to be running *neck and neck*.

off and running (to be) *exp.* to be acting with enthusiasm and energy.

EXAMPLE: From the moment Sylvester got approval to begin the project, he **was off and running** and never stopped until he finished.

TRANSLATION: From the moment Sylvester got approval to begin the project, he **acted with enthusiasm and energy** and never stopped until he finished.

"REAL SPEAK": Fr'm the moment Sylvester god approval ta begin the project, he **w'z off 'n running** 'n never stopped until 'e finished.

Origin: When the gates open and the horses exit their chutes, the typical comment of the race announcer is, "And they're off 'n running!"

ICE SKATING

skating on thin ice (to be) *exp.* to be in a risky situation.

EXAMPLE: My girlfriend was angry with me for forgetting her birthday last year. I'm **skating on thin ice**. If I forget again this year, she'll kill me!

TRANSLATION: My girlfriend was angry with me for forgetting her birthday last year. I'm **in a risky situation**. If I forget again this year, she'll kill me!

"REAL SPEAK": My girlfrien' w'z angry w'th me fer fergedding 'er birthday last year. I'm **skading on thin ice**. If I ferged again this year, she'll kill me!

Origin: A skater must always be careful not to skate on thin ice, or he/she risks falling through it.

POOL

call the shots (to) *exp.* to be in charge and make decisions.

EXAMPLE: You've got to stop disagreeing with everything the boss does. He **calls the shots** around here, not you.

TRANSLATION: You've got to stop disagreeing with everything the boss does. He **calls the shots** around here, not you.

"REAL SPEAK": Ya godda stop disagreeing w'th ev'rything the boss does. He **calls the shots** aroun' here, not you.

Origin: In a game of pool, one must state into which pocket he or she intends to shoot the ball. This is called "calling the shots."

RACE CAR DRIVING

inside track (to have the) *exp.* to have an advantage over one's competition.

EXAMPLE: I think Caroline is going to get the job because she **has the inside track**. She's the only one with experience.

TRANSLATION: I think Caroline is going to get the job because she **has an advantage over her competition**. She's the only one with experience.

"REAL SPEAK": I think Caroline's gonna get the job b'cuz she **has the inside track**. She's the only one with experience.

Origin: In race car driving, there are several tracks which are each occupied by a single driver. The driver who is positioned in the track closest to the center of the race course, called *the inside track*, has less distance to travel.

pit stop (to make a) *exp.* to make a brief stop (while traveling or working) in order to use the lavatory facilities.

EXAMPLE: Do you mind pulling over at the next gas station? I need to **make a pit stop**.

TRANSLATION: Do you mind pulling over at the next gas station? I need to **use the lavatory**.

"REAL SPEAK": Ya min' pulling over 'it the nex' gas station? I need da **make a pit stop**.

Origin: During a race, occasionally race cars need to stop in what is known as the *pit*, in order to be serviced.

ROWING

not to have both oars in the water *exp.* (humorous) to be eccentric, to be a little crazy.

EXAMPLE: My new neighbor **doesn't have both oars in the water**. Every morning, I see her having a conversation with the tree in her front yard.

TRANSLATION: My new neighbor **is a little crazy**. Every morning, I see her having a conversation with the tree in her front yard.

"REAL SPEAK": My new neighber **doesn' have both oars 'n the wader**. Ev'ry morning, I see 'er having a conversation w'th the tree 'n 'er front yard.

Origin: When rowing, if both oars are not properly in the water, you will not being able to travel in a forward motion normally.

SAILING

smooth sailing [ahead] *exp.* said of a situation which presents no obstacles.

EXAMPLE: It was hard preparing all the food for the party but now it's **smooth sailing [ahead]**. All we have to do is clean the house and we'll be ready for the guests.

TRANSLATION: It was hard preparing all the food for the party but now it's **going to be easy from this point**. All we have to do is clean the house and we'll be ready for the guests.

"REAL SPEAK": It w'z hard praparing all the food fer the pardy b't now it's **smooth sailing [ahead]**. All we hafta do 'ez clean the house 'n we'll be ready fer the guests.

take the wind out of one's sails (to) *exp.* to cause someone to lose his or her enthusiasm.

EXAMPLE: Debbie **took the wind out of my sails** when she told me she was planning on marrying someone else.

TRANSLATION: Debbie **caused me to lose my enthusiasm** when she told me she was planning on marrying someone else.

"REAL SPEAK": Debbie **took the wind oudda my sails** when she tol' me she w'z planning on marrying someone else.

Origin: Without wind, a sailboat stops and cannot continue its course.

SWIMMING

go off the deep end (to) *exp.* to go crazy.

EXAMPLE: After working in a stressful job for twenty years, my uncle finally **went off the deep end**.

TRANSLATION: After working in a stressful job for twenty years, my uncle finally **went crazy**.

"REAL SPEAK": After working in a stressful job fer twen'y years, my uncle fin'lly **wen' off the deep end**.

Origin: This expression refers to going into a swimming pool at the deep end, where a non-swimmer could easily drown.

keep one's head above water (to) *exp.* to keep oneself from getting overwhelmed with work or risk "drowning."

EXAMPLE: Congratulations on your new job as an executive. It's going to be a lot more work for you, but I'm sure you'll **keep your head above water**.

TRANSLATION: Congratulations on your new job as an executive. It's going to be a lot more work for you, but I'm sure you'll **keep yourself from getting overwhelmed**.

"REAL SPEAK": C'ngradjalations on yer new job 'ez 'n execudive. It's gonna be a lot more work fer ya, b'd I'm sher ya'll **keep yer head above wader**.

make a splash (to) *exp.* to become very successful (and get a lot of attention as one would if jumping into a pool and making a big splash).

EXAMPLE: I hear that your brother **made a splash** in Hollywood! Is it true he's going to be in three movies?

TRANSLATION: I hear that your brother **became very successful** in Hollywood! Is it true he's going to be in three movies?

"REAL SPEAK": I hear th't cher brother **made a splash** 'n Hollywood! Izit true 'e's gonna be 'n three movies?

TRACK AND FIELD

good track record (to have a) *exp.* to have a personal history of being successful and experienced.

EXAMPLE: I think we should hire Nicholas for the job. He has a **good track record** in this type of work.

TRANSLATION: I think we should hire Nicholas for the job. He has a **personal history of being successful and experienced** in this type of work.

"REAL SPEAK": I think we should hire Nichalas fer the job. He 'as a **good track record** 'n this type 'a work.

MARGE IS THE BIGGEST KLUTZ!

Foreign Words Used in Everyday Conversation

THIS LESSON FEATURES 12 FOREIGN WORDS COMMONLY USED IN ENGLISH

LET'S WARM UP!

MATCH THE PICTURES

As a fun way to get started, see if you can guess the meaning of the new slang words and expressions on the opposite page by using the pictures below and following the context of the sentences.

1

2

3

4

5

I LOVE YOU BABY, BUT YOU BETTER LEAVE BEFORE MY WIFE COMES HOME!

6

7

1. Sharon and Irv are ***gung-ho*** about their new house!
   Definition: *"enthusiastic"*
   ❑ True ❑ False

2. My niece is already in ***kindergarten*** and she's only three years old.
   Definition: *"gardening school"*
   ❑ True ❑ False

3. Baking has always been Bertha's ***forte***. She bakes the most amazing cakes!
   Definition: *"skill at which she excels"*
   ❑ True ❑ False

4. My girlfriend works in a clothing ***boutique*** in Beverly Hills.
   Definition: *"factory"*
   ❑ True ❑ False

5. You won't believe what Ralph said to me today, and this is ***verbatim***...
   Definition: *"what he said more or less"*
   ❑ *True* ❑ *False*

6. Ever since Eric started bodybuilding, he thinks he's super ***macho***.
   Definition: *"manly in an aggressive and even exaggerated way"*
   ❑ True ❑ False

7. Laurie is so ***blasé*** about everything. Nothing gets her excited any more.
   Definition: *"happy"*
   ❑ True ❑ False

8. I felt tremendous ***angst*** during my job interview!
   Definition: *"joy"*
   ❑ True ❑ False

9. Tina is such a ***prima donna***. If she doesn't get everything she wants, including everyone's attention, she gets upset.
   Definition: *"temperamental and conceited person"*
   ❑ True ❑ False

10. All three of us are best friends. There was ***camaraderie*** between us instantly.
    Definition: *"friendship"*
    ❑ True ❑ False

11. My uncle is such a ***klutz***. He always has stupid, little accidents.
    Definition: *"genius"*
    ❑ True ❑ False

12. Our new boss expects everyone to ***kowtow*** to him. He really enjoys that kind of power!
    Definition: *"act in a very submissive and subservient manner"*
    ❑ True ❑ False

I LOVE YOU BABY, BUT YOU BETTER LEAVE BEFORE MY WIFE COMES HOME!

LET'S TALK!

A. DIALOGUE USING SLANG & IDIOMS

The words introduced on the first two pages are used in the dialogue below. See if you can understand the conversation. *Note:* The translation of the words in boldface is on the right-hand page.

CD-A: TRACK 22

Marge: I think I'm going to get that job working in the perfume **boutique**!

Carla: Really? And you weren't even very **gung-ho** about going to the interview. You were so **blasé** about it.

Marge: Are you kidding? I was full of **angst**. I always feel like such a **klutz** at interviews. And working behind a counter isn't exactly my **forte**.

Carla: So, what happened at the interview that makes you think you got the job?

Marge: Well, I figured it was going to be like all the other interviews I've been on this week. Either I'll be interviewed by a **prima donna** or some **macho** guy who thinks women should **kowtow** to the boss. Anyway, as soon as I walked in, the nicest woman greeted me. We had instant **camaraderie** and I kept having this feeling that I knew her. I can't tell you what we said **verbatim**, but after a few moments, we realized that we were best friends in **kindergarten**!

B. DIALOGUE TRANSLATED INTO STANDARD ENGLISH

LET'S SEE HOW MUCH YOU REMEMBER!
Just for fun, move around in random order to the words and expressions in boldface below. See if you can remember their slang equivalents without looking at the left-hand page!

Marge: I think I'm going to get that job working in the perfume **shop**!

Carla: Really? And you weren't even very **enthusiastic** about going to the interview. You were so **casual** about it.

Marge: Are you kidding? I was full of **anxiety**. I always feel like such an **awkward person** at interviews. And working behind a counter isn't exactly my **specialty**.

Carla: So, what happened at the interview that makes you think you got the job?

Marge: Well, I figured it was going to be like all the other interviews I've been on this week. Either I'll be interviewed by an **arrogant woman** or some **overly masculine** guy who thinks women should **act in a subserviant manner** to the boss. Anyway, as soon as I walked in, the nicest woman greeted me. We had instant **friendly feelings toward each other** and I kept having this feeling that I knew her. I can't tell you what we said **in the exact words**, but after a few moments, we realized that we were best friends in **our first year of primary school**!

C. DIALOGUE USING "REAL SPEAK"

The dialogue below demonstrates how the slang conversation on the previous page would *really* be spoken by native speakers!

CD-A: TRACK 22

Marge: I think I'm gonna get that job working in the perfume **boutique**!

Carla: Really? An' you wern' even very **gung-ho** about going ta the in'erview. You were so **blasé** aboud it.

Marge: You kidding? I w'z full 'ev **angst**. I ahweez feel like such a **klutz** 'id in'erviews. An' working behind a coun'er isn' exactly my **forte**.

Carla: So, what happened 'it the in'erview that makes ya think ya got the job?

Marge: Well, I figured it w'z gonna be like all the other in'erviews I've been on this week. Either a'll be in'erviewed by a **prima donna** 'r s'm **macho** guy 'oo thinks women should **kowtow** ta the boss. Anyway, as soon 'ez I walked in, the nicest woman greeded me. We had instant **camaraderie** an' I kept having this feeling th'd I knew 'er. I can't tell ya what we said **verbadim**, b'd after a few moments, we realized th't we were best friends 'n **kindergarden**!

LET'S LEARN!

VOCABULARY

The following words and expressions were used in the previous dialogues. Let's take a closer look at what they mean.

CD-A: TRACK 23

angst *n.* (from German) a feeling of anxiety.

EXAMPLE: I feel such **angst** whenever the boss comes to review the employees! He's always so critical!

TRANSLATION: I feel such **anxiety** whenever the boss comes to review the employees! He's always so critical!

"REAL SPEAK": I feel such **angst** whenever the boss comes ta review the employees! He's ahweez so cridical!

NOW YOU DO IT. COMPLETE THE PHRASE ALOUD:
I also feel such anst whenever I...

blasé *adj.* (from French) indifferent, uninterested.

EXAMPLE: Nothing impresses Elizabeth anymore. She is **blasé** about everything.

TRANSLATION: Nothing impresses Elizabeth anymore. She is **indifferent** about everything.

"REAL SPEAK": Nothing impresses Elizabeth anymore. She's **blasé** aboud ev'rything.

NOW YOU DO IT. COMPLETE THE PHRASE ALOUD:
How could you possibly be blasé about...?

boutique *n.* (from French) a small shop that sells specialty items.

EXAMPLE: My mother works in a clothing **boutique** in Beverly Hills. She meets movie stars every day!

TRANSLATION: My mother works in a clothing **shop** in Beverly Hills. She meets movie stars every day!

"REAL SPEAK": My mother works 'n a clothing **boutique** 'n Beverly Hills. She meets movie stars ev'ry day!

NOW YOU DO IT. COMPLETE THE PHRASE ALOUD:
I always buy... at the boutique down the street.

camaraderie *n.* (from French) a feeling of friendship among people.

EXAMPLE: The **camaraderie** of our entire staff is what makes this company function so efficiently and successfully.

TRANSLATION: The **feeling of friendship** of our entire staff is what makes this company function so efficiently and successfully.

"REAL SPEAK": The **camaraderie** 'ev 'ar entire staff 'ez what makes this comp'ny function so efficiently 'n successfully.

NOW YOU DO IT. COMPLETE THE PHRASE ALOUD:
I admire the camaraderie between...and...

forte *n.* (from Italian – pronounced "fortay" or "fort") a skill at which a person excels.

EXAMPLE: Baking has always been my aunt's **forte**. For my birthday, she made me a cake that was 12 feet tall!

TRANSLATION: Baking has always been my aunt's **skill at which she excels**. For my birthday, she made me a cake that was 12 feet tall!

"REAL SPEAK": Baking's ahweez been my aunt's **fortay**. Fer my birthday, she made me a cake that w'z 12 feet tall!

Note: The noun *forte* is often mispronounced by Americans, who typically say "for-tay" instead of "forte" which, according to the dictionary, is the correct pronunciation. "For-tay" is only correct when used in a musical context in which it means to perfom the music "loudly."

NOW YOU DO IT. COMPLETE THE PHRASE ALOUD:
... is my forte!

gung-ho *adj.* (from Chinese) enthusiastic.

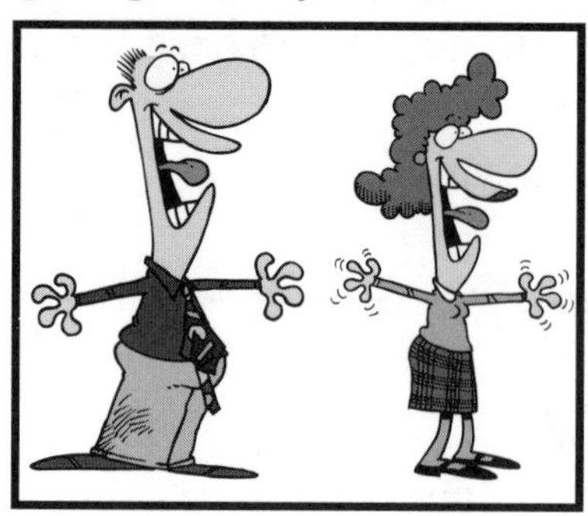

EXAMPLE: We're all **gung-ho** about the camping trip this weekend. It's going to be so much fun!

TRANSLATION: We're all **enthusiastic** about the camping trip this weekend. It's going to be so much fun!

"REAL SPEAK": W'r all **gung-ho** about the camping trip this weekend. It's gonna be so much fun!

NOW YOU DO IT. COMPLETE THE PHRASE ALOUD:
I'm really gung-ho about...

kindergarten *n.* (from German) a pre-first grade program for four-year-old to six-year-old children that serves as an introduction to school.

EXAMPLE:: My grandson goes to a **kindergarten** for exceptional children. He can already read and write. In fact, he just started to write a novel!

TRANSLATION: My grandson goes to a **pre-first grade school** for exceptional children. He can already read and write. In fact, he just started to write a novel!

"REAL SPEAK": My gran'son goes to a **kindergarden** fer exceptional children. He c'n ahready read 'n write. In fact, 'e jus' started ta wride a novel!

NOW YOU DO IT. COMPLETE THE PHRASE ALOUD:
Ralph is going to start kindergarten in...

klutz *n.* (from Yiddish) a clumsy person.

EXAMPLE: Clifford is such a **klutz**! He spilled coffee all over his new computer!

TRANSLATION: Clifford is such a **clumsy person**! He spilled coffee all over his new computer!

"REAL SPEAK": Clifford's such a **klutz**! He spilled coffee all over 'is new c'mpuder!

NOW YOU DO IT. COMPLETE THE PHRASE ALOUD:
I'm such a klutz! Today I...

kowtow [to someone] (to) *v.* (from Chinese) to act in a very submissive and subservient manner.

EXAMPLE: Our new boss expects everyone to **kowtow** to him. Our old boss treated everyone as equals.

TRANSLATION: Our new boss expects everyone to **act in a very submissive and subservient manner t**oward him. Our old boss treated everyone as equals.

"REAL SPEAK": 'Ar new boss expec's ev'ryone ta **kowtow** to 'im. 'Ar ol' boss treaded ev'ryone 'ez equals.

NOW YOU DO IT. COMPLETE THE PHRASE ALOUD:
I'm tired of being expected to kowtow to...

macho *adj.* (from Spanish) manly in an aggressive and even exaggerated way.

EXAMPLE: Ever since Ed started getting muscular, he's been acting so **macho**! I prefer a guy who is sensitive, sweet, and not afraid to show his emotions.

TRANSLATION: Ever since Ed started getting muscular, he's been acting so **manly in an aggressive and even exaggerated way**! I prefer a guy who is sensitive, sweet, and not afraid to show his emotions.

"REAL SPEAK": Ever since Ed starded gedding musculer, he's been acting so **macho**! I prefer a guy who's sensidive, sweet, 'n nod afraid ta show 'is emotions.

NOW YOU DO IT. COMPLETE THE PHRASE ALOUD:
...acts so macho all the time! I think he acts that way out of insecurity.

prima donna *n.* (from Italian) a temperamental and conceited person (either man or woman) • (lit.): the principal female singer in an opera company.

EXAMPLE: We were going to ask Gladys to be part of our community theater but she is such a **prima donna** that she can't get along with anyone.

TRANSLATION: We were going to ask Gladys to be part of our community theater but she is such a **temperamental and conceited person** that she can't get along with anyone.

"REAL SPEAK": We were gonna ask Gladys ta be pard 'ev 'ar communidy theeder b't she's such a **preema donna** th't she can't ged along with anyone.

Synonym: **diva** *n.*

NOW YOU DO IT. COMPLETE THE PHRASE ALOUD:
Janet is such a prima donna! Last night...

verbatim *adv.* (from Latin) in the exact words.

EXAMPLE: I repeated what Nicholas said **verbatim** without changing a word of it.

TRANSLATION: I repeated what Nicholas said **in his exact words** without changing a word of it.

"REAL SPEAK": I repeaded what Nicholas said **verbadim** without changing a word 'ev it.

NOW YOU DO IT. COMPLETE THE PHRASE ALOUD:
When I asked Brad how he was feeling, here's what he said verbatim...

LET'S PRACTICE!

CD-A: TRACK 24

A. I KNOW THE ANSWER, BUT WHAT'S THE QUESTION?

Read the answer and place a check next to the correct question.

1.

The answer is...

Yes, he's very gung-ho about it!

Questions:

- ☐ Is Ed excited about starting his new job?
- ☐ Did your father finally arrive?
- ☐ Has your uncle been in town long?

2.

The answer is...

Because she's a prima donna and has to have everything her way!

Questions:

- ☐ Why is Erin laughing?
- ☐ Why is Michelle yelling at everyone?
- ☐ How does Carol stay in such good shape?

3.

The answer is...

Yes. My brother must have dropped something. He's such a klutz!

Questions:

- ☐ Is that music I hear coming from upstairs?
- ☐ Are you getting hungry?
- ☐ Did you just hear a loud crash?

4.

The answer is...

Because I feel terrible angst. I have to go to Boston tomorrow and I hate flying!

Questions:

- ☐ Why are you so happy?
- ☐ Why are you sweating?
- ☐ Why are you working on the computer?

5.

The answer is...

Yes! Baking is my forte!

Questions:

- ☐ Did you take these pictures yourself?
- ☐ Did you decorate your house yourself?
- ☐ Did you make this chocolate cake yourself?

6.

The answer is...

Because I make them all kowtow to me.

Questions:

- ☐ Why are all your employees so happy?
- ☐ Why are your employees nervous around you?
- ☐ Why do so many people want to work for your company?

B. FIND YOUR PERFECT MATCH

Write the number of the slang term or idiom from Column A next to its matching picture in Column B as well as next to the matching definition in Column C.

COLUMN A	COLUMN B	COLUMN C
1. kowtow	☐ 	☐ a clumsy person
2. gung-ho	☐ 	☐ to act in a very submissive and subservient manner
3. kindergarten	☐ 	☐ enthusiastic
4. klutz	☐ 	☐ manly in an aggressive and even exaggerated way
5. macho	☐ 	☐ a pre-first grade program for four-year-old to six-year-old children

C. YOU'RE THE AUTHOR

Complete the dialogue using the words below. When you're finished, perform the dialogue out loud.

CD-A: TRACK 25

ANGST	**FORTE**	**KOWTOW**
BLASÉ	**GUNG-HO**	**MACHO**
BOUTIQUE	**KINDERGARTEN**	**PRIMA DONNA**
CAMARADERIE	**KLUTZ**	**VERBATIM**

Maggie: When I was a little girl, I had so much ________________ about going to ______________________. I tried to act ________________ about it so that my parents wouldn't be upset, but subtlety was never my ________________, even as a child. You should have heard me screaming as we drove to the school. I had never been separated from my parents before. Also I was scared that the other kids would make fun of me because I was big for my age and a total ________________. I kept falling all the time!

Susan: What about your twin brother? Was he screaming, too?

Maggie: No, my brother seemed really ________________ about it but looking back on it, I think he was just trying to be ________________ and not let everyone know that he was just as scared. Our parents kept telling us that it would be fun and that there would be a sense of ____________________ among all the kids...and they were right!

Susan: I found that, too. The worst part for me was the teacher. I'll never forget what she looked like. She wore tons of make-up and looked like she had just come from a cosmetics ________________! She was this ________________________ who used to teach at an exclusive school for rich kids but had to move with her husband. She hated being at our school. She expected all the kids to ________________ to her. The first words that came out of her mouth were, "I am your teacher and you will do exactly as I say and nothing more." And that's ____________________.

Maggie: She sounds truly charming!

More Foreign Words Used in Everyday Conversation

Millions of immigrants live in the United States and certainly millions more come to visit. In fact, many native-born Americans have grandparents from other countries who migrated here years ago. With such a **mélange** (French: "mixture") of **émigrés** (French: "immigrants"), the list of foreign words used commonly in the English language goes on **ad infinitum** (Latin: "forever"). Note that the pronunciation given is how Americans pronounce these foreign words, not how they would be pronounced by speakers from their country of origin!

FRENCH

Note: In the following examples, all spellings are presented as they would appear in an American English dictionary, *usually* without the typical French accent marks. However, some do retain the French accent marks!

a la carte *exp.* (pronounced: *ah la kahrt*) refers to each item priced separately on a menu.

EXAMPLE: A salad doesn't come with your dinner, but you can order one **a la carte**.

TRANSLATION: A salad doesn't come with your dinner, but you can order one **separately**.

"REAL SPEAK": A salad doesn' come w'th yer dinner, b't 'chu c'n order one **ah la kahrt**.

ambiance *n.* (pronoucned: *ahm-b'yahns*) the mood created by a particular environment.

EXAMPLE: The lighting in this restaurant creates a romantic **ambiance**.

TRANSLATION: The lighting in this restaurant creates a romantic **mood**.

"REAL SPEAK": The liding 'n th's rest'rant creates a roman(t)ic **ahm-b'yahns**.

apropos *adj.* (pronounced: *ah-proh-poh*) appropriate.

EXAMPLE: Considering Meg is so nasty, Barbara's sarcastic remarks about her were **apropos**.

TRANSLATION: Considering Meg is so nasty, Barbara's sarcastic remarks about her were **appropriate**.

"REAL SPEAK": C'nsidering Meg is so nasty, Barb'ra's sarcastic remarks aboud 'er were **ah-proh-poh**.

"A toute a l'heure!" *exp.* (pronounced: *toodaloo* by Americans) "See you later!"

EXAMPLE: I have to leave now. **Toodaloo**!

TRANSLATION: I have to leave now. **See you later**!

"REAL SPEAK": I hafta leave now. **Toodaloo**!

Note: In an attempt to pronounce this expression, Americans corrupted the French pronunciation of *ah toot ah ler* to *toodaloo* which has become popular usage.

Variation: **Toodles!**

attaché *n.* (pronounced: *ah-tah-shay*) a diplomatic official.

EXAMPLE: I am going to be sent as an **attaché** to three different countries this year.

TRANSLATION: I am going to be sent as a **diplomatic official** to three different countries this year.

"REAL SPEAK": I'm gonna be sent 'ez 'n **ah-tah-shay** da three diff'rent countries th's year.

Also: **attaché case** *exp.* a flat, rectangular briefcase used for carrying business papers and documents.

avant-garde *adj.* (pronounced: *ah-vahn-gard*) radically new and original.

EXAMPLE: Stravinsky was considered **avant-garde** in his day but now he sounds conservative compared to new music.

TRANSLATION: Stravinsky was considered **radically new and original** in his day but now he sounds conservative compared to new music.

"REAL SPEAK": Stravinsky w'z considered **ah-vahn-gard** 'n 'is day b't now 'e sounz conservadive compared da new music.

"Bon voyage!" *exclam.* (pronounced: *bohn vwah-yaj*) "Have a good trip!"

EXAMPLE: Don't forget to write. **Bon voyage**!

TRANSLATION: Don't forget to write. **Have a good trip**!

"REAL SPEAK": Don't ferget ta write. **Bohn-vwah-yaj**!

bourgeois *adj.* (pronounced: *boor-jwah*) middle-class and materialistic.

EXAMPLE: Pam's parents are so **bourgeois**. All they ever do is talk about their money.

TRANSLATION: Pam's parents are so **middle-class and materialistic**. All they ever do is talk about their money.

"REAL SPEAK": Pam's parents 'er so **boor-jwah**. All they ever do 'ez talk about their money.

Note: In English, *bourgeois* does not add an "e" at the end of the word, as it does in French to denote a woman, *bourgeoise*.

carte blanche *exp.* (pronounced: *kart-blahnsh*) permission to do anything one wants without asking • (lit.): white card (or blank piece of paper) that one may fill in as one pleases.

EXAMPLE: My mom gave me **carte blanche** to redecorate her house however I want.

TRANSLATION: My mom gave me **permission** to redecorate her house however I want.

"REAL SPEAK": My mom gamme **kart-blahnsh** ta redecorade 'er house however I want.

"C'est la vie" *exp.* (pronounced: *seh-lah-vee*) "Oh, well. Such is life" • (lit.): That's life.

EXAMPLE: I lost my favorite watch when I was on vacation. **C'est la vie**.

TRANSLATION: I lost my favorite watch when I was on vacation. **Oh, well. Such is life**.

"REAL SPEAK": I lost my fav'rit watch wh'n I w'z on vacation. **Seh-lah-vee**.

chateau *n.* (pronounced: *shah-toh*) castle.

EXAMPLE: Have you seen our new corporate headquarters? It's huge! It looks more like a **chateau** than an office building.

TRANSLATION: Have you seen our new corporate headquarters? It's huge! It look more like a **castle** than an office building.

"REAL SPEAK": Have ya seen 'ar new corp'rit headquarders? It's huge! It looks more like a **shah-toh** th'n 'n office building.

collage *n.* (pronounced: *kohl-ahj*) a picture made by sticking together pieces of paper, photographs, objects, etc.

EXAMPLE: The artist created her portrait in a **collage** using pieces of newspapers and tin cans.

TRANSLATION: The artist created her portrait in a **work made up of various pieces of materials glued together** using newspapers and tin cans.

"REAL SPEAK": The ardist creaded 'er portred in a **kohl-aj** using pieces 'ev newspapers 'n tin cans.

concierge *n.* (pronounced: *kon-see'air'j*) staff member of a hotel, office building, or apartment who is in charge of special services for guests.

EXAMPLE: I'm going to call the **concierge** and ask him to get me two tickets for the opera this evening.

TRANSLATION: I'm going to call the **member of the hotel staff who is in charge of special services for guests** and ask him to get me two tickets for the opera this evening.

"REAL SPEAK": I'm gonna call the **kon-see'air'j** 'n ask 'im da get me two tickets fer the opera th's ev'ning.

connoisseur *n.* (pronounced: *kon-eh-ser*) an expert who appreciates a particular field such as fine arts, food, wine, etc.

EXAMPLE: Frederick is a **connoisseur** of artwork. He owns a very rare collection of fine paintings.

TRANSLATION: Frederick is an **expert and enthusiast** of artwork. He owns a very rare collection of fine paintings.

"REAL SPEAK": Fred'rick's a **kon-eh-ser** 'ev artwork. He owns a very rare collection 'ev fine pain(t)ings.

debut (pronounced: *day-b'yoo*) • **1.** *n.* first public appearance • **2.** *v.* to give something or someone a first public appearance.

EXAMPLE 1: Fox TV's newest comedy show made its **debut** last week.

TRANSLATION: Fox TV's newest comedy show made its **first public appearance** last week.

"REAL SPEAK": Fox TV's newest comedy show made its **day-b'yoo** las' week.

EXAMPLE 2: Today we are hoping to **debut** our new products before our competition.

TRANSLATION: Today we are hoping to **give a first public appearance to** our new products before our competition.

"REAL SPEAK": Taday w'r hoping da **day-b'yoo** 'ar new produc's b'fore 'ar competition.

deja vu *exp.* (pronounced: *day-jah voo*) the illusion of having experienced something before • (lit.): already seen.

EXAMPLE: I had a sense of **deja vu** when I visited Egypt. Maybe I was there in a past life!

TRANSLATION: I had a sense of **having already been there** when I visited Egypt. Maybe I was there in a past life!

"REAL SPEAK": I had a sense 'ev **day-jah voo** wh'n I visided Egypt. Maybe I w'z there 'n a pas' life!

double entendre *exp.* (pronounced: *duh-b'l ahn-tahn-druh*) double meaning (one of which is often suggestive and sexual).

EXAMPLE: Every time I walk into my manager's office, he gives me strange looks and everything he says has a **double entendre**.

TRANSLATION: Every time I walk into my manager's office, he gives me strange looks and everything he says has a **double meaning**.

"REAL SPEAK": Ev'ry time I walk inda my manager's office, he gives me strange looks 'n ev'rything 'e says has a **duh-b'l ahn-tahn-druh**.

Note: Strangely enough, the expression *double entendre* does not even exist in French! Americans simply invented it. Instead, the French simply say *double sens*, literally meaning "double sense."

echelon *n.* (pronounced: *eh-shah-lahn*) level of authority or management in a business.

EXAMPLE: My company cut half its staff this year but the upper **echelon** got huge bonuses.

TRANSLATION: My company cut half its staff this year but the upper **level of management** got huge bonuses.

"REAL SPEAK": My comp'ny cut half its staff this year b't the upper **eh-shah-lahn** 'ev officers got huge bonuses.

eclair *n.* (pronounced: *ee-klair*) a narrow pastry filled with custard and topped with chocolate icing.

EXAMPLE: My favorite pastry is an **eclair**. I like to eat the ends off first, then eat my way toward the middle where I'll find the most custard.

TRANSLATION: My favorite pastry is a **narrow pastry filled with custard and topped with chocolate icing**. I like to eat the ends off first then, eat my way toward the middle where I'll find the most custard.

"REAL SPEAK": My fav'rit pastry's 'n **ee-klair**. I like ta eat the enz off first, th'n eat my way tord the middle where a'll fin' the mos' custard.

elite (pronounced: *ee-leet*) • **1.** *n.* the highest class of people • **2.** *adj.* specially selected as the best.

EXAMPLE 1: Only the **elite** attended the opening night of the opera.

TRANSLATION: Only the **highest class of people** attended the opening night of the opera.

"REAL SPEAK": Only the **ee-leed** attended the opening night 'a the op'ra.

EXAMPLE 2: An **elite** group of performers was invited to contribute to the opening of the new performing arts building.

TRANSLATION: A **specially selected** group of performers was invited to contribute to the opening of the new performing arts building.

"REAL SPEAK": An **ee-leet** group 'a performers w'z invided ta contribute ta the opening 'a the new performing arts building.

en route *exp.* (pronounced: *on root*) on the way.

EXAMPLE: We were **en route** to the airport when I remembered that I left the plane tickets at home!

TRANSLATION: We were **on the way** to the airport when I remembered that I left the plane tickets at home!

"REAL SPEAK": We were **on root** ta the airport wh'n I remembered th'd I left the plane tickets 'it home!

ennui *n.* (pronounced: *on-wee*) boredom, weariness and discontent.

EXAMPLE: Nothing interests me anymore. I'm filled with complete **ennui**.

TRANSLATION: Nothing interests me anymore. I'm filled with complete **ennui**.

"REAL SPEAK": Nothing int'ress me anymore. I'm filled w'th complede **on-wee**.

ensemble *n.* (pronounced: *on-sahm-bl*) • **1.** a coordinated set of clothing • **2.** a small music of performing musicians.

EXAMPLE 1: Ann always buys inexpensive, used clothing but her **ensembles** always look great!

TRANSLATION: Ann always buys inexpensive, used clothing but her **coordinated sets of clothing** always look great!

"REAL SPEAK": Ann ahweez buys inexpensive, used clothing bud 'er **on-sahm-blz** ahweez look great!

EXAMPLE 2: David performs with his **ensemble** at several nightclubs in the city.

TRANSLATION: David performs with his **small music group** at several nightclubs in the city.

"REAL SPEAK": David performs with his **ensemble** at several nightclubs in the city.

entree *n.* (pronounced: *on-tray*) • **1.** the main course of a meal • **2.** means of entry • (lit.): entrance.

EXAMPLE 1: The **entree** was a leg of lamb which was delicious but the vegetables were overcooked.

TRANSLATION: The **main course** was a leg of lamb which was delicious but the vegetables were overcooked.

"REAL SPEAK": The **on-tray** w'z a leg 'a lamb which w'z delicious b't the veggies were overcooked.

EXAMPLE 2: Ted's friendship with Senator Olson was his **entree** into the world of politics.

TRANSLATION: Ted's friendship with Senator Olson was his **means of entry** into the world of politics.

"REAL SPEAK": Ted's frien'ship w'th Senader Olson was 'is **on-tray** inta the world 'ev politics.

faux pas *exp.* (pronounced: *foh-pah*) an embarrassing mistake made in one's manners or social conduct • (lit.): false step.

EXAMPLE: Gordon made the **faux pas** of burping in front of the president of our company!

TRANSLATION: Gordon made the **embarrassing mistake in his manners** of burping in front of the president of our company!

"REAL SPEAK": Gordon made the **foh-pah** 'ev burping in fronna the president 'ev 'ar comp'ny!

finesse *n.* (pronounced: *fin-es*) delicacy and skill in managing a sensitive situation.

EXAMPLE: We hired Jim to work in our complaint department because of his **finesse** in speaking with unhappy customers.

TRANSLATION: We hired Jim to work in our complaint department because of his **delicacy and skill** in speaking with unhappy customers.

"REAL SPEAK": We hired Jim da work 'n 'ar complaint department b'cuz 'ev 'is **fin-es** 'n speaking w'th unhappy custamers.

gauche *adj.* (pronounced: *gohsh*) socially insensitive • (lit.): left.

EXAMPLE: I'll never take Jerry to an elegant party again. He asked the hostess how much she paid for her pearl necklace! He's so **gauche**.

TRANSLATION: I'll never take Jerry to an elegant party again. He asked the hostess how much she paid for her pearl necklace! He's so **socially insensitive**.

"REAL SPEAK": A'll never take Jerry to 'n elegant pardy again. He ast the hostess how much she paid fer her pearl necklace! He's so **gohsh**.

gourmet • (pronounced: *goor-may*) **1.** *n.* a person devoted to fine food and drink • **2.** *adj.* pertaining to fine food and dining.

EXAMPLE 1: A **gourmet** like Philip is used to eating in the best restaurants in the world but he'll always join his friends for a hamburger.

TRANSLATION: A **lover of fine food and drink** like Philip is used to eating in the best restaurants in the world but he'll always join his friends for a hamburger.

"REAL SPEAK": A **goor-may** like Philip's usta eading 'n the best rest'rants 'n the world b'd 'e'll ahweez join 'is frenz fer a burger.

EXAMPLE 2: You'll find that one of the benefits of being an executive with our company is access to our **gourmet** dining room for entertaining clients.

TRANSLATION: You'll find that one of the benefits of being an executive with our company is access to our **fine food** dining room for entertaining clients.

"REAL SPEAK": You'll find th't one 'a the benefits 'ev being 'n execudive w'th 'ar comp'ny is access ta 'ar **goor-may** dining room fer en(t)ertaining clients.

haute couture *exp.* (pronounced: *oht-koo-toor*) high fashion.

EXAMPLE: Lily indulges herself and buys one **haute couture** dress per year.

TRANSLATION: Lily indulges herself and buys one **high fashion** dress per year.

"REAL SPEAK": Lily indulges 'erself 'n buys one **oht-koo-toor** dress per year.

Also: **haute cuisine** *exp.* (pronounced: *oht-kwi-zeen*) gourmet cooking or food.

hors d'oeuvre *exp.* (pronounced: *or-durv*) appetizer, food used to stimulate the appetite before dinner.

EXAMPLE: I sure hope they're going to serve **hors d'oeuvres** since we aren't going to have dinner for an hour!

TRANSLATION: I sure hope they're going to serve **appetizers** since we aren't going to have dinner for an hour!

"REAL SPEAK": I sher hope they're gonna serve **or-durvz** since we aren't gonna have dinner fer 'n hour!

je ne sais quoi *exp.* (pronounced: *je-ne-say-kwah*) an indescribable (usually pleasing) quality • (lit.): I don't know what.

EXAMPLE: Mark has charmed our whole family with his special **je ne sais quoi**.

TRANSLATION: Mark has charmed our whole family with his special **indescribable quality**.

"REAL SPEAK": Mark 'iz charmed 'ar whole fam'ly with 'is special **je-ne-say-kwah**.

joie de vivre *exp.* (pronounced: *jwah-de-veev*) a joy of being alive • (lit.): joy of living.

EXAMPLE: Carol's positive attitude and **joie de vivre** are what keep her young.

TRANSLATION: Carol's positive attitude and **joy of being alive** are what keep her young.

"REAL SPEAK": Carol's posidive additude 'n **jwah-de-veev** 'er what keep 'er young.

laissez-faire *exp.* (pronounced: *leh-say-fair*) a policy of noninterference.

EXAMPLE: Our new boss has a **laissez-faire** attitude about his employees. He gives them assignments and then never interferes with how they get them done.

TRANSLATION: Our new boss has a **policy of noninterference** about his employees. He gives them assignments and then never interferes with how they get them done.

"REAL SPEAK": 'Ar new boss has a **leh-say-fair** additude about 'is employees. He gives 'em assignments 'n then never in'erferes with how they get 'em done.

maitre d'hotel *exp.* (pronounced: *may-der-dee* because Americans always drop the word *hotel* from this expression) headwaiter • (lit.): master of the establishment.

EXAMPLE: The restaurant is full but don't worry. The **maitre d'hotel** knows me well and always finds me a table.

TRANSLATION: The restaurant is full but don't worry. The **headwaiter** knows me well and always finds me a table.

"REAL SPEAK": The rest'rant's full b't don' worry. The **may-der-dee** knows me well 'n ahweez finz me a table.

malaise *n.* (pronounced: *mah-lez*) mental or physical discomfort.

EXAMPLE: This **malaise** I've been feeling for the last week makes me think I'm getting sick.

TRANSLATION: This **physical discomfort** I've been feeling for the last week makes me think I'm getting sick.

"REAL SPEAK": The **mah-lez** I' been feeling fer the las' week makes me think I'm getting sick.

Mardi Gras *exp.* (pronounced: *mahr-dee-grah*) a celebration climaxing the day before Lent, famous in some cities such as New Orleans and Rio de Janeiro where the festivities are wild and attract huge crowds • (lit.): fat Tuesday (the day before Ash Wednesday).

EXAMPLE: I partied for three days straight at **Mardi Gras** in New Orleans last year.

TRANSLATION: I partied for three days straight at **the celebration just before Lent** in New Orleans last year.

"REAL SPEAK": I pardied fer three days straight 'it **mahr-dee-grah** 'n New Orleens last year.

melee *n.* (pronounced: *may-lay*) a noisy, disorderly fight among several people.

EXAMPLE: A **melee** erupted when the police tried to hold back the demonstrators.

TRANSLATION: A **noisy, disorderly fight** erupted when the police tried to hold back the demonstrators.

"REAL SPEAK": A **may-lay** erupted when the palice tried da hold back the demonstraders.

menage a trois *exp.* (pronounced: *may-naj ah twah*) an arrangement in which three people have sexual relations • (lit.): household of three.

EXAMPLE: I thought Al was having an affair with the nanny but his wife is involved, too. They're having a **menage a trois**!

TRANSLATION: I thought Al was having an affair with the nanny but his wife is involved, too. They're having a **three-way sexual relationship**!

"REAL SPEAK": I thod Al w'z having 'n affair w'th the nanny b'd 'is wife's involve', too. They're having a **may-naj ah twah**!

milieu *n.* (pronounced: *meel-yoo*) one's environment.

EXAMPLE: Francine is arrogant because she grew up in a **milieu** of rich people. Her father is one of the richest men in the city.

TRANSLATION: Francine is arrogant because she grew up in an **environment** of rich people. Her father is one of the richest men in the city.

"REAL SPEAK": Francine's arrag'nt b'cuz she grew up 'n a **meel-yoo** 'ev rich people. Her father's one 'a the richest men 'n the cidy.

naive *adj.* (pronounced: *nah-yeev*) • **1.** simple and unsophisticated • **2.** inexperienced in life.

EXAMPLE 1: Ted is very **naive**. He trusts everyone.

TRANSLATION: Ted is very **simple and unsophisticated**. He trusts everyone.

"REAL SPEAK": Ted's very **nah-yeev**. He truss' ev'ryone.

EXAMPLE 2: Larry needs to travel the world for a while in order to grow up. He's still very **naive**.

TRANSLATION: Larry needs to travel the world for a while in order to grow up. He's still very **inexperienced in life**.

"REAL SPEAK": Larry needs ta travel the world fer a while 'n order da grow up. He's still very **nah-yeev**.

Note: In French, *naïve* is the feminine form of the word, while *naïf* is the masculine form. However, in English only the feminine form is used, without the accent mark.

Also: **naivete** or **naivety** *n.* (pronounced: *nah-eev-tay*) a lack of sophistication or experience of life.

nom de plume *exp.* (pronounced: *nohm-de-ploom*) a name a writer invents when he/she doesn't want to be known by his/her real name • (lit.): pen name.

EXAMPLE: A lot of authors write books and want to keep their identity unknown. That's why they use a **nom de plume**.

TRANSLATION: A lot of authors write books and want to keep their identity unknown. That's why they use an **invented name**.

"REAL SPEAK": A lot 'ev authers write books 'n wanna keep their iden'idy unknown. That's why they use a **nohm-de-ploom**.

nouveau riche *exp.* (pronounced: *noo-voh reesh*) a person who has gained his/her wealth relatively recently • (lit.): new rich.

EXAMPLE: Don't you find that many of the **nouveaux riches** like to show off their wealth?

TRANSLATION: Don't you find that many of the **newly rich** like to show off their wealth?

"REAL SPEAK": Dontcha fine th't many 'a the **noo-voh reesh** like ta show off their wealth?

Note: Whether in the singular form, *nouveau riche*, or plural form, *nouveaux riches*, the pronunciation is the same!

nouvelle cuisine *exp.* (pronounced: *noo-vel kwee-zeen*) a modern, healthier style of French cooking.

EXAMPLE: **Nouvelle cuisine** is lighter than traditional French food, but the portions are so small that I'm still hungry at the end of the meal!

TRANSLATION: **The modern style of French cooking** is lighter than traditional French food but the portions are so small that I'm still hungry at the end of the meal!

"REAL SPEAK": I like the fac' th't **noo-vel kwee-zeen**'s lider th'n traditional French food b't the portions 'er so small th'd I'm still hungry 'it the end 'a the meal!

passé *adj.* (pronounced: *pah-say*) out-of-date, no longer fashionable • (lit.): past.

EXAMPLE: You still listen to disco music? That's so **passé**!

TRANSLATION: You still listen to disco music? That's so **unfashionable**!

"REAL SPEAK": Ya still listen da disco music? That's so **pah-say**!

pièce de résistance *exp.* (pronounced: *pee'yes de ray-zees-tahns*) the outstanding item in a collection.

EXAMPLE: The new production of *Carmen* is the **pièce de résistance** of the opera season.

TRANSLATION: The new production of *Carmen* is the **most outstanding feature** of the opera season.

"REAL SPEAK": The new praduction 'ev *Carmen's* the **pee'yes de ray-zees-tahns** 'ev the op'ra season.

potpourri *n.* (pronounced: *poh-poo-ree*) • **1.** a mixture of unrelated elements • **2.** a mixture of dried flowers and spices kept in a special jar or bowl and left open in a room for their fragrance • (lit.): rotten pot.

EXAMPLE 1: We went to a concert last night and heard a **potpourri** of musical compositions, each one very different from the other.

TRANSLATION: We went to a concert last night and heard a **mixture** of musical compositions, each one very different from the other.

"REAL SPEAK": We went to a concert las' nide 'n heard a **poh-poo-ree** 'ev musical compasitions, each one very diff'rent fr'm the other.

EXAMPLE 2: Rita always keeps a bowl of **potpourri** in her house to make everything smell nice.

TRANSLATION: Rita always keeps a bowl of **dried flowers and spices** in her house to make everything smell nice.

"REAL SPEAK": Reeda ahweez keeps a bowl 'a **potpourri** 'n 'er house ta make ev'rything smell nice.

respondez s'il vous plait *exp.* always written as *R.S.V.P.* and used on an invitation to indicate that the favor of a reply is requested • (lit.): respond please.

EXAMPLE: We need to **R.S.V.P.** to Susan's invitation by this Wednesday.

TRANSLATION: We need to **respond** to Susan's invitation by this Wednesday.

"REAL SPEAK": We need da **R.S.V.P.** da Susan's invitation by this Wen'sday.

risqué *adj.* (pronounced: *ris-kay*) sexually suggestive.

EXAMPLE: The play we saw wasn't obscene enough for the authorities to close it down but it sure was **risqué**.

TRANSLATION: The play we saw wasn't obscene enough for the authorities to close it down but it sure was **sexually suggestive**.

"REAL SPEAK": The play we saw wasn' abscene enuf fer the athoridies ta close it down b'd it sher w's **ris-kay**.

salon *n.* (pronounced *suh-lahn*) a shop offering a specific service or product.

EXAMPLE: My mother goes to the beauty **salon** every week. That's why her hair always looks so perfect.

TRANSLATION: My mother goes to the beauty **shop** every week. That's why her hair always looks so perfect.

"REAL SPEAK": My mother goes da the beaudy **suh-lahn** ev'ry week. That's why 'er hair ahweez looks so perfect.

savoir-faire *exp.* (pronounced: *sah-vwah-fair*) an ability to say or do the appropriate thing in any situation • (lit.): to know what to do.

TRANSLATION: Clint is a great person to travel with because he has tremendous **savoir-faire** and can handle any cultural misunderstanding.

TRANSLATION: Clint is a great person to travel with because he has tremendous **ability to say or do the appropriate thing** and can handle any cultural misunderstanding.

"REAL SPEAK": Clint's a great person da travel with cuz 'e 'as tremendous **sah-vwah-fair** 'n c'n handle any cultural misunderstanding.

Also: **savvy** *n.* (pronounced: *sa-vee* — an American variation of the French *savoir-faire*) practical understanding and common sense.

soupe du jour *exp.* (pronounced: *soup doo joor*) a soup featured by a restaurant on a particular day • (lit.): soup of the day.

EXAMPLE: Have the **soupe du jour**. It's a chicken noodle today and it's delicious.

TRANSLATION: Have the **soup of the day**. It's a chicken noodle today and it's delicious.

"REAL SPEAK": Have the **soop doo joor**. It's a chicken noodle taday 'n it's delicious.

souvenir *n.* (pronounced: *soo-ven-eer*) an object that one purchases while on vacation as a reminder of the trip • (lit.): from French, *souvenir*, meaning "to remember."

EXAMPLE: When I went to Italy, I bought a little plastic replica of the Leaning Tower of Pizza. It will be a nice **souvenir**.

TRANSLATION: When I went to Italy, I bought a little plastic replica of the Leaning Tower of Pizza. It will be a nice **object that will remind me of my trip**.

"REAL SPEAK": When I went ta Idaly, I bod a liddle plastic replica of the Leaning Tower 'ev Pizza. Id'll be a nice **soo-ven-eer**.

tête-à-tête *exp.* (pronounced: *tay'd-ah-tay't*) a private conversation, usually between two people.

EXAMPLE: I have something important to talk about with you. I think it would be better to go to my office where we can be alone and have a **tête-à-tête**.

TRANSLATION: I have something important to talk about with you. I think it would be better to go to my office where we can be alone and have a **private conversation**.

"REAL SPEAK": I 'ave something import'nt ta talk about w'th you. I think it'd be bedder da go da my office where we c'n be alone 'n have a **tay'd-ah-tay't**.

"Touché!" *excl.* (pronounced: *too-chay*) an exclamation used to acknowledge a clever remark.

EXAMPLE:
– Is Marilyn stupid?! She has to get smarter to be considered stupid!
– **Touché**!

TRANSLATION:
– Is Marilyn stupid?! She has to get smarter to be considered stupid!
– **What a clever remark**!

"REAL SPEAK":
– Is Marilyn stupid?! She hasta get smarder da be considered stupid!
– **Tou-chay**!

Origin: A fencing expression used as an exclamation by one fencer who touches the other fencer with the sword.

"Voilà!" *exclam.* (pronounced: *vwah-lah*) an exclamation used to express success or satisfaction • (lit.): "There."

EXAMPLE: **Voilà**! That's my entire plan for getting the money to buy a new house. So, what do you think?

TRANSLATION: **There**! That's my entire plan for getting the money to buy a new house! So, what do you think?

"REAL SPEAK": **Vwah-lah**! That's my entire plan fer gedding the money da buy a new house! So, whaddy ya think?

Note: This exclamation is commonly used by magicians just as they reveal the magic trick.

GERMAN

ersatz *adj.* (pronounced: *er-zahts*) artificial, imitation.

EXAMPLE: I never buy cakes from the supermarket because they always use **ersatz** ingredients. I prefer a cake that's homemade.

TRANSLATION: I never buy cakes from the supermarket because they always use **artificial** ingredients. I prefer a cake that's homemade.

"REAL SPEAK": I never buy cakes fr'm the supermarket b'cuz they ahweez use **er-zatz** ingredients. I prafer a cake that's homemade.

"Gesundheit!" *exclam.* (pronounced: *geh-zun-tah'eet*) an expression used to wish someone good health, especially after that person has just sneezed • (lit.): health.

EXAMPLE: That was a big sneeze! **Gesundheit**! I hope you're not catching a cold.

TRANSLATION: That was a big sneeze! **Good health**! I hope you're not catching a cold.

"REAL SPEAK": That w'z a big sneeze! **Geh-zun-tah'eet**! I hope y'r not catching a cold.

kaput (to go) *exp.* (pronounced: *kah-put*) to break, to stop functioning.

EXAMPLE: Ed doesn't have much luck. Everything he touches seems to **go kaput**!

TRANSLATION: Ed doesn't have much luck. Everything he touches seems to **break**!

"REAL SPEAK": Ed doesn' have much luck. Ev'rything 'e touches seems da **go kah-put**!

verboten *adj.* (pronounced: *ver-boh-ten* or *fer-boh-ten*, as pronounced by a native speaker of German) forbidden.

EXAMPLE: I told our guests that smoking is **verboten** in our house.

TRANSLATION: I told our guests that smoking is **forbidden** in our house.

"REAL SPEAK": I told 'ar guests th't smoking 'ez **ver-boh-ten** 'n 'ar house.

wunderkind *n.* (pronounced: *wun-der-kint*) a prodigy, a person who succeeds at something at a relatively early age.

EXAMPLE: Any child who finishes college at ten and starts an Internet business is truly a **wunderkind**.

TRANSLATION: Any child who finishes college at ten and starts an Internet business is truly a **child prodigy**.

"REAL SPEAK": Any child 'oo finishes college 'it ten 'n stard 'n In(t)ernet bizness 'ez truly a **wun-der-kint**.

ITALIAN

a cappella *exp.* (pronounced: *ah kah-peh-lah*) without instrumental accompaniment • (lit.): in the manner of a chapel choir.

EXAMPLE: The singer performed the concert **a cappella**. He didn't even need a band!

TRANSLATION: The singer performed the concert **without instrumental accompaniment**. He didn't even need a band!

"REAL SPEAK": The singer performed the concerd **ah kah-peh-lah**. He didn' even need a band!

al dente *exp.* (pronounced: *ahl den-tay*) referring to pasta or vegetables that have been cooked so that they are firm to the bite and not too soft • (lit.): to the tooth.

EXAMPLE: Pasta needs to be cooked **al dente** or it may get soft.

TRANSLATION: Pasta needs to be cooked **so that it has some firmness** or it may get soft.

"REAL SPEAK": Pasta needs ta be cooked **ahl den-tay** 'r it may get soft.

aria *n.* (pronounced: *ah-ree-ya*) a melody sung solo, usually in an opera.

EXAMPLE: Violetta's big **aria** is at the end of the first act of *La Traviata*.

TRANSLATION: Violetta's big **solo** is at the end of the first act of *La Traviata*.

"REAL SPEAK": Violetta's big **ah-ree-ya**'s 'it the end 'a the first act 'ev *La Traviata*.

caffe latte *exp.* (pronounced: *cah-fay lah-tay*) a drink of strong espresso and steamed milk.

EXAMPLE: I prefer **caffe latte** to regular American coffee, which is a lot weaker.

TRANSLATION: I prefer **strong espresso coffee and steamed milk** to regular American coffee, which is a lot weaker.

"REAL SPEAK": I prefer **cah-fay lah-tay** ta regular American coffee, which 'ez a lot weaker.

Note: A *caffe latte* is commonly shortened to *latte*.

cappuccino *n.* (pronounced: *kap-ah-chee-noh*) a drink of strong espresso and milk often with cinnamon, nutmeg, and whipped cream.

EXAMPLE: I love having a good **cappuccino** after dinner. It's almost like dessert!

TRANSLATION: I love having a good **strong coffee with steamed milk, cinnamon, nutmeg, and whipped cream** after dinner. It's almost like dessert!

"REAL SPEAK": I love having a good **kap-ah-chee-noh** afder dinner. It's almos' like dessert!

espresso *n.* (pronounced: *es-pres-oh*) a strong coffee prepared by forcing steam under pressure through the ground beans.

EXAMPLE: I don't like the taste of regular coffee. It's so weak! I prefer a cup of strong **espresso**.

TRANSLATION: I don't like the taste of regular coffee. It's so weak! I prefer a cup of strong **coffee steamed under pressure**.

"REAL SPEAK": I don' like the taste 'a reguler coffee. It's so weak! I prafer a cup 'a strong **es-pres-oh**.

maestro *n.* (pronounced: *mah'ees-troh*) an accomplished and respected artist, usually a musical composer or conductor.

EXAMPLE: Leonard Bernstein was a great **maestro** and admired as a composer and conductor.

TRANSLATION: Leonard Bernstein was a great, **accomplished and respected musician** and admired as a composer and conductor.

"REAL SPEAK": Leonard Bernstein w'z a great **ma'ees-troh** and admired 'ez a c'mposer 'n c'nducter.

virtuoso • (pronounced: *ver-choo-oh-soh*) **1.** *n.* a person who has exceptional skill or knowledge in a field, particularly music • **2.** *adj.* extremely skilled.

EXAMPLE 1: Alexandra is a **virtuoso** as a pianist. She was accepted to the best music academy when she was only twelve years old!

TRANSLATION: Alexandra is a **sensation** as a pianist. She was accepted to the best music academy when she was only twelve years old!

"REAL SPEAK": Alexandra's a **ver-choo-oh-soh** 'ez a pianist. She w'z accepted to the best music academy wh'n she w's only twelve years old!

EXAMPLE 2: Bill studied at the Juilliard School of Music and is now a **virtuoso** violinist.

TRANSLATION: Bill studied at the Juilliard School of Music and is now an **exceptional** violinist.

"REAL SPEAK": Bill studied 'it the Juilliard School 'ev Music 'n is now a **ver-choo-oh-so** violinist.

LATIN

ad infinitum *exp.* (pronounced: *ad in-fin-eye-dum*) endlessly.

EXAMPLE: Mr. Devlin can lecture **ad infinitum** on his favorite subjects.

TRANSLATION: Mr. Devlin can lecture **endlessly** on his favorite subjects.

"REAL SPEAK": Mr. Devlin c'n lecture **ad in-fin-eye-dum** on 'is fav'rit subjects.

ad lib (to) *v.* (pronounced: *ad-lib*) to improvise.

EXAMPLE: I didn't have time to prepare my speech, so I have to **ad lib**.

TRANSLATION: I didn't have time to prepare my speech, so I have to **improvise**.

"REAL SPEAK": I didn' have time da prepare my speech, so I hafta **ad-lib**.

alma mater *exp.* (pronounced: *ahl-mah mah-der*) a former school (usually a college or university) one has attended • (lit.): nourishing mother.

EXAMPLE: My son will probably study at my **alma mater**, especially if I keep donating money to it.

TRANSLATION: My son will probably study at my **former university**, especially if I keep donating money to it.

"REAL SPEAK": My son'll prob'ly sudy 'it my **ahl-mah-mah-der**, espeshly if I keep donading money to it.

alter ego *exp.* (pronounced: *ahl-ter ee-goh*) • **1.** a second self, a perfect substitute • **2.** another side or aspect of oneself • **3.** an inseparable friend.

EXAMPLE 1: My wife knows me so well that when I go out of town, she acts as my **alter ego** at work.

TRANSLATION: My wife knows me so well that when I go out of town, she acts as my **perfect substitute** at work.

"REAL SPEAK": My wife knows me so well th't when I go oudda town, she aks 'ez my **ahl-ter ee-goh** 'it work.

EXAMPLE 2: If Calvin is being nasty to you, that's his **alter ego** talking. He's usually very sweet.

TRANSLATION: If Calvin is being nasty to you, that's the **other side of his personality** talking. He's usually very sweet.

"REAL SPEAK": If Calvin's being nasty da you, that's 'is **ahl-ter ee-goh** talking. He's ujally very sweet.

EXAMPLE 3: Deborah and I have known each other so long and so well that we are **alter egos** now.

TRANSLATION: Deborah and I have known each other so long and so well that we are **inseparable friends** now.

"REAL SPEAK": Deb'rah 'n I 'ev known each other so long 'n so well th't w'r **ahl-ter ee-gohz** now.

alumnus *n.* (pronounced: *ah-luhm-nuhs* • plural form is *alumni*, pronounced: *ah-luhm-n'eye*) a graduate of a school, college, or university.

EXAMPLE: Once a year, the **alumni** of my school get together for a reunion at the local park.

TRANSLATION: Once a year, the **graduates** of my school get together for a reunion at the local park.

"REAL SPEAK": Once a year, the **ah-luhm-n'eye** 'ev my school get tagether fer a reunion 'it the local park.

Note: The feminine form of *alumnus* is *alumna* (pronounced: *ah-luhm-nuh*), and the plural of *alumna* is *alumnae* (pronounced: *ah-luhm-n'eye*). However, educational institutions usually use *alumni* for graduates of both sexes.

bona fide *exp.* (pronounced: *bon-ah fah'eed*) • **1.** done or presented in good faith • **2.** authentic, genuine • (lit.): good faith.

EXAMPLE 1: Bill and Janet gave me a **bona fide** assurance that they would buy my house. That's why I didn't sell it to the next people who wanted to buy it.

TRANSLATION: Bill and Janet gave me a **good faith** assurance that they would buy my house. That's why I didn't sell it to the next people who wanted to buy it.

"REAL SPEAK": Bill 'n Janet gave me a **bona fide** assurance th't they'd buy my house. That's why I didn' sell it ta the next people who wan'ed da buy it.

EXAMPLE 2: An art expert told me that I have a **bona fide** Diego Rivera painting!

TRANSLATION: An art expert told me that I have an **authentic** Diego Rivera painting!

"REAL SPEAK": An ard expert told me th'd I have a **bon-ah f'eyed** Diego Rivera pain(t)ing!

cum laude *exp.* (pronounced: *kuhm-lah'oo-dee*) with honors (used in the granting of diplomas) • (lit.): with praise.

EXAMPLE: Scott was always a good student and graduated **cum laude**.

TRANSLATION: Scott was always a good student and graduated **with honors**.

"REAL SPEAK": Scott w'z always a good student 'n gradjuaded **kuhm-lah'oo-dee**.

Also 1: **magna cum laude** *exp.* (pronounced: *mag-nuh kuhm-lah'oo-dee*) with great praise or honor.

Also 2: **summa cum laude** *exp.* (pronounced: *soo-muh kuhm-lah'oo-dee*) with greatest praise or honor.

e.g. *exp.* (pronounced: *ee-gee*) an abbreviation of *exempli gratia*, literally meaning "for example."

EXAMPLE: Stella's garden is full of so many different kinds of flowers, **e.g.**, roses, violets, lilacs, and daisies.

TRANSLATION: Stella's garden is full of so many different kinds of flowers, **such as** roses, violets, lilacs, and daisies.

"REAL SPEAK": Stella's garden's full 'a so many diff'rent kinz 'a flowers, **ee-gee**, roses, vi'lets, lilacs, 'n daisies.

ego *n.* (pronounced: *ee-goh*) pride in oneself often to the point of being conceited.

EXAMPLE: Grant's **ego** has gotten out of control now that he is rich and famous. I don't even like being near him anymore!

TRANSLATION: Grant's **self-pride** has gotten out of control now that he is rich and famous. I don't even like being near him anymore!

"REAL SPEAK": Grant's **ego**'s gotten oudda control now th'd 'e's rich 'n famous. I don' even like being near 'im anymore!

etc. *exp.* (pronounced: *et seht-rah*) a common abbreviation of *et cetera* meaning "and more."

EXAMPLE: We sell all sorts of household supplies, like brooms, mops, vacuum cleaners, **etc.**

TRANSLATION: We sell all sorts of household supplies, like brooms, mops, vacuum cleaners, **and more**.

"REAL SPEAK": We sell all sorts 'ev household supplies, like brooms, mops, vacuum cleaners, **et seht-rah**.

i.e. *exp.* (pronounced: *eye-ee*) a common abbreviation of *id est* literally meaning "that is."

EXAMPLE: I'm only interested in socializing with people who have the same interests as I do, **i.e.**, people interesed in health and natural living.

TRANSLATION: I'm only interested in socializing with people who have the same interests as I do, **that is**, people interesed in health and natural living.

"REAL SPEAK": I'm only int'rested 'n soshalizing w'th people 'oo 'ave the same int'rests 'ez I do, **eye-ee**, people int'rested 'n health 'n natural living.

incognito *adv.* (pronounced: *in-cog-nee-doh*) with one's real identity concealed, as with a disguise or a false name.

EXAMPLE: I hear there is a movie star staying in our hotel, but not many people know it because he is traveling **incognito**.

TRANSLATION: I hear there is a movie star staying in our hotel, but not many people know it because he is traveling **with his real identity concealed**.

"REAL SPEAK": I hear there's a movie star staying 'n 'ar hotel, b't not many people know it cuz 'e's trav'ling **in-cog-nee-doh**.

libido *n.* (pronounced: *li-bee-doh*) sexual drive • (lit.): desire.

EXAMPLE: Connie and Ernest are a bad pair. She has a huge **libido** and he doesn't like sex.

TRANSLATION: Connie and Ernest are a bad pair. She has a huge **sex drive** and he doesn't like sex.

"REAL SPEAK": Connie 'n Ernest 'er a bad pair. She 'as a huge **li-bee-doh** an' he doesn' like sex.

per se *exp.* (pronounced: *per-say*) with respect to itself • (lit.): itself.

EXAMPLE: Gold **per se** has little value for me unless it is part of something that has sentimental value.

TRANSLATION: Gold **itself** has little value for me unless it is part of something that has sentimental value.

"REAL SPEAK": Gold **per-say** has liddle value fer me unless it's pard 'a something th't has sen'imen'al value.

persona *n.* (pronounced: *per-sohn-ah*) one's public image or personality, as opposed to one's true personality.

EXAMPLE: My brother is a comedian but he's very different from his **persona**. He's really quiet and serious.

TRANSLATION: My brother is a comedian but he's very different from his **public personality**. He's really quiet and serious.

"REAL SPEAK": My brother's a c'median bud 'e's very diff'rent from 'is **per-sohn-ah**. He's really quiet 'n serious.

quantum leap *exp.* (pronounced: *kwahn-tuhm*) significant or large (as in amount).

EXAMPLE: Sally has made a **quantum leap** in her studies. She used to fail all her subjects but now she gets perfect grades.

TRANSLATION: Sally has made a **significant leap** in her studies. She used to fail all her subjects but now she gets perfect grades.

"REAL SPEAK": Sally's made a **kwahn-tuhm leap** 'n 'er studies. She usta fail all 'er subjec's b't now she gets perfect grades.

status *n.* (pronounced: *sta-dus* or *stay-dus*) • **1.** a position of authority • **2.** the current condition of something.

EXAMPLE 1: Grant has a low **status** in the company and will not be considered for promotion for another year.

TRANSLATION: Grant has a low **position of authority** in the company and will not be considered for promotion for another year.

"REAL SPEAK": Grant has a low **sta-dus** 'n the comp'ny 'n won't be considered fer pramotion fer another year.

EXAMPLE 2: What is the **status** of your report? I need it by today.

TRANSLATION: What is the **current condition** of your report? I need it by today.

"REAL SPEAK": What's the **sta-dus** 'ev yer report? I need it by daday.

status quo *exp.* (pronounced: *sta-dus/stay-dus kwoh*) the existing state of affairs or conditions.

EXAMPLE: I think it's better to maintain the **status quo** and wait before making any changes to our personnel.

TRANSLATION: I think it's better to maintain the **existing state of affairs** and wait before making any changes to our personnel.

"REAL SPEAK": I think it's bedder da maintain the **sta-dus kwoh** 'n wait b'fore making any changes ta 'ar personnel.

vice versa *exp.* (pronounced: *v'eyess-ver-sah*) in the reverse order of how something was stated.

EXAMPLE: I think very highly of Rochelle and **vice versa**.

TRANSLATION: I think very highly of Rochelle and **Rochelle thinks very highly of me**.

"REAL SPEAK": I think very highly 'ev Rochelle 'n **v'eyess-ver-sah**.

SPANISH

aficionado *n.* (pronounced: *ah-fish-ah-nah-doh*) a fan, an enthusiast.

EXAMPLE: Rick is an **aficionado** of American football. He watches all the games!

TRANSLATION: Rick is an **enthusiast** of American football. He watches all the games!

"REAL SPEAK": Rick's 'n **a-fish-a-nah-doh** 'ev American football. He watches all the games!

cantina *n.* (pronounced: *kan-tee-nah*) a bar or other small establishment where one can buy refreshments.

EXAMPLE: There aren't many places to get lunch around here but we can get a sandwich and a beer at the **cantina**.

TRANSLATION: There aren't many places to get lunch around here but we can get a sandwich and a beer at the **bar**.

"REAL SPEAK": There aren't many places ta get lunch aroun' here b'd we c'n ged a san'wich 'n a beer 'it the **kan-tee-nah**.

Chicano/a *n. & adj.* (pronounced: *chi-kah-noh*) Mexican-American.

EXAMPLE: Southern California has lots of **Chicanos** whose ancestors immigrated from Mexico.

TRANSLATION: Southern California has lots of **Mexican-Americans** whose ancestors immigrated from Mexico.

"REAL SPEAK": Southern California has lots 'ev **chi-kah-nohz** whose ancesters immigraded fr'm Mexico.

Hasta la vista! *exp.* (pronounced: *ah-stah lah vee-stah*) See you later!

EXAMPLE: I've got to leave now. **Hasta la vista**!

TRANSLATION: I've got to leave now. **See you later**!

"REAL SPEAK": I've godda leave now. **Ah-stah lah vee-stah**!

Also 1: **Hasta luego!** *exp.* (pronounced: *ah-stah l'way-goh*) See you later!

Also 2: **Hasta mañana!** *exp.* (pronounced: *ah-stah mahn-yahn-ah*) See you tomorrow!

incommunicado *adj.* (pronounced: *in-co-m'yoon-i-cah-doh*) unable to be contacted.

EXAMPLE: I got a flat tire in the desert and was **incommunicado** for eight hours.

TRANSLATION: I got a flat tire in the desert and was **unable to be contacted** for eight hours.

"REAL SPEAK": I god a flat tire 'n the desert 'n w'z **in-co-m'yoon-i-cah-doh** fer aid hours.

mucho *adv.* (pronounced: *moo-choh*) very.

EXAMPLE: You really like Bert? He's **mucho** strange!

TRANSLATION: You really like Bert? He's **very** strange!

"REAL SPEAK": Ya really like Bert? He's **moo-choh** strange!

padre *n.* (pronounced: *pah-dray*) father (in reference to a priest or member of the clergy), a chaplain in the military service.

EXAMPLE: When I was in the army, I used to tell all my problems to the **padre**.

TRANSLATION: When I was in the army, I used to tell all my problems to the **military chaplain**.

"REAL SPEAK": When I w'z 'n the army, I usta tell all my problems ta the **pah-dray**.

poncho *n.* (pronounced: *pahn-choh*) a blanket-like garment with a hole in the center for the head to go through, now often made of waterproof material and used as a raincoat.

EXAMPLE: If I wear a hat and boots with my **poncho**, I stay completely dry when it rains.

TRANSLATION: If I wear a hat and boots with my **blanket-like raincoat**, I stay completely dry when it rains.

"REAL SPEAK": If I wear a hat 'n boots with my **pahn-choh**, I stay completely dry wh'n it rains.

pronto *adv.* (pronounced: *prahn-toh*) fast, right away.

EXAMPLE: Ed thought it would be best to leave the neighbors' yard **pronto** after meeting their new pet.

TRANSLATION: Ed thought it would be best to leave the neighbors' yard **right away** after meeting their new pet.

"REAL SPEAK": Ed thod id'ed be bes' ta leave the neighber's yard **prahn-toh** after meeding their new pet.

Que sera sera! *exp.* (pronounced: *kay seh-rah seh-rah*) What will be will be! (an expression of resignation).

EXAMPLE: I want to get that job but **que sera sera**!

TRANSLATION: I want to get that job but **what will be will be**!

"REAL SPEAK": I wanna get that job b't **kay seh-rah seh-rah**!

YIDDISH

bagel *n.* (pronounced: *bay-g'l*) a ring-shaped bread roll.

EXAMPLE: Make sure you get **bagels**, doughnuts, muffins, and coffee for the breakfast meeting.

TRANSLATION: Make sure you get **ring-shaped bread rolls**, doughnuts, muffins, and coffee for the breakfast meeting.

"REAL SPEAK": Make sher ya get **bay-g'lz**, doughnuts, muffins, 'n coffee fer the breakfast meeding.

nosh *n.* (pronounced: *nosh*) snack.

EXAMPLE: I've got to have a **nosh** or I won't survive until dinner!

TRANSLATION: I've got to have a **snack** or I won't survive until dinner!

"REAL SPEAK": I've godda have a **nosh** 'r I won't servive 'til dinner!

Oy! *eclam.* (pronounced: *oh'ee*) used to express surprise, fear, sadness, or most other negative reactions (the equivalent in English being *Oh!*).

EXAMPLE: **Oy**! Is this giving me a headache!

TRANSLATION: **Oh**! Is this giving me a headache!

"REAL SPEAK": **Oh'ee**! Iziss giving me a headache!

shlep (pronounced: *shlehp*) • **1.** *v.* to carry something heavy • **2.** *v.* to take a long time to do something • **3.** *n.* a sloppy-looking person.

EXAMPLE 1: Don't **shlep** those heavy boxes. You'll hurt yourself. Let me do it for you.

TRANSLATION: Don't **carry** those heavy boxes. You'll hurt yourself. Let me do it for you.

"REAL SPEAK": Don't **shlep** those heavy boxes. Ya'll hurt cherself. Lemme do it for ya.

EXAMPLE 2: Quit **shlepping** like an old man or we'll never make it to the movie on time.

TRANSLATION: Quit **walking so slowly** like an old man or we'll never make it to the movie on time.

"REAL SPEAK": Quit **shlehping** like 'n ol' man 'er we'll never make it ta the movie on time.

EXAMPLE 3: Helene used to be so elegant but ever since she got married, she's become such a **shlep**.

TRANSLATION: Helene used to be so elegant but ever since she got married, she's become such a **sloppy-looking person**.

"REAL SPEAK": Helene usta be so elegant b'd ever since she got married, she's b'come such a **shlehp**.

shlock *n.* (pronounced: *shlahk*) poorly made or defective merchandise.

EXAMPLE: I would never buy my clothes from that store. All they sell is **shlock**!

TRANSLATION: I would never buy my clothes from that store. All they sell is **poorly made merchandise**!

"REAL SPEAK": I'd never buy my clothes fr'm that store. All they sell 'ez **shlahk**!

schmaltzy *adj.* (pronounced: *shmahlt-see*) excessively sentimental.

EXAMPLE: My mother always gets very emotional every year when we give her a **schmaltzy** birthday card.

TRANSLATION: My mother always get very emotional every year when we give her an **excessively sentimental** birthday card.

"REAL SPEAK": My mother ahweez get very emotional ev'ry year when we give 'er a **shmahlt-see** birthday card.

Also: **schmaltz** *n.* excessive sentimentality.

shtick *n.* (pronounced: *shtik*) a person's style or behavior.

EXAMPLE: Don't be fooled by how sweet Maryanne is. I think that's just her **shtik** when she wants something from you.

TRANSLATION: Don't be fooled by how sweet Maryanne is. I think that's just her **personal style** when she wants something from you.

"REAL SPEAK": Don't be fooled by how sweet Maryanne is. I think that's just 'er **shtik** when she wants something from you.

tchotchke *n.* (pronounced: *chah'tch-kee*) a little, unimportant, inexpensive object.

EXAMPLE: Bertha's house is so full of **tchotchkes**. I don't know how she keeps them all clean. It's even hard to find a place to sit down!

TRANSLATION: Bertha's house is so full of **little objects**. I don't know how she keeps them all clean. It's even hard to find a place to sit down!

"REAL SPEAK": Bertha's house 'ez so full 'ev **chah'tch-keez**. I dunno how she keeps 'em all clean. It's even hard da find a place ta si' down!

verklempt *adj.* (pronounced: *fer-klempt*) emotional.

EXAMPLE: What a beautiful, romantic movie! I'm getting so **verklempt** I can hardly speak!

TRANSLATION: What a beautiful, romantic movie! I'm getting so **emotional** I can hardly speak!

"REAL SPEAK": Whad a beaudiful, romantic movie! I'm gedding so **fer-klempt** I c'n hardly speak!

Note: This adjective was popularized by the well known TV show *Saturday Night Live* where one of the characters was known for using this term regularly.

KAREN WENT ON AND ON ABOUT HER KNICK-KNACKS!

Alliterations & Repeating Words

THIS LESSON FEATURES 14 NEW SLANG WORDS & IDIOMS

LET'S WARM UP!

MATCH THE PICTURES

As a fun way to get started, see if you can guess the meaning of the new slang words and expressions on the opposite page by using the pictures below and following the context of the sentences.

1. Frances told me the same story ***over and over*** about how she got robbed on vacation.
   ❑ very loudly
   ❑ repeatedly

2. If you look closely at my new dress, you can see a ***criss-cross*** pattern on it.
   ❑ crossing-line
   ❑ round-dot

3. After Don was told he won the lottery, he couldn't stop ***grinning from ear to ear***!
   ❑ smiling a little
   ❑ smiling widely

4. Did you see the party dress Mary is wearing? It's so ***froufrou***!
   ❑ overly decorated
   ❑ increasing rapidly

5. I have a ***mishmash*** of reports I have to read by tomorrow morning!
   ❑ mixture
   ❑ dirty home

6. I met Karen on the Internet. Tomorrow we're going to meet ***face to face***.
   ❑ in public
   ❑ in person

7. My uncle's house is always ***spic-and-span***. You'll never find dirt in his house!
   ❑ completely clean
   ❑ very dirty

8. My aunt's house is filled with ***knick-knacks***. It's hard to find a place to sit!
   ❑ little things that she has collected
   ❑ expensive furniture

9. I never wear shoes to the beach. I always wear my ***flip-flops***.
   ❑ rubber sandals
   ❑ boots

10. Don't believe everything a car salesperson tells you. They're not always ***on the up and up***.
    ❑ tall
    ❑ honest

11. Every time I see Lucy, she ***goes on and on*** about how talented she is and how she wants to be an actress.
    ❑ talks briefly
    ❑ talks nonstop

12. Did you meet the new employee this morning? He's ***an out and out*** idiot! He can't do anything right.
    ❑ a total
    ❑ an occasional

13. I saw Ernie at the office party last night. We ***chit-chatted*** for almost two hours.
    ❑ had a casual conversation
    ❑ ate

14. Carl eats ice cream and potato chips all day. He's a real ***junk food junkie***!
    ❑ lover of unhealthy food
    ❑ lover of healthy food

LET'S TALK!

A. DIALOGUE USING SLANG & IDIOMS

The words introduced on the first two pages are used in the dialogue below. See if you can understand the conversation. *Note:* The translation of the words in boldface is on the right-hand page.

Peggy: I finally met the new neighbors **face to face** today. Their names are Karen and Alan. We **chit-chatted** for about an hour.

David: I kept promising myself **over and over** that I'd introduce myself, but I just haven't had the chance. So, what is their house like?

Peggy: It's a little **froufrou** for my taste. But I was surprised that with all the **knick-knacks** they collect, the house is so **spic-and-span**. And you should have seen their furniture. It's a **mishmash** of every style. Karen **went on and on** about how some of the furniture is worth thousands of dollars because it dates back to the 19th Century. At first, I thought she was an **out and out** liar, but when I took a closer look, she was **on the up and up**! I'd never seen such amazing antiques in my life!

David: I can't wait to see for myself! So, what do they look like?

Peggy: Well, Karen is always **grinning from ear to ear** and is very pretty. She came to the door wearing a cute dress with a **criss-cross** pattern on it. And Alan was wearing a big tee shirt and **flip-flops**. It's obvious he's a **junk food junkie**. He never stopped eating the entire time I was there.

David: Ah... my kind of friend!

B. DIALOGUE TRANSLATED INTO STANDARD ENGLISH

LET'S SEE HOW MUCH YOU REMEMBER!
Just for fun, move around in random order to the words and expressions in boldface below. See if you can remember their slang equivalents without looking at the left-hand page!

Peggy: I finally met the new neighbors **in person** today. Their names are Karen and Alan. We **had a friendly conversation** for about an hour.

David: I kept promising myself **many times** that I'd introduce myself, but I just haven't had the chance. So, what is their house like?

Peggy: It's a little **overly decorated** for my taste. But I was surprised that with all the **little objects** they collect, the house is so **totally clean**. And you should have seen their furniture. It's a **disorganized mixture** of every style. Karen **talked nonstop** about how some of the furniture is worth thousands of dollars because it dates back to the 19th Century. At first, I thought she was a **complete** liar, but when I took a closer look, she was **telling the truth**! I'd never seen such amazing antiques in my life!

David: I can't wait to see for myself! So, what do they look like?

Peggy: Well, Karen is always **smiling very widely** and is very pretty. She came to the door wearing a cute dress with a **crossing-line** pattern on it. And Alan was wearing a big tee shirt and **backless rubber sandals**. It's obvious he's **addicted to junk food**. He never stopped eating the entire time I was there.

David: Ah... my kind of friend!

C. DIALOGUE USING "REAL SPEAK"

The dialogue below demonstrates how the slang conversation on the previous page would *really* be spoken by native speakers!

CD-B: TRACK 1

Peggy: I fin'lly met the new neighbers **face ta face** taday. Their names 'er Karen 'n Alan. We **chit-chadded** fer aboud 'n hour.

David: I kep' promising myself **over 'n over** th'd I'd intraduce myself, b'd I just haven't had the chance. So, what's their house like?

Peggy: It's a liddle **froufrou** fer my taste. B'd I w'z saprised th't with all the **knick-knacks** they collect, the house 'ez so **spic-'n-span**. An' ya should 'a seen their furniture. It's a **mishmash** 'ev ev'ry style. Karen **wen' on 'n on** about how some 'a the furniture's worth thousands 'a dollers b'cuz it dates back ta the 19th Century. At first, I thought she w'z 'n **out 'n out** liar, b't when I took a closer look, she w'z **on the up 'n up**! I'd never seen such amazing antiques 'n my life!

David: I can't wait ta see fer myself! So, wha'do they look like?

Peggy: Well, Karen's always **grinning fr'm ear da ear** an' 'ez very preddy. She came ta the door wearing a cute dress with a **criss-cross** paddern on it. An' Alan w'z wearing a big tee shirt 'n **flip-flops**. It's obvious he's a **junk food junkie**. He never stopped eading the entire time I w'z there.

David: Ah... my kind 'a friend!

LET'S LEARN!

VOCABULARY

The following words and expressions were used in the previous dialogues. Let's take a closer look at what they mean.

CD-B: TRACK 2

chit-chat (to) • **1.** *v.* to converse casually • **2.** *n.* light, casual conversation.

EXAMPLE 1: Every morning, I stop at my uncle's house to **chit-chat** a little before going to work.

TRANSLATION: Every morning, I stop at my uncle's house to **converse casually** a little before going to work.

"REAL SPEAK": Ev'ry morning, I stop 'it my uncle's house ta **chit-chad** a liddle b'fore going ta work.

EXAMPLE 2: I had a nice **chit-chat** with the new neighbor today.

TRANSLATION: I had a nice **casual conversation** with the new neighbor today.

"REAL SPEAK": I had a nice **chit-chat** with the new neighbor today.

NOW YOU DO IT. COMPLETE THE PHRASE ALOUD:
Carol and I spent over an hour on the phone chit-chatting about...

criss-cross • **1.** *n.* a pattern or design of crossing lines • **2.** *v.* to move back and forth across or over • **3.** *v.* to draw or form a pattern of crossing lines.

EXAMPLE 1: Joan's new dress has a **criss-cross** of lines.

TRANSLATION: Joan's new dress has a **design of crossing** lines.

"REAL SPEAK": Joan's new dress has a **criss-cross** 'ev lines.

EXAMPLE 2: The soldiers **criss-crossed** over the field.

TRANSLATION: The soldiers **moved back and forth** over the field.

"REAL SPEAK": The soljers **criss-crossed** over the field.

EXAMPLE 3: The beams on the ceiling **criss-cross** over the room.

TRANSLATION: The beams on the ceiling **form a pattern of crossing lines** over the room.

"REAL SPEAK": [no change]

NOW YOU DO IT. COMPLETE THE PHRASE ALOUD:
I bought a... with a criss-cross pattern on it.

face to face *adv.* in person.

EXAMPLE: Ann and I have been communicating through the Internet for several months and we're finally going to meet **face to face** next week.

TRANSLATION: Ann and I have been communicating through the Internet for several months and we're finally going to meet **in person** next week.

"REAL SPEAK": Ann 'en I 'ev been communicading through the In'ernet fer sev'ral months 'n w'r fin'lly gonna meet **face ta face** nex' week.

NOW YOU DO IT. COMPLETE THE PHRASE ALOUD:
I'm meeting my boss face to face to tell him...

flip-flop • **1.** *n.* a flat rubber sandal without a back that is secured to the foot by a rubber thong between the first two toes • **2.** *v.* to make a sudden reversal (of attitude, policy, belief, direction, etc.).

EXAMPLE 1: I just bought new yellow **flip-flops** to match my bathing suit.

TRANSLATION: I just bought new yellow **backless, rubber sandals** to match my bathing suit.

"REAL SPEAK": I jus' bought new yellow **flip-flops** ta match my bathing suit.

EXAMPLE 2: My boss **flip-flopped** again on his vacation policy. Now, I have only two weeks of vacation a year instead of three.

TRANSLATION: My boss **made a sudden reversal** again on his vacation policy. Now, I have only two weeks of vacation a year instead of three.

"REAL SPEAK": My boss **flip-flopped** again on 'is vacation policy. Now, I have only two weeks of vacation a year instead 'ev three.

NOW YOU DO IT. COMPLETE THE PHRASE ALOUD:
Jack wore flip-flops to...? How embarrassing!

froufrou *adj.* overly decorated.

EXAMPLE: Angela's taste is not subtle. Her new dress is so **froufrou**! I get a headache every time I look at her!

TRANSLATION: Angela's taste is not subtle. Her new dress is so **overly decorated**! I get a headache every time I look at her!

"REAL SPEAK": Angela's taste isn't sud'l. Her new dress 'ez so **froufrou**! I ged a headache ev'ry time I look ad 'er!

NOW YOU DO IT. COMPLETE THE PHRASE ALOUD:
Did you see...? It's so froufrou!

grin from ear to ear (to) *exp.* to smile very widely.

EXAMPLE: When I told my father that I'd been accepted to medical school, he **grinned from ear to ear**.

TRANSLATION: When I told my father that I'd been accepted to medical school, he **smiled widely.**

"REAL SPEAK": When I told my father th'd I'd been accepted ta medical school, he **grinned fr'm ear da ear**.

Variation: **smile from ear to ear (to)** *exp.*

NOW YOU DO IT. COMPLETE THE PHRASE ALOUD:
Maria grinned from eat to ear when she found out that...

junk food junkie *exp.* a person who eats a lot of unhealthy foods that are high in salt, sugar, or fat such as potato chips, candy, cookies, cakes, etc.

EXAMPLE: Mark is a **junk food junkie**. Every day, he eats a whole bag of cookies and candy.

TRANSLATION: Mark is an **overeater of unhealthy foods**. Every day, he eats a whole bag of cookies and candy.

"REAL SPEAK": Mark's a **junk food junkie**. Ev'ry day, he eats a whole bag 'ev cookies 'n candy.

NOW YOU DO IT. COMPLETE THE PHRASE ALOUD:
I think Tessa is a junk food junkie because...

knick-knack *n.* an ornamental object that one has collected.

EXAMPLE: Eadie has cluttered her house with all of the **knick-knacks** she's collected on her travels.

TRANSLATION: Eadie has cluttered her house with all of the **ornamental objects** she's collected on her travels.

"REAL SPEAK": Eadie's cluddered 'er house with all 'a the **knick-knacks** she's collected on 'er travels.

NOW YOU DO IT. COMPLETE THE PHRASE ALOUD:
Some of my favorite knick-knacks I've collected over the years are...

mishmash *n.* a confused mess.

EXAMPLE: How do you think I can get any work done with this **mishmash** of papers on my desk?!

TRANSLATION: How do you think I can get any work done with this **confused mess** of papers on my desk?!

"REAL SPEAK": Howdy ya think I c'n ged any work done with this **mish-mash** 'ev papers on my desk?!

Synonym: **Hodge-podge** *n.*

NOW YOU DO IT. COMPLETE THE PHRASE ALOUD:
Did you taste the... that Janet made? I can't describe the taste. It's a mishmash of flavors.

on and on (to go) *exp.* to talk endlessly about something.

EXAMPLE: Jan **went on and on** about her husband, her children, her big, beautiful house and all the vacations they take. After thirty minutes, I was ready to stuff a sock in her mouth!

TRANSLATION: Jan **talked endlessly** about her husband, her children, her big, beautiful house and all the vacations they take. After thirty minutes, I was ready to stuff a sock in her mouth!

"REAL SPEAK": Jan **wen' on 'n on** aboud 'er husband, her children, her big, beaudiful house an' all the vacations they take. After thirdy minutes, I w'z ready da stuff a sock 'n 'er mouth!

NOW YOU DO IT. COMPLETE THE PHRASE ALOUD:
Liz went on and on about...

out and out *adj.* complete, total.

EXAMPLE: Our new boss is an **out and out** idiot. He poured paint in his coffee thinking it was cream!

TRANSLATION: Our new boss is a **complete** idiot. He poured paint in his coffee thinking it was cream!

"REAL SPEAK": 'Ar new boss 'ez 'n **oud 'n oud** idiot. He poured paint 'n 'is coffee thinking it w'z cream!

NOW YOU DO IT. COMPLETE THE PHRASE ALOUD:
Did you know that Glen is an out-and-out...?!

over and over *adv.* repeatedly.

EXAMPLE: Every time I see Pat, she tells me the same joke **over and over**. Her memory is getting terrible!

TRANSLATION: Every time I see Pat, she tells me the same joke **repeatedly**. Her memory is getting terrible!

"REAL SPEAK": Ev'ry time I see Pat, she tells me the same joke **over 'n over**. Her mem'ry's gedding terr'ble!

Variation: **over and over again** *exp.*

NOW YOU DO IT. COMPLETE THE PHRASE ALOUD:
I've told you over and over not to...

spic-and-span *adj.* completely clean.

EXAMPLE: Bernie loves to clean. Every time I visit him, his apartment is **spic-and-span**.

TRANSLATION: Bernie loves to clean. Every time I visit him, his apartment is **completely clean.**

"REAL SPEAK": Bernie loves ta clean. Ev'ry time I visid 'im, his apartment's **spic-'n-span**.

NOW YOU DO IT. COMPLETE THE PHRASE ALOUD:

My mother always makes sure that her... is spic-and-span.

up and up (to be on the) *exp.* to be honest, frank and sincere.

EXAMPLE: I bought a used car yesterday, but I don't think the salesperson was **on the up and up**. He said it was the only car in its color and today I saw a dozen exactly like it!

TRANSLATION: I bought a used car yesterday, but I don't think the salesperson was **honest**. He said it was the only car in its color and today I saw a dozen exactly like it!

"REAL SPEAK": I bod a used car yesterday, b'd I don't think the salesperson w'z **on the up 'n up**. He said it w'z the only car 'n its coler an' taday I saw a dozen exactly like it!

NOW YOU DO IT. COMPLETE THE PHRASE ALOUD:

I don't think John is on the up and up because...

LET'S PRACTICE!

A. THE UNFINISHED CONVERSATION

Read the conversations, then fill in the last line with your own words in response to what you've just read. Make sure to use the suggested words in your response. Your response can be in the form of a question or a statement.

CD-B: TRACK 3

1

Jodi: Don asked Alice to marry him today!

Angela: Finally! They've been dating each other for five years. Was she excited?

Jodi: ______________________

use: ***grinning from ear to ear***

2

Mark: Did you see Tim at the party last night?

Al: I sure did. He's really changed! He's gained so much weight!

Mark: ______________________

use: ***junk food junkie***

3

Kim: I just got back from a long vacation to Paris. It was absolutely wonderful!

Doug: Did you buy anything while you were there?

Kim: ______________________

use: ***knick-knacks***

4

Tessa: I'm going to buy a new car today! My neighbor works for a car dealership and he said he could get me a good price.

Nick: Are you sure you can trust him?

Tessa: ______________________

use: ***on the up and up***

5

Carl: I can't believe the way you decorated my house!

Mitch: Do you like it?

Carl: ______________________

use: ***froufrou***

B. CHOOSE THE RIGHT WORD

Underline the word that best completes the phrase.

CD-B: TRACK 4

1. Tim went (**up and up**, **on and on**, **face to face**) about how much he hates his job. If he doesn't like his job, he should just quit!

2. My mother loves to clean. That's why her house is always so spic and (**span**, **spin**, **spun**)!

3. You shouldn't go outside with nothing on your feet. The pavement is too hot! Put on my flip-(**fleas**, **floss**, **flops**).

4. Why are you grinning from (**face to face**, **toe to toe**, **ear to ear**)? Did you get the job you wanted?

5. I could eat cookies, candies, and potato chips for every meal. I'm a real junk food (**junkie**, **junket**, **junkyard**)!

6. You'll never guess who I saw in the market today. Lee Murphy! We haven't seen each other in years! We spent two hours chit-(**chanting**, **chewing**, **chatting**) in the parking lot!

7. I went to the modern art museum today and saw some interesting paintings. One of them was different colored lines going in all directions. They formed an interesting (**cross**, **criss**, **crest**)-cross pattern.

8. You can definitely trust that car salesperson. He's on the (**on and on**, **up and up**, **over and over**).

9. I brought you this gift from my trip to Rome. It's just a little knick-(**knack**, **knock**, **neck**) that I thought you would like.

10. I don't like this painting. It's nothing but a big mish(**mush**, **mouse**, **mash**) of colors. My eyes can't even focus anywhere!

11. I've told you (**over and over**, **up and up**, **spic-and-span**) not to borrow my clothes without my permission!

12. Rob told you he was a millionaire?! That guy is an (**up and up**, **over and over**, **out and out**) liar. He has no money at all!

C. COMPLETE THE STORY

Use the illustrations to help you fill in the blanks with the correct slang terms from the list below.

CD-B: TRACK 5

FACE-TO-FACE	KNICK-KNACKS	OUT AND OUT	FLIP-FLOPS
CHIT-CHAT	SPIC-AND-SPAN	UP AND UP	JUNK FOOD JUNKIE
OVER AND OVER	MISHMASH	EAR TO EAR	
FROUFROU	ON AND ON	CRISS-CROSS	

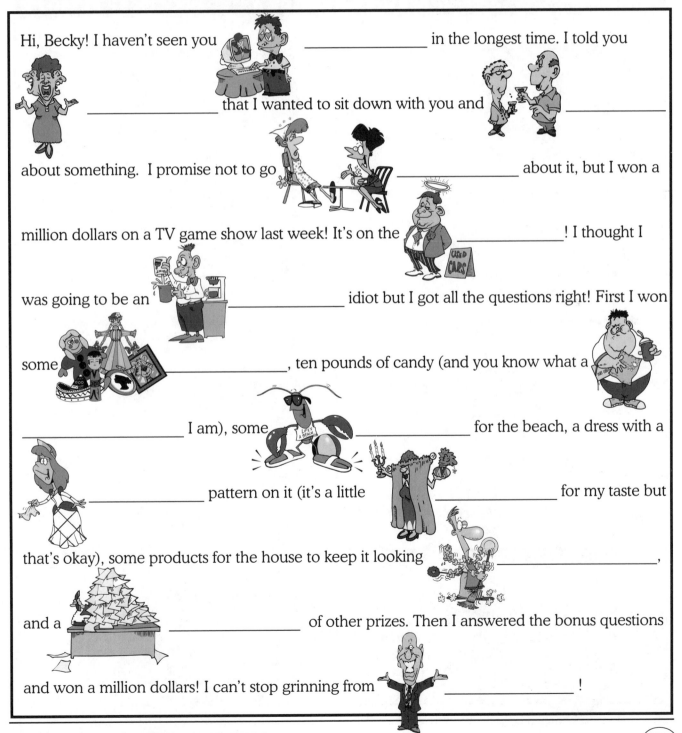

Hi, Becky! I haven't seen you ______________ in the longest time. I told you ______________ that I wanted to sit down with you and ______________ about something. I promise not to go ______________ about it, but I won a million dollars on a TV game show last week! It's on the ______________! I thought I was going to be an ______________ idiot but I got all the questions right! First I won some ______________, ten pounds of candy (and you know what a ______________ I am), some ______________ for the beach, a dress with a ______________ pattern on it (it's a little ______________ for my taste but that's okay), some products for the house to keep it looking ______________, and a ______________ of other prizes. Then I answered the bonus questions and won a million dollars! I can't stop grinning from ______________!

D. CREATE YOUR OWN SENTENCE

Read Person A's questions aloud, then use the suggested words to create your answer for Person B.

CD-B: TRACK 6

	PERSON A	PERSON B
1.	Why don't you ever believe anything Jim says to you?	use: **out and out**
2.	You've spoken with Tony hundreds of times, but you don't know what he looks like?	use: **face to face**
3.	Did you see all the ice cream and potato chips Tina ate at the party?	use: **junk food junkie**
4.	I heard you saw Tom Manne yesterday! Did you have a chance to talk with him?	use: **chit-chatted**
5.	What makes you think Bill was happy today?	use: **grinning from ear to ear**
6.	Why are you so angry at Peggy for borrowing your sweater?	use: **over and over**
7.	It's too hot to walk by the pool in your bare feet!	use: **flip-flops**
8.	What did you think of Irene's new home?	use: **spic-and-span**
9.	Do you think that I can believe everything that salesperson is telling me?	use: **up and up**
10.	Is it true that Sharon's house is like a museum?	use: **knick-knacks**

More Alliterations and Repeating Words

You'll no doubt be **gaga** *(excessively enthusiastic)* over this great **hodge-podge** *(mixture)* of alliterations and repeating words. Once you've learned them all, your knowledge of these types of words will be **tip-top** *(excellent)*!

ALLITERATIONS

bric-a-brac *n.* a collection of small objects arranged and displayed for their decorative or sentimental value.

EXAMPLE: I know my house is cluttered but all this **bric-a-brac** is important to me.

TRANSLATION: I know my house is cluttered but all these **small articles that I've collected** are important to me.

"REAL SPEAK": I know my house 'ez cluddered b'd all this **bric-a-brac** is important to me.

clip-clop *n.* the sound of horses' hooves on pavement.

EXAMPLE: Do you hear that **clip-clop**? I think there's a horse coming this way!

TRANSLATION: Do you hear that **sound of horses' hooves on pavement**? I think there's a horse coming this way!

"REAL SPEAK": Ya hear that **clip-clop**? I think there's a horse coming this way!

coochie-coo *exp.* words that indicate that someone is being tickled.

EXAMPLE: Are you ticklish? **Coochie-coo**!

TRANSLATION: Are you ticklish? **Tickle, tickle**!

"REAL SPEAK": Are ya ticklish? **Coochie-coo**!

Variation: **goochie-goo** *exp.*

ding-dong *n.* the sound made by a bell.

EXAMPLE: I just heard something go **ding-dong**. I think there's someone at your front door.

TRANSLATION: I just heard something make **a sound like a bell**. I think there's someone at your front door.

"REAL SPEAK": I jus' heard something go **ding-dong**. I think there's someone 'it cher front door.

ping-pong (to) *v.* (from Ping-Pong — a game of table tennis in which a ball is paddled back and forth over a net on a table) to move back and forth rapidly from one place or occupation to another.

EXAMPLE: Jack keeps **ping-ponging** from one job to another. He's never had a job for more than a month!

TRANSLATION: Jack keeps **rapidly changing** from one job to another. He's never had a job for more than a month!

"REAL SPEAK": Jack keeps **ping-ponging** fr'm one job to another. He's never had a job fer more th'n a month!

pitter-patter *n.* the sound of light taps in rapid succession, such as rain, footsteps, etc.

EXAMPLE: I like to lie in bed and listen to the **pitter-patter** of the rain in the morning.

TRANSLATION: I like to lie in bed and listen to the **tapping noise** of the rain in the morning.

"REAL SPEAK": I like ta lie 'n bed 'n listen ta the **pidder-padder** 'a the rain 'n the morning.

riffraff *n.* derogatory term for common people with a low social standing.

EXAMPLE: The thing I like about Barry's parties is that he invites both the people of the highest social classes and the **riffraff**.

TRANSLATION: The thing I like about Barry's parties is that he invites both the people of the highest social classes and **common people with a low social standing**.

"REAL SPEAK": The thing I like about Barry's pardies 'ez thad 'e invites both the people of the highest social classes an' the **riffraff**.

right as rain *exp.* (used primarily in the south) perfectly fine.

EXAMPLE: After being gone for so long, I was afraid of what I'd find when I got home. I was relieved to see that everything was **right as rain**.

TRANSLATION: After being gone for so long, I was afraid of what I'd find when I got home. I was relieved to see that everything was **perfectly fine**.

"REAL SPEAK": After being gone fer so long, I w'z afraid 'ev whad I'd find when I got home. I w'z relieve' ta see th'd ev'rything w'z **ride 'ez rain**.

seesaw • **1.** *n.* a game in which two children are each seated on opposite sides of a board raised under its middle so that the children can take turns going up and down • **2.** *v.* to change one's mind or attitude continually.

EXAMPLE 1: I'm not going to let Timmy play on a **seesaw** anymore. I'm afraid he'll fall off.

TRANSLATION: I'm not going to let Timmy play on **a board raised under its middle so that children can take turns going up and down** anymore. I'm afraid he'll fall off.

"REAL SPEAK": I'm not gonna let Timmy play on a **seesaw** anymore. I'm afraid 'e'll fall off.

EXAMPLE 2: Edgar can't stop **seesawing** about whether or not he's going to buy that house.

TRANSLATION: Edgar can't stop **changing his mind** about whether or not he's going to buy that house.

"REAL SPEAK": Edgar can't stop **seesawing** about whether 'er nod 'e's gonna buy that house.

Synonym: **teeter-totter** *n. & v.*

shipshape *adj.* very orderly.

EXAMPLE: Okay, boys. When I return, I want to see that you've cleaned up your room and made it **shipshape**.

TRANSLATION: Okay, boys. When I return, I want to see that you've cleaned up your room and made it **very orderly**.

"REAL SPEAK": Okay, boys. When I return, I wanna see th't chou've cleaned up yer room 'n made it **shipshape**.

singsong *adj.* said of someone's voice that goes up and down in a repetitious and monotonous fashion.

EXAMPLE: Every time a flight attendant makes the safety speech at the beginning of the flight, it's always **singsong**!

TRANSLATION: Every time a flight attendant makes the safety speech at the beginning of the flight, it's always **spoken in a voice going up and down in a repetitious and monotonous style**!

"REAL SPEAK": Ev'ry time a flide attendant makes the safety speech 'it the beginning 'a the flight, it's ahweez **singsong**!

ticktock • *n.* an alternating ticking sound, such as that made by a clock.

EXAMPLE: The **ticktock** of the grandfather clock in the hall kept me awake all night.

TRANSLATION: The **alternating ticking sound** of the grandfather clock in the hall kept me awake all night.

"REAL SPEAK": The **ticktock** 'a the gran'father clock 'n the hall kep' me awake all night.

Variation: **ticktocking** *n.*

tiptop • **1.** *adv.* at the highest point • **2.** *adj.* excellent.

EXAMPLE 1: I am going to place the star at the **tiptop** of the Christmas tree.

TRANSLATION: I am going to place the star at the **highest point** of the Christmas tree.

"REAL SPEAK": I'm gonna place the star 'it the **tiptop** 'a the Chris'mas tree.

EXAMPLE 2: My grandmother is in amazing health. She's always in **tiptop** condition.

TRANSLATION: My grandmother is in amazing health. She's always in **excellent** condition.

"REAL SPEAK": My gran'mother's in amazing health. She's ahweez 'n **tiptop** condition.

vim and vigor *exp.* energy and strength.

EXAMPLE: My father has exercised every day for the last fifty years. He is full of **vim and vigor**.

TRANSLATION: My father has exercised every day for the last fifty years. He is full of **energy and strength**.

"REAL SPEAK": My father's exercised ev'ry day fer the las' fifdy years. He's full 'a **vim 'n viger**.

wishy-washy *adj.* indecisive.

EXAMPLE: Stop being so **wishy-washy**. Just make up your mind!

TRANSLATION: Stop being so **indecisive**. Just make up your mind!

"REAL SPEAK": Stop being so **wishy-washy**. Jus' make up yer mind!

yakety-yak (to) *v.* to talk nonstop about nothing.

EXAMPLE: Every time my aunt calls, I know I'm going to be on the phone for at least an hour listening to her **yakety-yak**.

TRANSLATION: Every time my aunt calls, I know I'm going to be on the phone for at least an hour listening to her **talk nonstop about nothing**.

"REAL SPEAK": Ev'ry time my aunt calls, I know I'm gonna be on the phone fer 'it least 'n hour lis'ening to 'er **yakedy-yak**.

Variation: **yak (to)** *v.*

REPEATING WORDS

again and again *adv.* Repeatedly.

EXAMPLE: I've told you **again and again** not to borrow my sweater without my permission!

TRANSLATION: I've told you **repeatedly** not to borrow my sweater without my permission!

"REAL SPEAK": I've told 'ju **again 'n again** not ta borrow my sweader without my permission!

boo-boo *n.* • **1.** an insignificant, little mistake • **2.** a minor injury (used in talking to a small child or in jest when speaking to an adult).

EXAMPLE 1: This bill is way too high! I think the waiter made a **boo-boo** in his math.

TRANSLATION: This bill is way too high! I think the waiter made a **little mistake** in his math.

"REAL SPEAK": This bill's way too high! I think the waider made a **boo-boo** 'n 'is math.

EXAMPLE 2: Oh! Did Ernie fall down when he went skiing and get a **boo-boo**?!

TRANSLATION: Oh! Did Ernie fall down when he went skiing and get a **minor injury**?!

"REAL SPEAK": Oh! Did Ernie fall down when 'e went skiing 'n ged a **boo-boo**?!

bye-bye *exp.* • **1.** (informal) good-bye • **2. bye-bye (to go)** to leave (used in talking to a small child).

EXAMPLE 1: I have to go now. **Bye-bye**.

TRANSLATION: I have to go now. **Good-bye**.

"REAL SPEAK": I hafta go now. **Buh-bye**.

EXAMPLE 2: Does Baby want to **go bye-bye**?

TRANSLATION: Does Baby want to **leave**?

"REAL SPEAK": Does Baby wanna **go bye-bye**?

cheek-to-cheek *adv./adj.* one person's cheek pressed against another person's cheek.

EXAMPLE: I think Rick and Shawn are falling in love. They were dancing **cheek-to-cheek** all night!

TRANSLATION: I think Rick and Shawn are falling in love. They were dancing **with their cheeks pressed up against each other** all night!

"REAL SPEAK": I think Rick 'n Shawn 'er falling 'n love. They were dancing **cheek-ta-cheek** all night!

choo-choo *n.* (baby talk) train.

EXAMPLE: I want to ride on the **choo-choo**!

TRANSLATION: I want to ride on the **train!**

"REAL SPEAK": I wanna ride on the **choo-choo**!

Note 1: *Mommy* is children's language for "mother."

Note 2: Although it's actually redundant, children will also commonly say **choo-choo train**.

door-to-door • **1.** *adv./adj.* to go from one house to another, as in a salesperson who goes to people's homes to sell products • **2.** *adj.* describing a type of delivery which takes a package directly from a point of departure to a point of delivery.

EXAMPLE 1: After the crime, the police went **door-to-door** interviewing everyone in the neighborhood.

TRANSLATION: After the crime, the police went **from one house to another** interviewing everyone in the neighborhood.

"REAL SPEAK": After the crime, the police went **door-da-door** in'erviewing ev'ryone 'n the neighberhood.

EXAMPLE 2: We sent the package **door-to-door**. You should not have to go to the post office to pick it up.

TRANSLATION: We sent the package **directly from our place of business to your house**. You should not have to go to the post office to pick it up.

"REAL SPEAK": We sent the package **door-da-door**. Ya shouldn' hafta go da the post office ta pick id up.

eye to eye (to see) *exp.* to agree, to be of the same opinion.

EXAMPLE: Ed and I have been successful partners for ten years because we **see eye to eye** on everything.

TRANSLATION: Ed and I have been successful partners for ten years because we **agree** on everything.

"REAL SPEAK": Ed 'n I 'ev been successful partners fer ten years b'cuz we **see eye da eye** on ev'rything.

gaga over someone or something (to be) *exp.* • **1.** to be excessively, even foolishly enthusiastic • **2.** to be infatuated • **3.** to be senile from old age.

EXAMPLE 1: Many people are **gaga over** anything having to do with Elvis Presley.

TRANSLATION: Many people are **excessively and foolishly enthusiastic about** anything having to do with Elvis Presley.

"REAL SPEAK": Many people 'er **gaga over** anything having da do w'th Elvis Presley.

EXAMPLE 2: Poor Al. He's totally **gaga over** Clarice but she always ignores him.

TRANSLATION: Poor Al. He's totally **infatuated with** Clarice but she always ignores him.

"REAL SPEAK": Poor Al. He's todally **gaga over** Clarice b't she ahweez ignores 'im.

EXAMPLE 3: My grandfather is getting a little **gaga**. He thinks he's Superman!

TRANSLATION: My grandfather is getting a little **senile**. He thinks he's Superman!

"REAL SPEAK": My gran'father's gedding a liddle **gaga**. He thinks 'e's Superman!

"Ha ha!" *exp.* indicates laughter, but of a sarcastic nature in which one is laughing at another (and is voiced in a melodic style where the second "ha" lowers in pitch).

EXAMPLE: You flunked the English final? **Ha ha!** I got a perfect score!

TRANSLATION: You flunked the English final? **(Melodic laugh where the second "ha" has a loswer pitch than the first)**. I got a perfect score!

"REAL SPEAK": Ya flunked the English final? **Ha ha!** I god a perfect score!

hand in hand *adv.* together • (lit.): with one's hand holding another person's hand.

EXAMPLE: The actors and writers worked **hand in hand** to create a brilliant theatrical production.

TRANSLATION: The actors and writers worked **together** to create a brilliant theatrical production.

"REAL SPEAK": The acters 'n wriders worked **hand 'n hand** ta creade a brilliant theatrical praduction.

Variation: **hand in hand (to go)** *exp.* to happen at the same time • *Springtime and weddings go* ***hand in hand;*** Springtime and weddings ***happen at the same time***.

hand-to-hand *adj.* close to one's adversary.

EXAMPLE: Nowadays, battles are fought from the air but centuries ago, fighting was **hand-to-hand** combat.

TRANSLATION: Nowadays, battles are fought from the air but centuries ago, fighting was combat **close to one's adversary**.

"REAL SPEAK": Nowadays, baddles 'er fought fr'm the air b't centuries ago, fiding w'z **han'-da-han'** combat.

head-to-head (to go) *exp.* to battle verbally (as two rams ramming their horns together in combat).

EXAMPLE: Bret and Debbie **went head-to-head** the whole day over which one of them was going to name their new dog.

TRANSLATION: Bret and Debbie **battled verbally** the whole day over which one of them was going to name their new dog.

"REAL SPEAK": Bret 'n Debbie **went head-da-head** the whole day over which one 'ev 'em w'z gonna name their new dog.

heart-to-heart • **1.** *adj.* frank, sincere • **2.** *n.* a frank, sincere discussion, usually between two people.

EXAMPLE 1: Betty and I finally had a **heart-to-heart** talk about all our differences.

TRANSLATION: Betty and I finally had a **frank, sincere** talk about all our differences.

"REAL SPEAK": Beddy 'n I fin'lly had a **heart-ta-heart** talk aboud all 'ar diff'rences.

EXAMPLE 2: I need to have a **heart-to-heart** with Tom or he's going to lose his job.

TRANSLATION: I need to have a **frank, sincere talk** with Tom or he's going to lose his job.

"REAL SPEAK": I need da have a **heart-ta-heart** w'th Tom 'r 'e's gonna lose 'is job

"Hip hip hooray!" *exp.* a common cheer of approval.

EXAMPLE: Our team beat the opposing team and we won the tournament. **Hip hip hooray!**

TRANSLATION: Our team beat the opposing team and we won the tournament. **(Cheer of approval).**

"REAL SPEAK": 'Ar team beat the opposing team 'n we won the tournament. **Hip hip hooray!**

hush-hush *exp.* said of something being kept secret.

EXAMPLE: I'm planning a big surprise party next month for all the employees. Don't say anything to anyone. It's very **hush-hush**.

TRANSLATION: I'm planning a big surprise party next month for all the employees. Don't say anything to anyone. It's **a big secret**.

"REAL SPEAK": I'm planning a big saprise pardy nex' month fer all the employees. Don't say anything ta anyone. It's very **hush-hush**.

less and less • **1.** *adv.* increasingly seldom • **2.** *adj.* to a decreasing amount.

EXAMPLE 1: People are going to the theater **less and less** these days.

TRANSLATION: People are going to the theater **increasingly seldom** these days.

"REAL SPEAK": People 'er going ta the theeder **less 'n less** these days.

EXAMPLE 2: I'm spending **less and less** time at work because I'm doing most of my assignments at home on my computer.

TRANSLATION: I'm spending **a decreasing amount of** time at work because I'm doing most of my assignments at home on my computer.

"REAL SPEAK": I'm spending **less 'n less** time 'it work b'cuz I'm doing most 'a my assignments 'it home on my c'mpuder.

Antonym: **more and more** • **1.** *adv.* increasingly frequently • **2.** *adj.* to an increasing degree.

mouth-to-mouth *exp.* (short for *mouth-to-mouth resuscitation*) a respiration technique used on someone who has stopped breathing, involving placing one's mouth over the mouth of the injured person and blowing air into his/her lungs.

EXAMPLE: Quick! Give him **mouth-to-mouth** or he's going to die!

TRANSLATION: Quick! Give him **mouth-to-mouth resuscitation** or he's going to die!

"REAL SPEAK": Quick! Give 'im **mouth-ta-mouth** 'er 'e's gonna die!

"Naughty naughty!" *exp.* (child language) "That's very bad behavior!"

EXAMPLE: Did you just touch that after I told you not to? **Naughty naughty**!

TRANSLATION: Did you just touch that after I told you not to? **That's very bad behavior**!

"REAL SPEAK": Did'ju jus' touch thad after I told 'ju not to? **Nody nody**!

"Night-night" *exp.* • **1.** "Good night" • **2. night-night (to go)** to go to sleep (used when speaking to a child).

EXAMPLE 1: I'll see you tomorrow. **Night-night**.

TRANSLATION: I'll see you tomorrow. **Good night**.

"REAL SPEAK": See ya damorrow. **Night-night**.

EXAMPLE 2: It's time to **go night-night**. Go brush your teeth.

TRANSLATION: It's time to **go to sleep**. Go brush your teeth.

"REAL SPEAK": It's time da **go night-night**. Go brush yer teeth.

no-no *n.* (usually used when speaking to a child) something forbidden.

EXAMPLE: Billy, I told you that hitting your sister is a **no-no**.

TRANSLATION: Billy, I told you that hitting your sister is **forbidden**.

"REAL SPEAK": Billy, I tol'ju th't hidding yer sister's a **no-no**.

"Now, now" *n.* "Take a moment to regain control of your emotions."

EXAMPLE:
– I can't believe Jan didn't call me to wish me happy birthday. I'm never speaking to her again!
– **Now, now**. She's always very busy at work. I'm sure she'll call tonight when she gets home.

TRANSLATION:
– I can't believe Jan didn't call me to wish me happy birthday. I'm never speaking to her again!
– **Take a moment to regain control of your emotions**. She's always very busy at work. I'm sure she'll call tonight when she gets home.

"REAL SPEAK":
– I can't believe Jan didn't call me da wish me happy birthday. I'm never speaking da her again!
– **Now, now**. She's ahweez very busy 'it work. I'm sher she'll call tanight wh'n she gets home.

peepee (to go) *exp.* (baby talk, also used in jest by adults) to urinate.

EXAMPLE: Okay, children. Everybody **go peepee** before we start our long drive.

TRANSLATION: Okay, children. Everybody **urinate** before we start our long drive.

"REAL SPEAK": Okay, children. Ev'rybody **go peepee** b'fore we stard 'ar long drive.

pompom *n.* an ornamental bunch of wool, feathers, or strips of colored paper used as decoration, particularly by cheerleaders.

EXAMPLE: Don't you think that cheerleader is flirting with me? She's shaking her **pompom** in my direction.

TRANSLATION: Don't you think that cheerleader is flirting with me? She's shaking her **bunch of colored paper strips** in my direction.

"REAL SPEAK": Dontcha think that cheerleader's flirding with me? She's shaking 'er **pompom** 'n my direction.

Variation: **pompon** *n.*

pooh-pooh (to) *v.* (with emphasis on the second syllable) to show a lack of respect for something and then to reject it.

EXAMPLE: My colleagues **pooh-poohed** my idea of allowing the employees to dress casually every Friday.

TRANSLATION: My colleagues **showed disrespect in rejecting** my idea of allowing the employees to dress casually every Friday.

"REAL SPEAK": My colleagues **pooh-poohed** my idea 'ev allowing the employees ta dress casually ev'ry Friday.

Note: The term **pooh-pooh** has two *very* different meanings depending on where you place the stress. If you put the stress on the second syllable, the meaning is "to show a lack of respect for something and then to reject it." However if the stress is on the first syllable, the meaning is a child's word for "defecation"!

R and R *exp.* (originally a military term) rest and recreation, rest and recuperation, or rest and relaxation.

EXAMPLE: I've been working over fifty hours every week. Next month I'm going to Hawaii for some **R and R**.

TRANSLATION: I've been working over fifty hours every week. Next month I'm going to Hawaii for some **rest and recreation**.

"REAL SPEAK": I've been working over fifdy hours ev'ry week. Nex' month I'm going ta Hawaii fer s'm **R 'n R**.

same old, same old *exp.* the usual.

EXAMPLE:
– Hi, Ken. What's new?
– **Same old, same old**. Nothing new and exciting ever happens in my life.

TRANSLATION:
– Hi, Ken. What's new?
– **The usual**. Nothing new and exciting ever happens in my life.

"REAL SPEAK":
– Hi, Ken. What's new?
– **Same ol', same old**. Nothing new 'n exciding ever happens 'n my life.

so-and-so *n.* • **1.** someone whose identity is not definitely named • **2.** euphemistic usage to replace a vulgar noun pertaining to someone.

EXAMPLE 1: Let's say **so-and-so** came into the store. What would be the first thing you would do?

TRANSLATION: Let's say **someone whose identity is not definitely named** came into the store. What would be the first thing you would do?

"REAL SPEAK": Let's say **so-'n-so** came inta the store. What'd be the first thing ya'd do?

EXAMPLE 2: I never liked Pat. He's nothing but an old **so-and-so**.

TRANSLATION: I never liked Pat. He's nothing but an old **(vulgar noun)**.

"REAL SPEAK": I never liked Pat. He's nothing bud 'n ol' **so-'n-so**.

so-so *adj.* neither very good nor very bad, just okay.

EXAMPLE:
– What did you think of the movie?
– **So-so**. It's the kind of movie I've seen a thousand times.

TRANSLATION:
– What did you think of the movie?
– **Just okay**. It's the kind of movie I've seen a thousand times.

"REAL SPEAK":
– Whad'ja think 'a the movie?
– **So-so**. It's the kinda movie I've seen a thousan' times.

"Ta ta!" *exp.* "Good-bye!"

EXAMPLE: Hope to see you again soon. Give my best to your family. **Ta ta**.

TRANSLATION: Hope to see you again soon. Give my best to your family. **Good-bye**.

"REAL SPEAK": Hope ta see ya again soon. Best ta yer fam'ly. **Ta ta**.

Note: On occasion, you may hear people shortened this expression to *"Ta!"*

"There, there" *exp.* (said when comforting someone who is crying) "Everything is going to be alright."

EXAMPLE: **There, there**. I know that ending a relationship with someone is never easy, but it's all for the best.

TRANSLATION: **Everything is going to be alright**. I know that ending a relationship with someone is never easy, but it's all for the best.

"REAL SPEAK": **There, there**. I know th'd ending a relationship w'th someone's never easy, b'd it's all fer the best.

through and through *adv.* completely.

EXAMPLE: I walked a half hour in the rain and now I'm wet **through and through**.

TRANSLATION: I walked a half hour in the rain and now I'm **completely** wet.

"REAL SPEAK": I walked a half hour 'n the rain 'n now I'm wet **thru 'n thru**.

toe-to-toe • **1.** *adv.* in an attitude of direct confrontation • **2.** *adj.* in constant disagreement.

EXAMPLE 1: When Joe and Bob argue, they go **toe-to-toe** for hours.

TRANSLATION: When Joe and Bob argue, they do it **in an attitude of direct confrontation** for hours.

"REAL SPEAK": When Joe 'n Bob argue, they go **toe-da-toe** fer hours.

EXAMPLE 2: Those two are **toe-to-toe** on every matter. I wish they'd agree on something.

TRANSLATION: Those two are **in constant disagreement** on every matter. I wish they'd agree on something.

"REAL SPEAK": Those two 'er **toe-da-toe** on ev'ry matter. I wish they'd agree on something.

JENNY BECOMES A FIREFIGHTER!

How to be Politically Correct or "PC"

THIS LESSON FEATURES 14 NEW SLANG WORDS & IDIOMS

LET'S WARM UP!

READING

MATCH THE PICTURES

As a fun way to get started, see if you can guess the meaning of the new slang words and expressions on the opposite page by using the pictures below and following the context of the sentences.

1 2 3 4 5 6 7 8

WAKY news

- ☐ 1. Those are my favorite ***actors***! I'm going to get their autographs!
- ☐ 2. My sister is a ***flight attendant***. She travels everywhere!
- ☐ 3. If we're not careful about protecting the earth, ***humankind*** could be in terrible trouble!
- ☐ 4. Jack and Irene became ***husband and wife*** fifty years ago.
- ☐ 5. George is a great ***comedian***. He's so funny!
- ☐ 6. If anyone wants information about our company, Janice is our ***spokesperson***.
- ☐ 7. Al is ***a self-made person***. He built a big company by himself.
- ☐ 8. I just saw Brad on television reporting the news. He's an ***anchor*** on a big television station.
- ☐ 9. There's a fire in that building! Call a ***firefighter***! Hurry!
- ☐ 10. My first day as a ***police officer***, I arrested a major criminal!
- ☐ 11. I'm only a ***frosh*** in college. I have another three years to go.
- ☐ 12. I'm going to let you ***run*** the company while I'm on vacation.
- ☐ 13. Where's the ***mail carrier***? I'm expecting an important letter.
- ☐ 14. We don't have enough ***personnel*** to finish all this work.

A. passenger-assistant who works in an airplane
B. representative
C. on-camera person who reports the news
D. movie (television or theatrical) performers
E. an entrepreneur
F. person hired by the city to make sure that the laws are being enforced
G. student in my first year
H. a married couple
I. operate
J. person whose occupation is to deliver the mail
K. performer of funny stories and jokes
L. employees
M. all the inhabitants of the earth
N. person whose occupation is to extinguish fires

LET'S TALK!

A. DIALOGUE USING SLANG & IDIOMS

The words introduced on the first two pages are used in the dialogue below. See if you can understand the conversation. *Note:* The translation of the words in boldface is on the right-hand page.

CD-B: TRACK 7

Jodi: So, who is in this movie?

Nancy: It's starring Susie Jones.

Jodi: You mean the **actor** who was discovered when she was a **flight attendant**? Sure, I know her. She's a really funny **comedian**.

Nancy: Well in this, she plays the part of a **self-made person** named Jenny, who becomes a **firefighter** although she's only a **frosh** in college. So she's at this huge fire, **running** the water pump, when suddenly, the entire building collapses and she gets trapped! Unfortunately, there's not enough **personnel** to rescue everyone. Luckily, a **mail carrier** and **police officer** are nearby to help. During all this, an **anchor** is interviewing a **spokesperson** from the fire department who tells us that there's a bomb in the building which could explode at any moment! When the police officer hears this, he rushes into the building, rescues Jenny and disables the bomb. By the end of the story, Jenny and the police officer become **husband and wife** and all of **humankind** is saved!

B. DIALOGUE TRANSLATED INTO STANDARD ENGLISH

Just for fun, move around in random order to the words and expressions in boldface below. See if you can remember their slang equivalents without looking at the left-hand page!

Note: The non-politically correct (or non-PC) version and translation are given.

READING

Jodi: So, who is in this movie?

Nancy: It's starring Susie Jones.

Jodi: You mean the **actress** *(a woman who has a speaking part in a television, movie, or theatrical performance)* who was discovered when she was a **stewardess** *(a woman whose occupation is to assist passengers in an airplane)*? Sure, I know her. She's a really funny **comedienne** *(a woman who performs a humorous monologue)*.

Nancy: Well in this, she plays the part of a **self-made man** *(a man who starts his own company)* named Jenny, who becomes a **fireman** *(a man whose job it is to extinguish fires)* although she's only a **freshman** *(a student in his first year of school)* in college. So she's at this huge fire, **manning** *(operating)* the water pump, when suddenly, the entire building collapses and she gets trapped! Unfortunately, there's not enough **manpower** *(personnel who help perform a duty as a team)* to rescue everyone. Luckily, a **postman** *(a man whose occupation is to deliver the mail to your home or office)* and **policeman** *(a man hired by the city to make sure that the laws are being enforced)* are nearby to help. During all this, an **anchorman** *(the on-camera male who reports the news)* is interviewing a **spokesman** *(a representative who speaks for someone else)* from the fire department who tells us that there's a bomb in the building which could explode at any moment! When the policeman hears this, he rushes into the building, rescues Jenny and disables the bomb. By the end of the story, Jenny and the policeman become **man and wife** *(a married couple)* and all of **mankind** *(the inhabitants of earth)* is saved!

C. DIALOGUE USING "REAL SPEAK"

The dialogue below demonstrates how the slang conversation on the previous page would *really* be spoken by native speakers!

CD-B: TRACK 7

Jodi: So, who's 'n this movie anyway?

Nancy: It's starring Susie Jones.

Jodi: Ya mean the **acter** who w'z discovered when she w'z a **flide attendant**? Sher, I know 'er. She's a really funny **comedian**.

Nancy: Well in this, she plays the pard 'ev a **self-made person** named Jenny, who b'comes a **fire fider** although she's only a **frosh** 'n college. So she's at this huge fire, **running** the water pump, when suddenly, the entire building collapses 'n she gets trapped! Unfortunately, there's nod anuf **personnel** da rescue ev'ryone. Luckily, a **mail carrier** 'n **police officer** are nearby da help. During all this, an **ancher** 's in'erviewing a **spokesperson** from the fire department who tells us th't there's a bomb 'n the building which could explode ad any moment! When the police officer hears this, he rushes inta the building, rescues Jenny 'n disables the bomb. By the end 'a the story, Jenny 'n the police officer become **husband 'n wife** 'n all 'ev **humankind** is saved!

LET'S LEARN!

VOCABULARY

The following words and expressions were used in the previous dialogues. Let's take a closer look at what they mean.

Note that in this lesson, terms that are followed by *m.* refer to a masculine noun, terms that are followed by *f.* refer to a feminine noun, and terms followed by *n.* indicate a noun that can be applied to both sexes.

CD-B: TRACK 8

actor *n.* one who has a speaking part in a television, movie, or theatrical performance; performer.

NON-PC VERSION: **actor** *m.* • **actress** *f.*

EXAMPLE: I just had the most exciting night of my life! I went to a movie opening and saw some of my favorite **actors**!

TRANSLATION: I just had the most exciting night of my life! I went to a movie opening and saw some of my favorite **performers**!

"REAL SPEAK": I just had the most exciding nide 'a my life! I went to a movie opening 'n saw some 'a my fav'rid **acters**!

NOW YOU DO IT. COMPLETE THE PHRASE ALOUD:
My favorite actor is... because...

anchor *n.* the on-camera person who reports the news.

NON-PC VERSION: **anchorman** *m.* • **anchorwoman** *f.*

EXAMPLE: My neighbor is a popular news **anchor** in Los Angeles.

TRANSLATION: My neighbor is a popular news **reporter** in Los Angeles.

"REAL SPEAK": My neighbor's a populer news **ancher** 'n L.A.

Synonym 1: **announcer** *n.*

Synonym 2: **newscaster** *n.*

NOW YOU DO IT. COMPLETE THE PHRASE ALOUD:
Today, I heard the anchor report a story about...

comedian *n.* one who performs a humorous monologue full of funny stories and jokes.

NON-PC VERSION: **comedian** *m.* • **comedienne** *f.*

EXAMPLE: Edward is so funny! He should be a **comedian**!

TRANSLATION: Edward is so funny! He should be a **person who performs alone, making people laugh**!

"REAL SPEAK": Edward's so funny! He should be a **camedian**!

Synonym: **comic** *n.*

NOW YOU DO IT. COMPLETE THE PHRASE ALOUD:
...is my favorite comedian!

firefighter *n.* one whose occupation is to extinguish fires.

NON-PC VERSION: **fireman** *m.*

EXAMPLE: My sister has been a **firefighter** for several years. She's considered one of the best in the city!

TRANSLATION: My sister has been a **person who extinguishes fires** for several years. She's considered one of the best in the city!

"REAL SPEAK": My sister's been a **firefider** fer sev'ral years. She's considered one 'a the best 'n the cidy!

Note: At one point in time, no feminine version existed because these professions were closed to women.

NOW YOU DO IT. COMPLETE THE PHRASE ALOUD:
It took... firefighters to put out the fire at...

flight attendant *n.* one whose occupation is to assist passengers in an airplane.

NON-PC VERSION: **steward** *m.* • **stewardess** / **air hostess** *f.*

EXAMPLE: If your seat isn't comfortable, just ask the **flight attendant** to bring you a few pillows to put behind your back.

TRANSLATION: If your seat isn't comfortable, just ask the **passenger-assistant who works in the airplane** to bring you a few pillows to put behind your back.

"REAL SPEAK": If yer sead isn't comf'tr'ble, just ask the **flide attendant** ta bring ya a few pillows ta put behin 'jer back.

NOW YOU DO IT. COMPLETE THE PHRASE ALOUD:
I want to be a flight attendant because...

frosh *n.* a student in his/her first year of school.

NON-PC VERSION: **freshman** *n.*

EXAMPLE: Grant is only fourteen years old and he's already a **frosh** at a major university.

TRANSLATION: Grant is only fourteen years old and he's already a **student in his first year** at a major university.

"REAL SPEAK": Grant's only fourteen years old 'n 'e's ahready a **frosh** 'id a majer universidy.

NOW YOU DO IT. COMPLETE THE PHRASE ALOUD:
...is a frosh at...

humankind *n.* all the inhabitants of the earth..

NON-PC VERSION: **mankind** *n.*

EXAMPLE: Scientists are constanly working toward a cure for cancer which will greatly benefit **humankind**.

TRANSLATION: Scientists are constanly working toward a cure for cancer which will greatly benefit **all the inhabitants of the earth**.

"REAL SPEAK": Scientists are constanly working toward a cure for cancer which will greatly benefit **humankind**.

NOW YOU DO IT. COMPLETE THE PHRASE ALOUD:
Humankind has greatly benefitted from the invention of...

husband and wife [or] **wife and husband** *m. & f.* a married couple, the label of a man and a woman who have just gotten married.

NON-PC VERSION: **man and wife** *m. & f.*
Note: This was the typical label of a man and a woman who just got married. The implication here is that they are not equal from the start since the term *wife* carries certain responsbilities toward the husband and the term *man* carries none.

EXAMPLE: And now, by the power vested in me, I now pronounce you **husband and wife**.

TRANSLATION: And now, by the power vested in me, I now pronounce you **a married couple.**

"REAL SPEAK": An' now, by the power vested 'n me, I now pranounce you **husband 'n wife**.

NOW YOU DO IT. COMPLETE THE PHRASE ALOUD:
... and ... are going to become husband and wife!

mail carrier *n.* one whose occupation is to deliver the mail to your home or office.

NON-PC VERSION: **mailman** *m.*

Note: At one point in time, no feminine version existed because these professions were closed to women.

EXAMPLE: I wonder what time the **mail carrier** is going to get here. I'm expecting an important letter from New York.

TRANSLATION: I wonder what time the **person who delivers our mail** is going to get here. I'm expecting an important letter from New York.

"REAL SPEAK": I wonder what time the **mail carrier**'s gonna get here. I'm expecting 'n important ledder fr'm New York.

Synonym 1: **letter carrier** *n,*

Synonym 2: **postal carrier** *n.*

NOW YOU DO IT. COMPLETE THE PHRASE ALOUD:
Our mail carrier just delivered a package from...

personnel *n.* employees.

NON-PC VERSION: **manpower** *m.*

EXAMPLE: Our hospital has the best **personnel** in the medical field. The patients always give us the best reviews.

TRANSLATION: Our hospital has the best **employees** in the medical field. The patients always give us the best reviews.

"REAL SPEAK": 'Ar hospid'l has the best **personnel** 'n the medical field. The patients ahweez give us the best reviews.

Synonym 1: **staff** *n.*

Synonym 2: **workforce** *n.*

NOW YOU DO IT. COMPLETE THE PHRASE ALOUD:
We need to hire some more personnel soon to help us ...

police officer *n.* one who is hired by the city to make sure that the laws are being enforced.

NON-PC VERSION: **policeman** *m.* • **policewoman** *f.*

EXAMPLE: One of the most important duties of a **police officer** is to keep the city safe from criminal activity.

TRANSLATION: One of the most important duties of a **person hired by the city to make sure that our laws are enforced** is to keep the city safe from criminal activity.

"REAL SPEAK": One 'a the most important dudies of a **police officer** is ta keep the cidy safe fr'm criminal activity.

Note: A *police officer* is referred to as a *cop* in slang, commonly used among police officers!

NOW YOU DO IT. COMPLETE THE PHRASE ALOUD:
Quick! We need to call a police officer because...

run something (to) *n.* to operate something.

NON-PC VERSION: **man (to)** *v.* (used for both sexes).

EXAMPLE: I need to find someone who can **run** my company while I'm on vacation.

TRANSLATION: I need to find someone who can **operate** my company while I'm on vacation.

"REAL SPEAK": I need da fine someone who c'n **run** my comp'ny while I'm on vacation.

Synonym 1: **run (to)** *v.*

Synonym 2: **staff (to)** *v.*

NOW YOU DO IT. COMPLETE THE PHRASE ALOUD:

I don't know how to run this...

self-made person *n.* an entrepreneur, one who has created his/her own company.

NON-PC VERSION: **self-made man** *m.*

Note: At one time, no feminine version existed because only men were given the opportunity to succeed in the business world.

EXAMPLE: Greg is a **self-made person**. He started his own Web design business and now he's a millionaire!

TRANSLATION: Greg is a **person who has started his own company**. He started his own Web design business and now he's a millionaire!

"REAL SPEAK": Greg's a **self-made person**. He starded 'is own Web design bizness 'n now 'e's a millionaire!

NOW YOU DO IT. COMPLETE THE PHRASE ALOUD:

Jennifer is a self-made person. She started her own...

spokesperson *n.* a representative who speaks for someone else.

NON-PC VERSION: **spokesman** *m.*

EXAMPLE: There is a newspaper reporter here who would like to interview us about our new fashions for women. Let's have Noah speak with the reporter. He's a great **spokesperson** for our products.

TRANSLATION: There is a newspaper reporter here who would like to interview us about our new fashions for women. Let's have Noah speak with the reporter. He's a great **representative** for our products.

"REAL SPEAK": There's a newspaper raporder here who'd like ta in'erview us aboud 'ar new fashions fer women. Let's have Noah speak with the raporder. He's a great **spokesperson** fer 'ar produc's.

NOW YOU DO IT. COMPLETE THE PHRASE ALOUD:

...is a spokesperson for...

LET'S PRACTICE!

A. "ACROSS" WORD PUZZLE

Fill in the crossword puzzle by choosing the correct word from the list below.

CD-B: TRACK 9

CARRIER	OFFICER
COMEDIAN	PERSONNEL
FROSH	RUNS
HUMANKIND	SELF-MADE

1. The police ________ arrested the bank robber.
2. Al is a ____-____ person. He started his own company!
3. Nancy is so funny! She should be a ________.
4. The mail ________ just left this letter for you.
5. My mother ________ a big company all by herself!
6. Dan is a ________ but he's graduating in two years!
7. The meteor missed us! ________ is saved!
8. Our company has become so busy that we need to hire more ________ soon!

B. CROSSWORD PUZZLE

Fill in the crossword puzzle by choosing the PC (politically correct) word from the list below.

CD-B: TRACK 10

ACTOR	FIGHTER	PERSONNEL
ANCHOR	FROSH	RUN
ATTENDANT	HUMANKIND	SELF
CARRIER	HUSBAND	SPOKESPERSON
COMEDIAN	OFFICER	

ACROSS

1. The non-PC expression, *man and wife*, has been replaced by ___ *and wife.*

13. The terms *policeman* and *policewoman* have been replaced by police ___.

18. A person who has created his/her own company is called a ___*-made person.*

19. A student in his/her first year of school is called a ___.

23. The PC version of *manpower* is ___.

27. The PC version of *mailman* is *postal* ___.

31. A person who performs a humorous monologue full of funny stories and jokes in order to make people laugh is called a ___.

36. The PC version of *actress* is ___.

41. ___ refers to all the inhabitants of the earth.

47. A *fireman* is now called a *fire* ___.

DOWN

3. A representative who speaks for someone else is called a ___.

20. *To man something* is the non-PC version of *to* ___ *something.*

32. The terms *steward*, *stewardess*, and *air hostess* are non-PC terms for flight___.

33. The on-camera person who reports the news is called an ___.

CROSSWORD PUZZLE

C. YOU'RE THE AUTHOR

Complete the dialogue using the words below. Note that each word can only be used one time.

CD-B: TRACK 11

ACTOR	HUMANKIND
ANCHOR	HUSBAND
ATTENDANT	OFFICER
CARRIER	PERSONNEL
COMEDIAN	RUN
FIGHTER	SELF-MADE
FROSH	SPOKESPERSON

Joe: I hear you're going to be a __________ next year! What kind of courses will you be taking when you start college?

David: Well, I haven't made a career choice yet. I've always enjoyed performing, so I could be an __________, or even a __________ since I love telling funny stories. But I do love traveling and as a flight __________, I could help people and see the world at the same time. Or maybe I could be a __________ for the travel industry.

Joe: That's true. But I also know that you've always wanted to do something for __________ and one of the best ways is to become a fire __________ or police __________. Actually, a mail __________ is probably a lot safer, except for the occasional angry dog!

David: I definitely don't want to do anything dangerous! Maybe I could become a __________ person like my mother and __________ my own company. I've always wanted to have my own publishing company. I just have to make sure that I get good __________! That would be the hardest part. I just don't know if I'd like being in an office all day.

Joe: I've got it! Since you like to perform and also help people, why don't you become a television __________ and report the news! Jim Manne used to report the news for years in Los Angeles until he fell in love with his producer. Now they're __________ and wife and live in San Diego. That could be you!

FROM THE SLANGMAN FILES

How to be Politically Correct or "P.C."

In recent American history, many careers and sports were not accessible to either one sex or another. For example, careers such as *nurse, manicurist, hairdresser, secretary, etc.* were thought of as "woman's work" and hiring a man for these positions was not even considered. And since it was regarded as being appropriate only for women to express themselves physically and emotionally, the world of ballet never created a male equivalent of the term *ballerina*. In addition, many careers that were closed to women actually included "man" within the job title such as *chair***man***, sales***man***, spokes***man***, etc.*

In order to include both sexes in the same career or sport, new labels needed to be created that were non-gender specific or "politically correct" (usually shorted to "P.C."). Some were already P.C. like *gymnast, swimmer, race car driver, etc.* However, most needed to be created, as seen in the following list. Pay particular attention to the non-PC versions of each entry. To the disappointment and frustration of feminists, many of the non-PC versions that you'll see after each entry are still commonly, yet ignorantly, used by Americans!

ancestors *n.* relatives of past generations.

NON-PC VERSION: **forefathers** *n.pl.*

EXAMPLE: My **ancestors** came to this country a hundred years ago.

TRANSLATION: My **relatives of past generations** came to this country a hundred years ago.

"REAL SPEAK": My **ancesters** came ta this country a hundred years ago.

artisan *n.* a professional whose work is always of the highest quality.

NON-PC VERSION: **craftsman** *n.*

EXAMPLE: Did you see the beautiful pottery Mark makes? He's a real **artisan**.

TRANSLATION: Did you see the beautiful pottery Mark makes? He's a real **professional whose work is always of the highest quality**.

"REAL SPEAK": Did'ja see the beaudiful poddery Mark makes? He's a real **ardiz'n**.

artisanship *n.* the quality of something that had been made.

NON-PC VERSION: **craftsmanship** *n.* • **workmanship** *n.*

EXAMPLE: Did you see the **artisanship** of this glass vase? It's beautiful!

TRANSLATION: Did you see the **quality** of this glass vase? It's beautiful!

"REAL SPEAK": Did'ja see the **ardisanship** 'a this glass vase? It's beaudiful!

ballet dancer *n.* one who dances in a classical style known as "ballet."

NON-PC VERSION: **ballerina** *f.*

Note: No masculine version existed because boys were not encouraged to participate in this type of dance.

EXAMPLE: Ever since I was four years old, I've wanted to be a **ballet dancer**. Now I dance with the San Francisco Ballet Company.

TRANSLATION: Ever since I was four years old, I've wanted to be a **dancer of the classical style known as "ballet."** Now I dance with the San Francisco Ballet Company.

"REAL SPEAK": Ever since I w'z four years old, I've wan'ed da be a **ballet dancer**. Now I dance w'th the San Fr'ncisco Ballet Comp'ny.

bartender *n.* one whose occupation is to prepare drinks (usually alcoholic) behind a bar.

NON-PC VERSION: **barman** *m.* • **barmaid** *f.*

EXAMPLE: In order to put herself through school, Debbie works as a **bartender** in the evenings.

TRANSLATION: In order to put herself through school, Debbie works as a **person who prepares drinks behind a bar** in the evenings.

"REAL SPEAK": In order da pud 'erself through school, Debbie works 'ez a **bartender** 'n the ev'nings.

bridal attendant *n.* a woman who helps a bride prepare for her wedding and is part of the wedding ceremony itself.

NON-PC VERSION: **bridesmaid** *f.*

EXAMPLE: At Kim's wedding, all the **bridal attendants** were girls she went to school with.

TRANSLATION: At Kim's wedding, all the **women who helped her prepare for her wedding** were girls she went to school with.

"REAL SPEAK": At Kim's wedding, all the **bridal attendants** were girls she went ta school with.

business person *n.* a person who has an ability to grow a business; an executive.

NON-PC VERSION: **businessman** *m.* • **businesswoman** *f.*

EXAMPLE: My father started his own company a year ago and now it's grown into a corporation. He's a great **business person**.

TRANSLATION: My father started his own company a year ago and now it's grown into a corporation. He's has a great **ability to grow a business**.

"REAL SPEAK": My father starded 'is own comp'ny a year ago 'n now it's grown into a corperation. He's a great **bizness person**.

camera operator *n.* one whose occupation is to operate a television or movie camera.

NON-PC VERSION: **cameraman** *m.*

EXAMPLE: My sister is working as the **camera operator** in a movie starring Tom Cruise.

TRANSLATION: My sister is working as the **person who operates the camera** in a movie starring Tom Cruise.

"REAL SPEAK": My sister's working 'ez the **cam'ra operader** 'n a movie starring Tom Cruise.

chairperson *n.* one who leads a meeting, group or organization.

NON-PC VERSION: **chairman** *m.* • **chairwoman** *f.*

EXAMPLE: Liz is the new **chairperson**. If you have anything you want to say during the meeting, be sure to direct your comments to her.

TRANSLATION: Liz is the new **leader of our meetings**. If you have anything you want to say during the meeting, be sher da direc' cher comments ta her.

"REAL SPEAK": Liz 'ez the new **chairperson**. If ya 'ave anything ya wanna say during the meeding, be sure da direct yer comments ta her.

Synonym: **chair** *n.*

Note: The officer in charge of a meeting is also referred to as the *chairman*. As more and more women became involved in business, originally considered a man's world, the term *chairwoman* was added. However, due to the Women's Liberation movement, many terms in business have been recreated to be non-gender specific (or *"politically correct,"* as it is called). Enter the word *chairperson*. Now here's where it gets confusing. Many businesspeople do their best to be politically correct and refer to officers in this position as a *chairperson*. However, according to Robert's Rules of Order which, again, sets the guidelines for this type of parliamentary procedure, when addressing the *chair* or *chairperson* in a meeting, one must still use *chairman*! And to make things even more gender-confusing, if the *chairperson* is a man, he is to be addressed as *Mr. Chairman;* if it's a woman, she is to be addressed as *Madame Chairman*!

cleaning person *n.* one whose occupation is to clean homes or offices.

NON-PC VERSION: **cleaning lady** *f.* • **cleaning girl** *f.*

EXAMPLE: My new **cleaning person** did an amazing job in my house. I've never seen it so clean!

TRANSLATION: My new **person who was hired to clean** did an amazing job in my house. I've never seen it so clean!

"REAL SPEAK": My new **cleaning person** did 'n amazing job 'n my house. I've never seen it so clean!

Synonym: **cleaner** *n.*

Note: The term *cleaning girl* is considered an extremely derogatory label for a woman who cleans one's home. This term came from a time when the majority of *cleaning people* were African-American women and never given the respect of an adult. Even the older African-Americans were addressed as "boy" or "girl," robbing them of their dignity. In addition, no masculine version existed because these professions were only available to women.

cleric *n.* one who has dedicated his/her life to religious service.

NON-PC VERSION: **clergyman** *m.*

Note: No feminine version existed because these professions were closed to women.

EXAMPLE: After working in a high pressure job for ten years, my brother decided to change careers. Now he's working as a **cleric** in a church close to where he lives.

TRANSLATION: After working in a high pressure job for ten years, my brother decided to change careers. Now he's **doing religious service** in a church close to where he lives.

"REAL SPEAK": After working 'n a high pressure job fer ten years, my brother decided da change careers. Now 'e's working 'ez a **cleric** 'n a church close ta where 'e lives.

Synonym: **member of the clergy** *n.*

drafting technician *n.* one whose occupation is to draw plans for structures that are going to be built.

NON-PC VERSION: **draftsman** *m.*

Note: No feminine version existed because these professions were closed to women.

EXAMPLE: My mother drew all the plans for our house. She's one of the best **drafting technicians** in the city!

TRANSLATION: My mother drew all the plans for our house. She's one of the best **technical illustrators** in the city!

"REAL SPEAK": My mother drew all the plans fer 'ar house. She's one 'a the bes' **drafting technicians** 'n the cidy!

Synonym: **draftsperson** *n.*

fair play *n.* a respect for the rules when competing in a sport.

NON-PC VERSION: **sportsmanship** *n.*

EXAMPLE: Greg always exhibits **fair play** when he competes in sports.

TRANSLATION: Greg always exhibits **respect for the rules** when he competes in sports.

"REAL SPEAK": Greg ahweez exhibits **fair play** when 'e c'mpetes 'n sports.

first voyage *n.* the first trip made by a ship.

NON-PC VERSION: **maiden voyage** *n.*

EXAMPLE: The Titanic sunk during its **first voyage**.

TRANSLATION: The Titanic sunk during its **first trip**.

"REAL SPEAK": The Titanic sunk during its **first voyage**.

fisher *n.* one whose hobby it is to go fishing.

NON-PC VERSION: **fisherman** *n.*

EXAMPLE: My mother has been a **fisher** all her life. You should have seen the salmon she caught last week!

TRANSLATION: My mother has been an **enthusiast of fishing** all her life. You should have seen the salmon she caught last week!

"REAL SPEAK": My mother's been a **fisher** all 'er life. Ya should'a seen the salmon she caught las' week!

Note: **fishing crew** *n.pl.* more than one fisher.

foreperson *n.* one who serves as the leader of a group of workers.

NON-PC VERSION: **foreman** *m.*

Note: No feminine version existed because these professions were closed to women.

EXAMPLE: The **foreperson** said we could all leave early today! I love working for this company!

TRANSLATION: The **leader of the workers** said we could all leave early today! I love working for this company!

"REAL SPEAK": The **foreperson** said we could all leave early taday! I love working fer this comp'ny!

Synonym: **supervisor** *n.*

handyperson *n.* one whose occupation is to do a variety of small tasks and repairs.

NON-PC VERSION: **handyman** *n.*
Note: No feminine version existed because these professions were closed to women, who had the reputation of being helpless and unskilled.

EXAMPLE: I found the best **handyperson**. She can fix anything!

TRANSLATION: I found the best **person who does small tasks and repairs**. She can fix anything!

"REAL SPEAK": I foun' the best **handyperson**. She c'n fix anything!

Synonym: **do-it-yourselfer** *n.*

heir *n.* one who inherits a title, position or money.

NON-PC VERSION: **heir** *m.* • **heiress** *f.*

EXAMPLE: Jennifer is **heir** to her father's fortune. When he dies, she's going to inherit 30 million dollars!

TRANSLATION: Jennifer is **the person who is going to inherit** her father's fortune. When he dies, she's going to inherit 30 million dollars!

"REAL SPEAK": Jennifer's **heir** do 'er father's fortune. When 'e dies, she's gonna inherit thirdy million dollers!

hero *n.* one who is greatly admired because of a remarkable accomplishment.

NON-PC VERSION: **hero** *m.* • **heroine** *f.*
Note: Yes, this is spelled and pronounced the same way as the drug "heroine"!

EXAMPLE: I had an important meeting at the office today and forgot my briefcase at home! Luckily, my husband brought it to me just in time! He's my **hero**!

TRANSLATION: I had an important meeting at the office today and forgot my briefcase at home! Luckily, my husband brought it to me just in time! He's the **person I admire most**!

"REAL SPEAK": I had 'n important meeding 'it the office taday 'n fergot my briefcase 'it home! Luckily, my husban' brod it ta me just 'n time! He's my **hero**!

homemaker *n.* one who takes care of one's home and family (typically describing someone who does not have a paying job but has a spouse who earns the living).

NON-PC VERSION: **housewife** *f.* / **househusband** *m.* (although not P.C., this term is becoming increasingly popular)..

EXAMPLE: Carl is a **homemaker**. He takes care of the children and the house while his wife, Sue, supports the family. She's an executive in one of the largest software companies in the U.S.

TRANSLATION: Carl is a **person who takes care of the home and family**. He takes care of the children and the house while his wife, Sue, supports the family. She's an executive in one of the largest software companies in the U.S.

"REAL SPEAK": Carl's a **homemaker**. He takes care 'a the children 'an the house while 'is wife, Sue, sapports the fam'ly. She's 'n executive 'n one 'a the larges' sof'ware comp'nies 'n the U.S.

host *n.* one who gives a party or event to which you are invited.

NON-PC VERSION: **host** *m.* • **hostess** *f.*

EXAMPLE: Irene is a wonderful **host**. She serves the best food and always has great entertainment.

TRANSLATION: Irene is a wonderful **party-giver**. She serves the best food and always has great entertainment.

"REAL SPEAK": Irene's a wonderful **host**. She serves the bes' food 'n ahweez has grade in(t)ertainment.

insurance agent *n.* one whose occupation is to sell insurance.

NON-PC VERSION: **insurance salesman** *m.*

Note: No feminine version existed because these professions were closed to women.

EXAMPLE: My **insurance agent** found me a great deal on car insurance. I'm going to be paying half of what I paid last year!

TRANSLATION: The **person who sells me insurance** found me a great deal on car insurance. I'm going to be paying half of what I paid last year!

"REAL SPEAK": My **insurance agent** foun' me a great deal on car insherance. I'm gonna be paying half 'a whad I paid last year!

Synonym: **insurance broker** *n.*

layperson *n.* an amateur.

NON-PC VERSION: **layman** *n.*

EXAMPLE: I know you're not a professional painter but for a **layperson**, your painting looks so realistic!

TRANSLATION: I know you're not a professional painter but for an **amateur**, your painting looks so realistic!

"REAL SPEAK": I know y'r nod a prafessional pain(t)er b't fer a **layperson**, yer pain(t)ing looks so realistic!

middleperson *n.* the contact or "intermediary" between two or more people.

NON-PC VERSION: **middleman** *n.*

EXAMPLE:
– You can tell Steve that if he wants to come to my party, he has to apologize to me.
– I'm not going to be the **middleperson** for you both. If you want to communicate with him, talk to him directly!

TRANSLATION:
– You can tell Steve that if he wants to come to my party, he has to apologize to me.
– I'm not going to be the **intermediary** for you both. If you want to communicate with him, talk to him directly!

"REAL SPEAK":
– Ya c'n tell Steve th'd if 'e wants ta come da my pardy, he hasta apolagize ta me.
– I'm not gonna be the **middleperson** fer you both. If ya wannna communicate with 'im, talk to 'im direc'ly!

modern society *n.* present-day civilization.

NON-PC VERSION: **modern man** *n.*

EXAMPLE: Two hundred years ago, air travel was considered impossible. Luckily, **modern society** invented airplanes!

TRANSLATION: Two hundred years ago, air travel was considered impossible. Luckily, **present-day society** invented airplanes!

"REAL SPEAK": Two hundred years ago, air travel w'z c'nsidered impossible. Luckily, **modern sasiedy** inven(t)ed airplanes!

nature lover *n.* one who loves being around nature and going on hikes and nature walks.

NON-PC VERSION: **outdoorsman** *m.*

Note: No feminine version existed because this type of activity wasn't considered proper for women.

EXAMPLE: My father is a real **nature lover**. He takes me on hikes every weekend!

TRANSLATION: My father is a real **enthusiast about nature**. He takes me on hikes every weekend!

"REAL SPEAK": My father's a real **nature lover**. He takes me on hikes ev'ry weekend!

paper carrier *n.* one whose occupation is to deliver the newspaper to your home or office.

NON-PC VERSION: **paperboy** *m.* • **papergirl** *f.*

EXAMPLE: Can you believe this? The **paper carrier** threw the newspaper into the water again!

TRANSLATION: Can you believe this? The **person who delivers the newspaper** threw the newspaper into the water again!

"REAL SPEAK": C'n you believe this? The **paper carrier** threw the paper inta the wader again!

patrol officer *n.* a police officer who controls a specific area.

NON-PC VERSION: **patrolman** *m.*

Note: No feminine version existed because these professions were closed to women.

EXAMPLE: I think someone is trying to break into that building. Quick! Find a **patrol officer**!

TRANSLATION: I think someone is trying to break into that building. Quick! Find a **police offer who controls this area**!

"REAL SPEAK": I think someone's trying ta break inta that building. Quick! Find a **patrol officer**!

person in the street *n.* the average person.

NON-PC VERSION: **man in the street** *n.* [or] **common man** *n.*

Note: No feminine version of these terms existed, which implies that only a man's opinion was important and there was no need to create a feminine version.

EXAMPLE: Before we create a new personal computer, we need to find out what people want. Let's interview the **person in the street** and get some opinions.

TRANSLATION: Before we create a new personal computer, we need to find out what people want. Let's interview the **average person** and get some opinions.

"REAL SPEAK": B'fore we creade a new pers'nal c'mpuder, we need da find out what people want. Let's in'erview the **person in the street** 'n get s'm opinions.

prehistoric people *n.* people who lived in the prehistoric time.

NON-PC VERSION: **early man** *n.*

Note: No feminine version existed because a woman's contribution to society was considered less important than that of a man's.

EXAMPLE: When **prehistoric people** invented the wheel, it was the beginning of numerous new inventions.

TRANSLATION: When **people who lived in the prehistoric time** invented the wheel, it was the beginning of numerous new inventions.

"REAL SPEAK": When **pre'istoric people** inven(t)ed the wheel, it w'z the beginning of numerous new inventions.

repairperson *n.* one whose occupation is to make repairs.

NON-PC VERSION: **repairman** *m.*
Note: No feminine version existed because these professions were closed to women.

EAMPLE: The television isn't working again. I think we need to call a **repairperson**.

TRANSLATION: The television isn't working again. I think we need to call a **person who makes repairs**.

"REAL SPEAK": The TV isn't working again. I think we need da call a **repairperson**.

sales representative *n.* one whose occupation is to sell merchandise.

NON-PC VERSION: **salesman** *m.* • **saleswoman** *f.* • **saleslady** *f.* • **salesgirl** *f.* •

EXAMPLE: If you're interested in buying a new carpet, I'd be happy to get a **sales representative** to help you.

TRANSLATION: If you're interested in buying a new carpet, I'd be happy to get a **person employed to sell merchandise** to help you.

"REAL SPEAK": If y'r int'rested 'n buying a new carped, I'd be happy da ged a **sales rep** ta help ya.

Synonym 1: **sales agent** *n.*

Synonym 2: **salesperson** *n.*

sharpshooter *n.* one who is extremely proficient at shooting a gun.

NON-PC VERSION: **rifleman** *m.* • **marksman** *m.*
Note: No feminine version existed because this type of activity was not considered proper for women.

EXAMPLE: My grandmother was known as being the only female **sharp-shooter** in her town. She could shoot a can off a fence a mile away!

TRANSLATION: My grandmother was known as being the only female **person who was extremely proficient at shooting a gun** in her town. She could shoot a can off a fence a mile away!

"REAL SPEAK": My gra'ma w'z known 'ez being the only female **sharpshooder** in 'er town. She could shood a can off a fence a mile away!

sporting *adj.* said of conduct that is expected of a good athlete such as courtesy and grace in losing.

NON-PC VERSION: **sportsmanlike** *adj.*

EXAMPLE: After Jeff lost the tennis match, he went up to the winner and congratulated him. That was very **sporting** of him.

TRANSLATION: After Jeff lost the tennis match, he went up to the winner and congratulated him. That was very **courteous sports behavior**.

"REAL SPEAK": After Jeff lost the tennis match, he wen' up ta the winner 'n c'ngradjaladed 'im. That w'z very **spording** of 'im.

waiter *n.* one whose occupation is to serve customers food in a restaurant.

NON-PC VERSION: **waiter** *m.* • **waitress** *f.*

EXAMPLE: Could you ask the **waiter** to bring us some more water?

TRANSLATION: Could you ask the **food-server** to bring us some more water?

"REAL SPEAK": Could'ja ask the **wader** da bring us s'm more wader?

Synonym: **server** *n.*

weather reporter *n.* the person on the news who reports the weather conditions for the day and the near future.

NON-PC VERSION: **weatherman** *n.*

Note: No feminine version existed because these professions were closed to women.

EXAMPLE: The **weather reporter** says it's going to rain tomorrow and I just washed my car!

TRANSLATION: The **person who reports the weather conditions on the news** says it's going to rain tomorrow and I just washed my car!

"REAL SPEAK": The **weather reporder** says it's gonna rain tamorrow 'n I jus' washed my car!

Synonym: **meteorologist** *n.*

worker *n.* one who is hired to do physical labor.

NON-PC VERSION: **workman** *m.*

Note: No feminine version existed because these professions were closed to women.

EXAMPLE: We need to hire some **workers** to build us a new roof. It leaks in here every time it rains!

TRANSLATION: We need to hire some **people who do physical labor** to build us a new roof. It leaks in here every time it rains!

"REAL SPEAK": We need da hire s'm **workers** ta build us a new roof. It leaks in here ev'ry time it rains!

yachter *n.* one who owns a yacht.

NON-PC VERSION: **yachtsman** *m.*

Note: No feminine version existed because yachting was considered a man's pastime.

EXAMPLE: Jim is a millionaire and owns several boats. He has been a **yachter** for thirty years.

TRANSLATION: Jim is a millionaire and owns several boats. He has been a **yacht-owner** for thirty years.

"REAL SPEAK": Jim's a millionaire 'n owns sev'ral boats. He's been a **yachter** fer thirdy years.

Synonym 1: **sailor** *n.*
Synonym 2: **yacht owner** *n.*

A BIG BREAK IN SHOW BIZ!

Television & Entertainment Slang

THIS LESSON FEATURES 15 NEW SLANG WORDS & IDIOMS

LET'S WARM UP!

MATCH THE PICTURES

As a fun way to get started, see if you can guess the meaning of the new slang words and expressions on the opposite page by using the pictures below and following the context of the sentences.

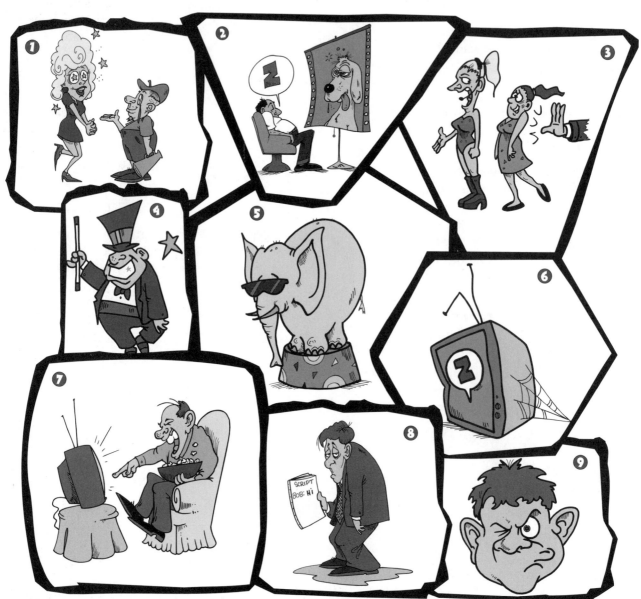

1. Donna has been trying to become an actor for years. Well, today she finally got her ***big break***! A producer offered her a big part in a movie!
   Definition: *"big opportunity"*
   ❑ True ❑ False

2. Why are you going to see that movie? I hear it's a real ***dog***!
   Definition: *"high quality work"*
   ❑ True ❑ False

3. Alice didn't get a big part. It was just a ***walk-on***.
   Definition: *"minor, non-speaking role"*
   ❑ True ❑ False

4. My dad's a performer. He's been in ***show biz*** all his life.
   Definition: *"the entertainment industry"*
   ❑ True ❑ False

5. When the elephants came out dressed as movie stars, it was a ***show-stopper***!
   Definition: *"boring moment in the show"*
   ❑ True ❑ False

6. I saw this episode already. It's a ***rerun***.
   Definition: *"rebroadcast"*
   ❑ True ❑ False

7. My uncle loves watching his favorite ***series*** every Wednesday night.
   Definition: *"commercials"*
   ❑ True ❑ False

8. Although Al only has a ***one-liner***, I know he'll get a huge reaction from the audience!
   Definition: *"very large part"*
   ❑ True ❑ False

9. Many silent film actors were known for ***mugging*** since there was no sound.
   Definition: *"using exaggerated facial expressions"*
   ❑ True ❑ False

10. That television ***pilot*** was great! I hope it becomes a regular program!
    Definition: *"test episode from a proposed television program"*
    ❑ True ❑ False

11. If a television show is really popular, oftentimes a ***spin-off*** is created.
    Definition: *"variation of the show based on the original"*
    ❑ True ❑ False

12. I love ***sitcoms*** because I love to laugh and be entertained.
    Definition: *"dramatic television programs"*
    ❑ True ❑ False

13. Did you see the ***spoof*** on *Raiders of the Lost Arc* last night? It was hilarious!
    Definition: *"humorous satire"*
    ❑ True ❑ False

14. John thinks he's a great actor but he's nothing but a ***ham***!
    Definition: *"bad actor who overacts"*
    ❑ True ❑ False

15. I don't like ***slapstick*** comedies. I prefer comedies that rely on great dialogue to make you laugh!
    Definition: *"physical"*
    ❑ True ❑ False

LET'S TALK!

A. DIALOGUE USING SLANG & IDIOMS

The words introduced on the first two pages are used in the dialogue below. See if you can understand the conversation. *Note:* The translation of the words in boldface is on the right-hand page.

CD-B: TRACK 12

Andrea: Did you see the television show last night about the actor who tries to get his **big break** in **show biz**?

Gary: I didn't see it, but I heard about it. Wasn't it a **rerun**?

Andrea: No. It was a television **pilot** for a **sitcom**. It was a **spin-off** of a **series** that used to be real popular a few years ago.

Gary: So, what did you think?

Andrea: It was a **spoof** about Hollywood, but it was way too **slapstick** for me. The star of the show was such a **ham**! He did nothing but **mug** all the time. And you won't believe who had a **walk-on**... Lee Murphy!

Gary: What was she doing in a **dog** like that?

Andrea: I don't know. She didn't even have a **one-liner**, but her reactions were a **show-stopper**!

B. DIALOGUE TRANSLATED INTO STANDARD ENGLISH

LET'S SEE HOW MUCH YOU REMEMBER!
Just for fun, move around in random order to the words and expressions in boldface below. See if you can remember their slang equivalents without looking at the left-hand page!

Andrea: Did you see the television show last night about the actor who tries to get his **exciting opportunity** in **the entertainment industry**?

Gary: I didn't see it, but I heard about it. Wasn't it a **repeat of a previous show**?

Andrea: No. It was a television **show that is presented one time to test people's reactions** for a **situation comedy**. It was a **version** of a **regular television program** that used to be real popular a few years ago.

Gary: So, what did you think?

Andrea: It was a **humorous satire** about Hollywood, but it was way too **physical and clownish** for me. The star of the show was such an **unskilled actor who overacts**! He did nothing but **make overly exaggerated facial expressions** all the time. And you won't believe who had a **small part**... Lee Murphy!

Gary: What was she doing in **something of such low quality** like that?

Andrea: I don't know. She didn't even have **one word or phrase to say**, but her reactions were **the best part of the show**!

C. DIALOGUE USING "REAL SPEAK"

The dialogue below demonstrates how the slang conversation on the previous page would *really* be spoken by native speakers!

CD-B: TRACK 12

Andrea: Did'ja see the TV show las' nide about the acter who tries da get 'is **big break** 'n **show biz**?

Gary: I didn't see it, b'd I heard aboud it. Wasn' id a **re-run**?

Andrea: No. It w'z a TV **pilot** fer a **sitcom**. It w'z a **spin-off** 'ev a **series** th't usta be real populer a few years ago.

Gary: So, whad'ja think?

Andrea: It w'z a **spoof** about Hollywood, b'd it w'z way too **slapstick** fer me. The star 'a the show w'z such a **ham**! He did nothing b't **mug** all the time. An' ja won't believe who had a **walk-on**... Lee Murphy!

Gary: What w'z she doing 'n a **dog** like that?

Andrea: I dunno. She didn' even have a **one-liner**, bud 'er reactions were a **show-stopper**!

LET'S LEARN!

VOCABULARY

The following words and expressions were used in the previous dialogues. Let's take a closer look at what they mean.

CD-B: TRACK 13

big break *exp.* exciting opportunity (most often heard in reference to the entertainment industry, but can also be used to describe an exciting opportunity in other careers).

EXAMPLE: Alice finally got her **big break**. There was a big Hollywood producer in the audience of her school play who hired her for his new movie!

TRANSLATION: Alice finally got her **exciting opportunity to advance in her career**. There was a big Hollywood producer in the audience of her school play who hired her for his new movie!

"REAL SPEAK": Alice fin'ly god 'er **big break**. There w'z a big Hollywood praducer 'n the audience 'ev 'er school play who hired 'er fer 'is new movie!

NOW YOU DO IT. COMPLETE THE PHRASE ALOUD:
My favorite actor is... because...

dog *n.* something of very low quality.

EXAMPLE: That movie was such a **dog**! I feel like getting my money back from the movie theater!

TRANSLATION: That movie was such **low quality**! I feel like getting my money back from the movie theater!

"REAL SPEAK": That movie w'z such a **dog**! I feel like gedding my money back fr'm the movie theeder!

Synonym: **turkey** *n.*

NOW YOU DO IT. COMPLETE THE PHRASE ALOUD:
The movie... was such a dog because...

ham *n.* a shortened version of *ham actor* which is an unskilled actor who overacts.

EXAMPLE: Bob's acting is completely unnatural and exaggerated. He's such a **ham**!

TRANSLATION: Bob's acting is completely unnatural and exaggerated. He's such an **unskilled actor who overacts**!

"REAL SPEAK": Bob's acting is c'mpletely unnatural 'n exaggeraded. He's such a **ham**!

NOW YOU DO IT. COMPLETE THE PHRASE ALOUD:
I think... is a big ham because...

mug (to) *v.* to make exaggerated facial expressions.

EXAMPLE: Tony's acting isn't believable at all. He keeps **mugging** to the camera!

TRANSLATION: Tony's acting isn't believable at all. He keeps **making exaggerated facial expressions** to the camera!

"REAL SPEAK": Tony's acting isn't believable 'id all. He keeps **mugging** ta the cam'ra!

NOW YOU DO IT. COMPLETE THE PHRASE ALOUD:
...mugs more than any performer I've ever seen!

one-liner *n.* • **1.** a very small part consisting of one word or sentence (known as a *line*) • **2.** a short joke usually told in one sentence.

EXAMPLE 1: After studying acting for ten years, I just got my first part in a movie. I should be happy but it's just a **one-liner**.

TRANSLATION: After studying acting for ten years, I just got my first part in a movie. I should be happy but it's just a **very smart part consisting of one word or sentence**.

"REAL SPEAK": After studying acting fer ten years, I jus' got my firs' pard 'n a movie. I should be happy bud it's just a **one-liner**.

EXAMPLE 2: Gil told a funny **one-liner** at my party. I laughed so hard!

TRANSLATION: Gil told a funny **short joke** at my party. I laughed so hard!

"REAL SPEAK": Gil told a funny **one-liner** 'it my pardy. I laughed so hard!

NOW YOU DO IT. COMPLETE THE PHRASE ALOUD:
Eric got his first one-liner in a...

pilot *n.* a test episode from a proposed television program presented to the public in order to get a general reaction.

EXAMPLE: I just got hired as an actor in a TV **pilot**. If it's approved, I'll have a regular part in a TV program!

TRANSLATION: I just got hired as an actor in a TV **test episode**. If it's approved, I'll have a regular part in a TV program!

"REAL SPEAK": I jus' got hired 'ez 'n actor 'n a TV **pilot**. If it's approved, a'll have a reguler pard 'n a TV program!

NOW YOU DO IT. COMPLETE THE PHRASE ALOUD:
I just got hired as an actor in a TV pilot about...

rerun *n.* a TV or radio program that has already been broadcast one or more times before.

EXAMPLE: I'm so excited! *Seinfeld* is on television tonight! Oh, wait. It's a **rerun** and I've already seen this episode.

TRANSLATION: I'm so excited! *Seinfeld* is on television tonight! Oh, wait. It's **already been broadcast before** and I've already seen this episode.

"REAL SPEAK": I'm so excided! *Seinfeld* 'ez on TV danight! Oh, waid. It's a **rerun** 'n I've ahready seen this episode.

NOW YOU DO IT. COMPLETE THE PHRASE ALOUD:
Last night, I saw a rerun of my favorite...

series *n.* a television program that is broadcast each week with a new episode.

EXAMPLE: *Friends* is one of America's longest-running **series**. It's been on television for over ten years!

TRANSLATION: *Friends* is one of America's longest-running **television programs that are broadcast each week with a new episode**. It's been on television for over ten years!

"REAL SPEAK": *Friends* 'ez one 'ev America's longes'-running **series**. It's been on TV fer over ten years!

NOW YOU DO IT. COMPLETE THE PHRASE ALOUD:
My favorite series is...because...

show biz *exp.* an abbreviation of *show business* which is common slang for "the entertainment industry."

EXAMPLE: Irene has been in **show biz** most of her life. She started acting when she was five years old.

TRANSLATION: Irene has been in **the entertainment industry** most of her life. She started acting when she was five years old.

"REAL SPEAK": Irene's been 'n **show biz** most 'ev 'er life. She starded acting when she w'z five years old.

Variation: **the biz** *exp.*

NOW YOU DO IT. COMPLETE THE PHRASE ALOUD:
My favorite actor is... because...

show-stopper *n.* a performance or performer that receives so much applause from the audience that the show is temporarily interrupted.

EXAMPLE: When the magician turned the mouse into an elephant, it was a **show-stopper**! I never saw anything like that before.

TRANSLATION: When the magician turned the mouse into an elephant, it was an **exciting moment where the applause from the audience temporarily interrupted the show**! I never saw anything like that before.

"REAL SPEAK": When the magician turned the mouse into 'n elephant, it w'z a **show-stopper**! I never saw anything like that before.

NOW YOU DO IT. COMPLETE THE PHRASE ALOUD:

Recently, I saw a great performance. But the part that was the show-stopper was...!

sitcom *n.* an abbreviation of *situation-comedy* which is a television show focusing on different comedic situations.

EXAMPLE: My favorite **sitcom** is a famous American television show called *I Love Lucy* starring Lucille Ball and Desi Arnaz.

TRANSLATION: My favorite **television show focusing on different comedic situations** is a famous American television show called *I Love Lucy* starring Lucille Ball and Desi Arnaz.

"REAL SPEAK": My fav'rit **sitcom** is a famous American TV show called *I Love Lucy* starring Lucille Ball and Desi Arnaz.

NOW YOU DO IT. COMPLETE THE PHRASE ALOUD:

My favorite sitcom is... because...

slapstick *adj.* said of a television show, movie, or play that contains a lot of physical comedy such as throwing pies in each other's face, exaggerated falls, comedic fighting, collisions, etc. • (lit.): a paddle designed to produce a loud noise when striking someone without causing injury.

EXAMPLE: One of America's most popular **slapstick** comedies was called *The Three Stooges,* where three eccentric men constantly hit and punched each other.

TRANSLATION: One of America's most popular **physical** comedies was called *The Three Stooges,* where three eccentric men constantly hit and punched each other.

"REAL SPEAK": One 'ev America's most populer **slapstick** comedies w'z called *The Three Stooges,* where three eccentric men constantly hit 'n punched each other.

NOW YOU DO IT. COMPLETE THE PHRASE ALOUD:

A performer from my country who is famous for doing slapstick is...

spin-off *n.* a variation of a television show based on the original.

EXAMPLE: *Frasier* was a **spin-off** of the popular television program called *Cheers* which was on television for over ten years!

TRANSLATION: *Frasier* was a **variation of a television show based on** the popular television program called *Cheers* which was on television for over ten years!

"REAL SPEAK": *Frasier* w'z a **spin-off** of the populer TV program called *Cheers* which w'z on TV fer over ten years!

NOW YOU DO IT. COMPLETE THE PHRASE ALOUD:
My favorite spin-off is based on...

spoof *n.* a humorous satire.

EXAMPLE: *The Mummy* with Brandan Frasier is a **spoof** of the original movie. It was hilarious! I've already seen it more than a dozen times!

TRANSLATION: *The Mummy* with Brandan Frasier is a **humorous satire** of the original movie. It was hilarious! I've already seen it more than a dozen times!

"REAL SPEAK": *The Mummy* w'th Brandan Frasier's a **spoof** of the original movie. It w'z hilarious! I've ahready seen it more th'n a dozen times!

NOW YOU DO IT. COMPLETE THE PHRASE ALOUD:
My favorite spoof is... because...

walk-on *n.* a minor non-speaking role.

EXAMPLE: Claudia told everyone that she had a part in the new Madonna movie but it was nothing more than a **walk-on**!

TRANSLATION: Claudia told everyone that she had a part in the new Madonna movie but it was nothing more than a **minor non-speaking role**!

"REAL SPEAK": Claudia told ev'ryone th't she had a pard 'n the new Madonna movie b'd it w'z nothing more th'n a **walk-on**!

Also 1: **cameo** *n.* short for *cameo role* which is a brief appearance by a well-known actor in a television show, movie, or play.

Also 2: **extra** *n.* a minor actor in a non-speaking role that is usually part of a crowd scene.

Synonym: **atmosphere** *n.*

NOW YOU DO IT. COMPLETE THE PHRASE ALOUD:
I'd love to have a walk-on on the TV show called...

LET'S PRACTICE!

A. CREATE YOUR OWN STORY - *(Part 1)*

Follow the instructions below and write down your answer in the space provided. When you have finished answering all the questions, transfer your answers to the story on the next page. Make sure to match the number of your answer with the numbered space in the story. Remember: The funnier your answers, the funnier your story will be!

1. Write down an adjective *(big, small, strange, etc.):* ______________________________

2. Write down a thing *(pencil, potato, toothbrush, etc.):* ______________________________

3. Write down a place *(restaurant, library, market, etc.):* ______________________________

4. Write down a thing in plural form *(pencils, potatoes, toothbrushes, etc.):* ____________________

5. Write down an adjective *(big, small, strange, etc.):* ______________________________

6. Write down a liquid *(water, glue, wine, etc.):* ______________________________

7. Write down a verb ending in "-ing" *(golfing, dancing, running, etc.):* ____________________

8. Write down any type of living creature *(rat, lizard, goldfish, etc.):* ____________________

9. Write down a piece of clothing in plural form *(hats, belts, shoes, etc.):* ____________________

10. Write down a body part in plural form *(feet, arms, eyes, etc.):* ____________________

11. Write down a noun *(footstool, piano, radio, etc.):* ______________________________

12. Write down a verb ending in "-ing" *(golfing, dancing, running, etc.):* ____________________

B. CREATE YOUR OWN STORY - *(Part 2)*

Once you've filled in the blanks, read your story aloud. If you've done Part 1 correctly, your story should be hilarious!

THE WEEKLY

Crimea River Gazette

TELL GABBY WHERE IT HURTS...

"Dear Gabby..."

by Gabby Blabber
Advice Columnist

Dear Gabby...

I finally got my **big break** in **show biz** last week. I know that I should be feeling very ______ (1.) about it, but I got hired to play the part of a ______ (2.) who works in a ______ (3.). I've studied acting from some of the best ______ (4.) in the world and the thought of having a **one-liner** in a ______ (5.) **sitcom** makes me want to drown myself in a pool of ______ (6.). The **pilot** is about a man who loves to go ______ (7.) with his pet ______ (8.) which is always wearing ______ (9.) on his ______ (10.). Doesn't that sound like a **dog** to you? I can't believe it's actually being turned into a **series**.

The **show-stopper** is when we see his pet eat an entire ______ (11.)! I certainly wouldn't mind doing a **walk-on** on a show that wasn't so **slapstick** and full of actors who are nothing but big **hams** and **mug** all the time! Am I wrong not to be ______ (12.) for joy?!

Signed,

Brad Pitts

C. WHAT WOULD YOU DO IF SOMEONE SAID...?

What would you do in response to the words in white italics?
Choose your answer by placing an "X" in the box.

CD-B: TRACK 14

		I would...
1. ***Jim is the biggest ham!***		☐ a. agree that he's a great actor ☐ b. agree that he's a terrible actor ☐ c. agree that he has been getting fat
2. ***Benny is doing a walk-on in the opening of a big Broadway play!***		☐ a. ask him how long he's been a golfer ☐ b. suggest he try running instead ☐ c. buy a ticket to see his performance
3. ***I just saw the biggest dog. Don't waste your money.***		☐ a. ask why he loved the movie so much ☐ b. go see the movie right away ☐ c. ask why he didn't like the movie
4. ***My mother has been in show biz for years!***		☐ a. ask what kind of business she's in ☐ b. ask if she meets a lot of movie stars ☐ c. ask if she has found a job yet
5. ***I love sitcoms!***		☐ a. ask why he prefers dramas ☐ b. ask why he prefers comedies ☐ c. ask why he prefers musicals
6. ***When the flying saucer landed on stage, it was a show-stopper!***		☐ a. ask to know more about it ☐ b. ask not to be told more about it ☐ c. wonder why they stopped the show
7. ***I saw a great TV pilot last night!***		☐ a. ask how many years it's been on TV ☐ b. hope it becomes a regular TV show ☐ c. think it's unsafe for pilots to watch TV
8. ***I'm so happy. I finally got my big break!***		☐ a. offer my congratulations ☐ b. offer my sympathies ☐ c. offer to call the paramedics
9. ***I just saw a spoof about Hollywood tonight.***		☐ a. ask if it was a serious documentary ☐ b. ask if it was scary ☐ c. ask if it was funny
10. ***Jason got a one-liner in a new movie! It's his first part!***		☐ a. congratulate him on his small role ☐ b. congratulate him on his big role ☐ c. ask him if he had a starring role

D. CREATE YOUR OWN SENTENCES

Read Person A's questions aloud, then use the suggested words to create your sentences for Person B.

1. **PERSON A:** Why is Nancy so happy?	**PERSON B:** [**big break**] [**one-liner**] [**show biz**]
2. **PERSON A:** Isn't that a famous actor over there?	**PERSON B:** [**sitcom**] [**show-stopper**] [**series**]
3. **PERSON A:** Is there anything to watch on TV tonight?	**PERSON B:** [**rerun**] [**mug**] [**dog**]
4. **PERSON A:** I've never heard of this TV show before.	**PERSON B:** [**spin-off**] [**slapstick**] [**big break**]
5. **PERSON A:** I heard you got a big role in a TV show.	**PERSON B:** [**walk-on**] [**spin-off**] [**show biz**]
6. **PERSON A:** What does Larry do for a living?	**PERSON B:** [**series**] [**ham**] [**mug**] [**slapstick**]

E. TRUE OR FALSE

Decide if the sentence is true or false.

1. A **walk-on** is a minor non-speaking role.
   ❑ True ❑ False
2. A **spin-off** is a long commercial.
   ❑ True ❑ False
3. **Slapstick** refers to a television show, movie, or play that contains a lot of physical comedy.
   ❑ True ❑ False
4. A **big break** is an exciting opportunity.
   ❑ True ❑ False
5. A **one-liner** is a very large and important part consisting of many words or sentences.
   ❑ True ❑ False
6. To **mug** means to make exaggerated facial expressions.
   ❑ True ❑ False
7. **Show biz** refers to people who like to be *showy* which is slang for "pretentious."
   ❑ True ❑ False
8. A **spoof** is a dramatic satire.
   ❑ True ❑ False
9. A **sitcom** is a television show focusing on different comedic situations.
   ❑ True ❑ False
10. A **rerun** is a television or radio program that is being broadcast for the first time.
    ❑ True ❑ False

More Television & Entertainment Slang

The following terms and expressions were taken directly from some of the most popular American television shows, so you can be sure they are extremely popular and used by almost everyone! In the U.S., some of our most loved and well-known television shows are situation comedies (known as *sitcoms*), daytime episodic dramas (known as *soaps*), police shows, medical shows, and law shows.

In addition, the following list will give you some of the most common terms used in music and the newspaper. Have fun learning them all! ***Break a leg***! (That's entertainment slang for "Good luck!")

TV SITCOMS

Note 1: *TV* and *sitcom* are popular abbreviations used by everyone:
- *TV* = "television"
- *sitcom* = "situation comedy" (a TV comedy focusing on a different situation each week).

Note 2: Because of the nature of TV sitcoms, you'll notice that many of the following terms and expressions are typically fun, light-hearted, and imaginative.

blowhard *n.* a person who is very talkative and brags constantly, a braggart.

EXAMPLE: Laurie does nothing but talk about her accomplishments all the time and most of what she says is a lie. She's such a **blowhard**!

TRANSLATION: Laurie does nothing but talk about her accomplishments all the time and most of what she says is a lie. She's such a **braggart**!

"REAL SPEAK": Laurie does nothing b't talk aboud 'er accomplishments all the time 'n most 'a what she says 'ez a lie. She's such a **blowhard**!

bore the pants off someone (to) *exp.* to bore someone so much that even the person's pants want to get away!

EXAMPLE: Emily talked to me for an entire hour about her surgery. After five minutes, she was **boring the pants off me**!

TRANSLATION: Emily talked to me for an entire hour about her surgery. After five minutes, she was **boring me terribly**!

"REAL SPEAK": Emily talk' ta me fer 'n entire hour aboud 'er surgery. After five minutes, she w'z **boring the pants off me**!

Synonym: **bore the living daylights out of someone (to)** *exp.*

brain dead (to go) *exp.* to forget something suddenly • (lit.): a medical condition said of someone whose brain is completely dead.

EXAMPLE: I forgot what I was talking about a moment ago. I just **went brain dead**!

TRANSLATION: I forgot what I was talking about a moment ago. I just **completely forgot what I was thinking**!

"REAL SPEAK": I fergot wh'd I w'z talking aboud a momen' ago. I jus' **went brain dead**!

butt naked (to be) *exp.* to be completely naked.

EXAMPLE: Did you see that? Our neighbor is running around outside **butt naked**!

TRANSLATION: Did you see that? Our neighbor is running around outside **completely naked**!

"REAL SPEAK": Did'ju see that? 'Ar neighber's running around outside **butt naked**!

Variation 1: **buck naked (to be)** *exp.*

Variation 2: **stark naked (to be)** *exp.*

cakewalk (to be a) *n.* said of something extremely easy.

EXAMPLE: I have to finish writing this book by next month. This is going to be a **cakewalk**. I'm already on chapter eight!

TRANSLATION: I have to finish writing this book by next month. This is going to be **extremely easy**. I'm already on chapter eight!

"REAL SPEAK": I hafta finish wriding this book by nex' month. This 'ez gonna be **a cakewalk**. I'm ahready on chapter eight!

Variation: **piece of cake (to be a)** *exp.*

"Catch my drift?" *exp.* "Do you understand what I'm really saying?"

EXAMPLE: I think Carol and Pat are more than just friends. **Catch my drift**?

TRANSLATION: I think Carol and Pat are more than just friends. **Do you understand what I'm really saying**?

"REAL SPEAK": I think Carol 'n Pad 'er more th'n jus' friends. **Catch my drift**?

Variation: **"Get my drift?"** *exp.*

chintzy *adj.* of very poor quality, cheap-looking.

EXAMPLE: Did you notice the furniture in Margaret's house? It's so **chintzy** and I know she's very rich!

TRANSLATION: Did you notice the furniture in Margaret's house? It's so **cheap-looking** and I know she's very rich!

"REAL SPEAK": Did 'ju nodice the furniture 'n Marg'ret's house? It's so **chintzy** 'n I know she's very rich!

Synonym: **schlocky** *adj.*

chow down (to) *exp.* to eat.

EXAMPLE: I'm hungry. Do you want to go **chow down** somewhere?

TRANSLATION: I'm hungry. Do you want to go **eat** somewhere?

"REAL SPEAK": I'm hungry. Wanna go **chow down** somewhere?

crack someone up (to) *exp.* to make someone laugh.

EXAMPLE: Cecily is the funniest person I know. She always **cracks me up**!

TRANSLATION: Cecily is the funniest person I know. She always **makes me laugh**!

"REAL SPEAK": Cecily's the funniest person I know. She ahweez **cracks me up**!

Also: **crack-up (a)** *n.* something very funny • *This movie is **a crack-up**!*; This movie is ***very funny***!

dressed to kill (to be) *exp.* to be dressed in beautiful clothes.

EXAMPLE: Where are you going tonight? **You're dressed to kill**!

TRANSLATION: Where are you going tonight? **You're dressed in beautiful clothes**!

"REAL SPEAK": Where'er ya going tanight? **Y'r dress' ta kill**!

Synonym: **dressed to the nines (to be)** *exp.*

flake *n.* someone unreliable.

EXAMPLE: Don't rely on Ed to remember to pick you up at the airport. He's such a **flake**.

TRANSLATION: Don't rely on Ed to remember to pick you up at the airport. He's such an **unreliable person**.

"REAL SPEAK": Don't rely on Ed da ramember da pick ya up 'it the airport. He's such a **flake**.

Also: **flake [out] (to)** *exp.* to be unreliable • *You promised you would water my plants while I was on vacation. You **totally flaked [out]**!*; You promised you would water my plants while I was on vacation. You ***were totally unreliable***!

laid back (to be) *exp.* said of someone whose disposition is calm and relaxed.

EXAMPLE: My mother never gets upset about little problems. She's very **laid back** about things like that.

TRANSLATION: My mother never gets upset about little problems. She's very **calm and relaxed** about things like that.

"REAL SPEAK": My mother never gets upsed about liddle problems. She's very **laid back** about things like that.

Synonym: **mellow (to be)** *adj.*

lose one's marbles (to) *exp.* to go crazy.

EXAMPLE: I think your neighbor finally **lost her marbles**. She's standing outside barking at people!

TRANSLATION: I think your neighbor finally **went crazy**. She's standing outside barking at people!

"REAL SPEAK": I think yer neighbor fin'lly **lost 'er marbles**. She's standing outside barking 'it people!

Synonym: **lose it (to)** *exp.* to go crazy or to explode with anger (depending on the context).

not to be all it's cracked up to be *exp.* not to meet one's expectations.

EXAMPLE: This job **isn't all it's cracked up to be**. I'm so bored.

TRANSLATION: This job **doesn't meet my expectations**. I'm so bored.

"REAL SPEAK": This job **isn' all it's cracked up ta be**. I'm so bored.

umpteenth time (for the) *exp.* a made-up number which represents an infinite number of times.

EXAMPLE: I've told you **for the umpteenth time** that Mark's birthday is today. I can't believe you forgot to buy him a present!

TRANSLATION: I've told you **countless times** that Mark's birthday is today. I can't believe you forgot to buy him a present!

"REAL SPEAK": I've told 'ja **fer the umpteenth time** th't Mark's birthday's taday. I can't believe ya fergot ta buy 'im a present!

Synonym: **for the kabillionth / kagillionth time** *exp.*

"SOAPS"

Note: This is a very common abbreviation of *soap operas* which are daytime episodic television shows, once sponsored by advertisers of soap products. *Soaps* are well known for their high drama and intense emotional relationships between characters. As a result, you'll notice that the following terms carry strong emotion.

"Break it up!" *interj.* "Stop fighting!"

EXAMPLE: **Break it up**! I won't allow you two to turn my home into a boxing ring!

TRANSLATION: **Stop fighting**! I won't allow you two to turn my home into a boxing ring!

"REAL SPEAK": **Break id up**! I won' allow you two da turn my home into a boxing ring!

cold fish *exp.* an unfriendly and unemotional person.

EXAMPLE: Brad's new wife is such a **cold fish**. When I went to their house, she never smiled once.

TRANSLATION: Brad's new wife is such an **unfriendly and unemotional person**. When I went to their house, she never smiled once.

"REAL SPEAK": Brad's new wife 'ez such a **cold fish**. When I went ta their house, she never smiled once.

drop a bombshell on someone (to) *exp.* to give someone some news that he/she is not prepared to hear.

EXAMPLE: Carla **dropped a bombshell** on her father when she told him she was moving to France.

TRANSLATION: Carla **gave** her father **some news that he wasn't prepared to hear** when she told him she was moving to France.

"REAL SPEAK": Carla **dropped a bombshell** on 'er father when she told 'im she w'z moving da France.

get all bent out of shape (to) *exp.* to get extremely upset.

EXAMPLE: Paula **got all bent out of shape** just because I was a little late picking her up at the airport.

TRANSLATION: Paula **got extremely upset** just because I was a little late picking her up at the airport.

"REAL SPEAK": Paula **god all ben' oudda shape** jus' b'cuz I w'z a liddle late picking 'er up 'it the airport.

get even with someone (to) *exp.* to retaliate.

EXAMPLE: So, Monica thinks she can steal my husband? Well, I'm going to **get even with her** if it's the last thing I do.

TRANSLATION: So, Monica thinks she can steal my husband? Well, I'm going to **retaliate** if it's the last thing I do.

"REAL SPEAK": So, Monica thinks she c'n steal my husband? Well, I'm gonna **ged even with 'er** if it's the last thing I do.

"Get lost!" *interj.* "Leave me alone!"

EXAMPLE: **Get lost**! I told you never to speak to me again!

TRANSLATION: **Leave me alone**! I told you never to speak to me again!

"REAL SPEAK": **Get lost**! I tol' ju never da speak ta me again!

have it in for someone (to) *exp.* to resent someone so much that you desire retaliation.

EXAMPLE: Connie has **had it in for me** ever since Jerry chose me over her. You should see how she looks at me.

TRANSLATION: Connie has **so much resentment toward me that she wants retaliation** ever since Jerry chose me over her. You should see how she looks at me.

"REAL SPEAK": Connie's **had id in fer me** ever since Jerry chose me over her. You should see how she looks 'it me.

jerk someone around (to) *exp.* to mislead someone.

EXAMPLE: Every few months, you tell me that you'll pay me back, but three years have already passed and I haven't received a dime from you. I think you're **jerking me around**.

TRANSLATION: Every few months, you tell me that you'll pay me back, but three years have already passed and I haven't received a dime from you. I think you're **misleading me**.

"REAL SPEAK": Ev'ry few munts, ya tell me th't chu'll pay me back, b't three years 'ev ahready passed 'n I haven't received a dime fr'm you. I think y'r **jerking me around**.

"Look who's talking!" *exp.* "You're just as guilty!"

EXAMPLE:
– You don't care about Tim and you know it.
– **Look who's talking**! When he was in the hospital, you never even came to visit.

TRANSLATION:
– You don't care about Tim and you know it.
– **You're just as guilty**! When he was in the hospital, you never even came to visit.

"REAL SPEAK":
– You don't care about Tim 'n you know it.
– **Look oo's talking**! When 'e w'z in the hospid'l, ya never even came da visit.

pull a fast one (to) *exp.* to do something dishonest.

EXAMPLE: Karen told all her friends she needed money for rent. In reality, she spent it all on gambling. She certainly **pulled a fast one**.

TRANSLATION: Karen told all her friends she needed money for rent. In reality, she spent it all on gambling. She certainly **was dishonest**.

"REAL SPEAK": Karen told all 'er friends she needed money fer rent. In realidy, she spen' id all on gambling. She certainly **pulled a fast one**.

slap in the face (a) *exp.* an insult.

EXAMPLE: When Don promoted Ed instead of me, that was a real **slap in the face**.

TRANSLATION: When Don promoted Ed instead of me, that was a real **insult**.

"REAL SPEAK": Wh'n Don pramoded Ed 'nstead 'a me, that w'z a real **slap 'n the face**.

tear jerker *exp.* (pronounced: *teer jer-ker*) a story that causes one to cry.

EXAMPLE: On my favorite soap today, Nancy's husband finally returned home after being lost at sea for five years! It was such a **tear jerker**!

TRANSLATION: On my favorite soap today, Nancy's husband finally returned home after being lost at sea for five years! It was such an **emotional story that made me cry**!

"REAL SPEAK": On my fav'rit soap taday, Nancy's husban' fin'lly returned home after being lost 'it sea fer five years! It w'z such a **tear jerker**!

"That's the last straw!" *interj.* "That's all I can tolerate!"

EXAMPLE: You lied to me again?! **That's the last straw**! Get out of my house.

TRANSLATION: You lied to me again?! **That's all I can tolerate**! Get out of my house.

"REAL SPEAK": You lied da me again?! **That's the las' straw**! Ged oudda my house.

touchy (to be) *exp.* to be quick to take offense.

EXAMPLE: Joanne is **touchy** today. I asked her how Jeff was and told me never to ask her that again!

TRANSLATION: Joanne is **quick to take offense** today. I asked her how Jeff was and she said told me never to ask her that again!

"REAL SPEAK": Joanne's **touchy** daday. I ast 'er how Jeff was 'n she said tol' me never da ask 'er thad again!

TV POLICE SHOWS

alibi *n.* an excuse that demonstrates that a suspect was away from the crime scene, proving his/her innocence.

EXAMPLE: Our suspect did not commit the murder. He has a good **alibi**. He was in the hospital at the time having surgery.

TRANSLATION: Our suspect did not commit the murder. He has a good **excuse**. He was in the hospital at the time having surgery.

"REAL SPEAK": 'Ar suspect didn' commit the murder. He has a good **alibi**. He w'z in the hospidle 'it the time having surgery.

come clean (to) *exp.* to tell the truth.

EXAMPLE: The Senator finally decided to **come clean** about his relationship with his secretary.

TRANSLATION: The Senator finally decided to **tell the truth** about his relationship with his secretary.

"REAL SPEAK": The Senader fin'lly decided da **come clean** aboud 'is relationship with 'is secretary.

crack a case (to) *exp.* to solve a case.

EXAMPLE: It's taken the detectives five years to **crack this case**, but they finally found the evidence they were looking for.

TRANSLATION: It's taken the detectives five years to **solve this case**, but they finally found the evidence they were looking for.

"REAL SPEAK": It's taken the detec'dives five years ta **crack this case**, b't they fin'lly foun' the evidence they were looking for.

do time (to) *exp.* to spend time in jail or prison.

EXAMPLE: If you get stopped for drinking and driving, you may **do time**.

TRANSLATION: If you get stopped for drinking and driving, you may **go to jail**.

"REAL SPEAK": If ya get stopped fer drinking 'n driving, ya may **do time**.

Synonym 1: **behind bars (to be)** *exp.*

Synonym 2: **cool one's heels (to)** *exp.*

Synonym 3: **in the slammer (to be)** *exp.*

framed (to get) *adj.* to get wrongfully accused because someone lied in order to make you take the blame.

EXAMPLE: I didn't commit any crime! I was **framed**!

TRANSLATION: I didn't commit any crime! I was **made to take the blame for something I didn't do**!

"REAL SPEAK": I didn't commid any crime! I w'z **framed**!

Synonym: **set up (to get)** *exp.*

Also 1: **pin something on someone (to)** *exp.* to blame something on someone.

Also 2: **take the heat for something (to)** *exp.* to take the blame for something.

Also 3: **take the rap for something (to)** *exp.* to take the blame for something.

go down (to) *exp.* to get arrested.

EXAMPLE: The criminal can run, but he can't hide. We're going to find him and when we do, he's **going down**.

TRANSLATION: The criminal can run, but he can't hide. We're going to find him and when we do, he's **getting arrested**.

"REAL SPEAK": The criminal c'n run, bud 'e can't hide. W'r gonna find 'im 'n when we do, he's **goin' down**.

hot on someone's heels (to be) *exp.* to be close to finding a suspect.

EXAMPLE: The suspect won't get far. We're **hot on his heels**.

TRANSLATION: The suspect won't get far. We're **close to finding him**.

"REAL SPEAK": The suspect won't get far. W'r **hod on 'is heels**.

Synonym: **close in on someone (to)** *exp.*

lead *n.* a clue leading to a possible solution.

EXAMPLE: A witness who actually saw the robbery just called us. This is our first **lead** in the case.

TRANSLATION: A witness who actually saw the robbery just called us. This is our first **clue that may lead us to a possible solution** in the case.

"REAL SPEAK": A witness 'oo akshelly saw the robbery jus' called us. This 'ez 'ar firs' **lead** 'n the case.

Synonym: **break** *n.* short for *break in the case.*

let someone off [the hook] (to) *exp.* to pardon someone from an offense.

EXAMPLE: I'm going to **let you off [the hook]** this once because I don't have any evidence against you. But if I see you around here again, you're in big trouble!

TRANSLATION: I'm going to **pardon you** this once because I don't have any evidence against you. But if I see you around here again, you're in big trouble!

"REAL SPEAK": I'm gonna **let' chu off [the hook]** this once b'cuz I don't have any evidence against you. B'd if I see you around here again, y'r 'n big trouble!

nab someone (to) *v.* to arrest someone.

EXAMPLE: The police **nabbed** the robber the moment he walked out of the bank.

TRANSLATION: The police **arrested** the robber the moment he walked out of the bank.

"REAL SPEAK": The police **nabbed** the robber the moment 'e walked oudda the bank.

Synonym 1: **haul in (to)** *v.*

Synonym 2: **nail (to)** *v.*

Synonym 3: **pick up (to)** *v.*

Synonym 4: **take in (to)** *v.*

on the lam (to be) *n.* to be running from the police.

EXAMPLE: The criminal is still **on the lam**? I thought he was arrested a long time ago.

TRANSLATION: The criminal is still **running from the police**? I thought he was arrested a long time ago.

"REAL SPEAK": The criminal's still **on the lam**? I thod 'e w'z arrested a long time ago.

Synonym: **on the run (to be)** *exp.*

rap sheet *n.* a police record of crimes committed by someone.

EXAMPLE: That criminal has been committing crimes for years. He has a **rap sheet** a mile long.

TRANSLATION: That criminal has been committing crimes for years. He has a **police record** a mile long.

"REAL SPEAK": That criminal's been commiding crimes fer years. He has a **rap sheed** a mile long.

take a lot of twists and turns (to) *exp.* said of a case that has new and unusual developments.

EXAMPLE: At first, we were positive that the mother was the murderer. But after finding some new evidence, we think it was actually the daughter who committed the murders. This case is **taking a lot of twists and turns**.

TRANSLATION: At first, we were positive that the mother was the murderer. But after finding some new evidence, we think it was actually the daughter who committed the murders. This case is **having a lot of new and unusual developments**.

"REAL SPEAK": At first, we were posidive th't the mother w'z the murderer. B'd after finding s'm new evidence, we think it w'z akshelly the dawder who commided the murders. This case 'ez **taking a lodda twiss 'n turns**.

TV LAW SHOWS

ambulance chaser *n.* a lawyer who looks for accidents in hope of making money, usually in an unethical way through lying.

EXAMPLE: Why are you letting that lawyer represent you in your accident? He's just an **ambulance chaser**!

TRANSLATION: Why are you letting that lawyer represent you in your accident? He's just a **lawyer who looks for accidents in hopes of making money unethically**!

"REAL SPEAK": Why 'er ya ledding that lawyer represen 'chu in yer accident? He's just 'n **ambulance chaser**!

case in point *exp.* a relevant example.

EXAMPLE:
- Do you think Susan's bad temper could ever make her do something violent?
- I doubt that. It's true that I did see her punch her fist in a wall once, but that was different.
- **Case in point**! If she could be violent then, she can be violent now.

TRANSLATION:
- Do you think Susan's bad temper could ever make her do something violent?
- I doubt that. It's true that I did see her punch her fist in a wall once, but that was different.
- **A relevant example**! If she could be violent then, she can be violent now.

"REAL SPEAK":
- Ya think Susan's bad temper could ever make 'er do something vi'lent?
- I doubt that. It's true th'd I did see 'er punch 'er fist 'n a wall once, b't that w'z diff'rent.
- **Case 'n point**! If she could be vi'lent then, she c'n be violent now.

hearsay *n.* information passed verbally from one person.

EXAMPLE:
- I'm going to testify that Jim wasn't at school when the teacher was robbed. He told me he was at a restaurant.
- But that's **hearsay**. You didn't actually see him at the restaurant, so the judge won't accept your testimony.

TRANSLATION:
- I'm going to testify that Jim wasn't at school when the teacher was robbed. He told me he was at a restaurant.
- But that's **just information passed along to you verbally**. You didn't actually see him at the restaurant, so the judge won't accept your testimony.

"REAL SPEAK": – I'm gonna testify th't Jim wasn' 'it school wh'n the teacher w'z robbed. He told me he w'z ad a resterant.

– B't that's **hearsay**. Ya didn' akshelly see 'im at the resterant, so the judge won' accep' cher testimony.

legalese *n.* referring to the incomprehensible legal language used by attorneys.

EXAMPLE: I can't understand this contract at all. It's written completely in **legalese**. Why can't attorneys just write in normal English?

TRANSLATION: I can't understand this contract at all. It's written completely in **legal language**. Why can't attorneys just write in normal English?

"REAL SPEAK": I can' understan' this contract 'id all. It's written completely in **legalese**. Why can' atterneys jus' wride 'n normal English?

loophole *n.* an error in a contract that makes the entire contract invalid.

EXAMPLE: I think we can get you out of the contract. I found a **loophole**.

TRANSLATION: I think we can get you out of the contract. I found an **error that will release you from the contract**.

"REAL SPEAK": I think we c'n get 'chu oudda the contract. I found a **loophole**.

manslaughter *n.* the unlawful killing of another human being, done without malice.

EXAMPLE: I just heard that Greg was convicted of **manslaughter**! He accidentally killed a woman with his car when he ran a red light.

TRANSLATION: I just heard that Greg was convicted of **killing someone accidentally**! He accidentally killed a woman with his car when he ran a red light.

"REAL SPEAK": I jus' heard th't Greg w'z convicted 'ev **mansloder**! He accident'lly killed a woman with 'is car when 'e ran a red light.

Note: This term comes from the verb *to slaughter* meaning "to kill" and "man" meaning, in this case, "person." Now you're probably thinking, *"But how can* ***man****slaughter be applied to a woman? Isn't that politically incorrect?!"* You're right! Although this term is definitely not P.C., to the anger of many feminists, the legal system has not yet created a non-gender specific replacement.

open and shut case *n.* a court case that is easily and quickly decided.

EXAMPLE: Of course you're going to win your case. Your neighbor admitted that he destroyed your car by accident. It's an **open and shut case**.

TRANSLATION: Of course you're going to win your case. Your neighbor admitted that he destroyed your car by accident. It's a **court case that is easily and quickly decided**.

"REAL SPEAK": Of course y'r gonna win yer case. Yer neighber admidded thad 'e destroyed jer car by accident. It's 'n **open 'n shut case**.

sign one's life away (to) *n.* to give away too much when negotiating a contract.

EXAMPLE: If you sign that contract, a percentage of everything you make as an author will belong to your agent forever! You're about to **sign your life away**!

TRANSLATION: If you sign that contract, a percentage of everything you make as an author will belong to your agent forever! You're about to **give away too much in your negotiation**!

"REAL SPEAK": If ya sign that contract, a percen'age 'ev ev'rything ya make 'ez 'n auther'll belong ta yer agent ferever! Y'r about ta **sign yer life away**!

sue the pants off someone (to) *exp.* to take someone to court and win everything that person owns (including his/her pants).

EXAMPLE: You're dating another woman?! I want a divorce and I'm going to **sue the pants off you**!

TRANSLATION: You're dating another woman?! I want a divorce and I'm going to **take you to court and win everything you own**!

"REAL SPEAK": Y'r dading another woman?! I wanna divorce 'n I'm gonna **sue the pants off you**!

"The jig is up" *exp.* "Your criminal activity has just ended."

EXAMPLE: Stop right there! **The jig is up**. Put down your gun slowly.

TRANSLATION: Stop right there! **Your criminal activity has just ended**. Put down your gun slowly.

"REAL SPEAK": Stop right there! **The jig 'ez up**. Put down yer gun slowly.

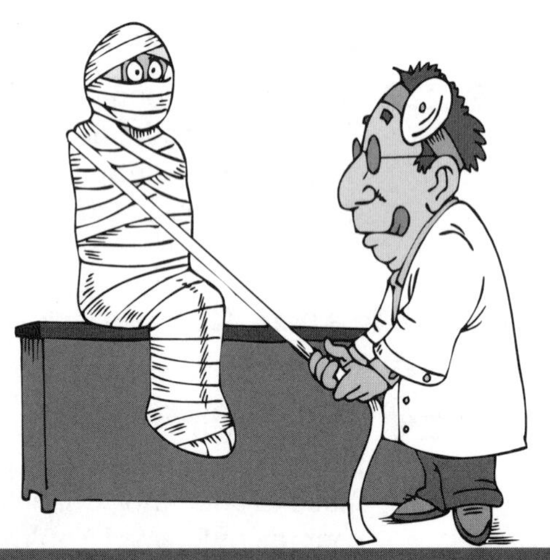

TV MEDICAL SHOWS

bedside manner *exp.* the way in which a doctor treats his/her patients.

EXAMPLE: My doctor is really unfriendly. He has the worst **bedside manner**.

TRANSLATION: My doctor is really unfriendly. He has the worst **attitude toward his patients**.

"REAL SPEAK": My doctor's really unfriendly. He 'as the worst **bedside manner**.

code blue *exp.* a medical emergency in which a team of medical personnel try to revive a patient whose heart has stopped.

EXAMPLE: We have a **code blue** in room five! Meet me there right away!

TRANSLATION: We have a **medical emergency in which a patient's heart has stopped** in room five! Meet me there right away!

"REAL SPEAK": We 'ave a **code blue** 'n room five! Meet me there ride away!

Variation: **code (to)** *v.* said of a patient whose heart has stopped.

come to (to) *exp.* to regain consciousness.

EXAMPLE: After being in a coma for more than a year, Joan finally **came to**.

TRANSLATION: After being in a coma for more than a year, Joan finally **regained consciousness**.

"REAL SPEAK": After being 'n a coma fer more th'n a year, Joan fin'lly **came to**.

crash cart *exp.* a table on wheels that carries special electrical paddles that are used to restart a patient's stopped heart.

EXAMPLE: Mr. Beehler's heart stopped! Get a **crash cart** over here fast!

TRANSLATION: Mr. Beehler's heart stopped! Get a **table on wheels that carries special electrical paddles** over here fast!

"REAL SPEAK": Mr. Beehler's heart stopped! Ged a **crash card** over here fast!

flat line (to) *exp.* said of a patient who registers a flat line on the electrocardiogram (which measures activity of the heart) indicating that the patient's heart has completely stopped.

EXAMPLE: Get a doctor, quick! The patient just started to **flat line**!

TRANSLATION: Get a doctor, quick! The patient just started to **indicate a stopped heart on the electrocardiogram**!

"REAL SPEAK": Ged a docter, quick! The patient jus' starded da **flat line**!

on the mend (to be) *exp.* to be getting better.

EXAMPLE: You're definitely **on the mend**. You can leave the hospital by tomorrow.

TRANSLATION: You're definitely **getting better**. You can leave the hospital by tomorrow.

"REAL SPEAK": Y'r definitely **on the mend**. You c'n leave the hospid'l by damorrow.

laid up (to be) *exp.* to be unable to move around normally while recovering (from illness, surgery, accident, etc.).

EXAMPLE: The doctor says I have to lie in bed for at least two weeks while I recover from surgery. Could you bring me some books since I'm going to be **laid up** for so long?

TRANSLATION: The doctor says I have to lie in bed for at least two weeks while I recover from surgery. Could you bring me some books since I'm going to be **unable to move around normally** for so long?

"REAL SPEAK": The doctor says I hafta lie 'n bed fer at leas' two weeks while I recover fr'm sergery. Could'ja bring me s'm books since I'm gonna be **laid up** fer so long?

pull the plug (to) *exp.* to turn off a patient's life-support machine.

EXAMPLE: The only way Mr. Jones can breathe is because he's being kept alive artificially. I think it's time to accept his situation and **pull the plug**.

TRANSLATION: The only way Mr. Jones can breathe is because he's being kept alive artificially. I think it's time to accept his situation and **turn off his life-support machine**.

"REAL SPEAK": The only way Mr. Jones c'n breathe 'ez b'cuz 'e's being kept alive ardificially. I think it's time da accept 'is situation 'n **pull the plug**.

put someone out (to) *exp.* to put someone to sleep with drugs in preparation for surgery.

EXAMPLE: I'm getting my tonsils removed next week. Luckily, the doctor is going to **put me out**, so I won't be aware of anything.

TRANSLATION: I'm getting my tonsils removed next week. Luckily, the doctor is going to **give me drugs to put me to sleep**, so I won't be aware of anything.

"REAL SPEAK": I'm gedding my tonsils removed nex' week. Luckily, the docter's gonna **put me out**, so I won't be aware 'ev anything.

Synonym 1: **knock someone out (to)** *exp.*

Synonym 2: **put someone under (to)** *exp.*

stat *adj.* immediately.

EXAMPLE: Get an X-ray of this man's chest **stat**. It looks to me like he may have pneumonia.

TRANSLATION: Get an X-ray of this man's chest **immediately**. It looks to me like he may have pneumonia.

"REAL SPEAK": Ged 'n X-ray 'ev this man's chest **stat**. It looks to me like he may have pneumonia.

triage *n.* a process of evaluting which patients need the most urgent medical attention.

EXAMPLE: As soon as you're admitted to the hospital, you'll go directly to **triage**. After that, you'll see a doctor.

TRANSLATION: As soon as you're admitted to the hospital, you'll go directly to **an area where the seriousness of your condition will be evaluated**. After that, you'll see a doctor.

"REAL SPEAK": As soon 'ez y'r admidded ta the hospid'l, you'll go directly da **triage**. After that, chu'll see a docter.

THEATRICAL PLAY OR CONCERT

booed (to get) *exp.* to show displeasure by shouting "Boooooooo!"

EXAMPLE: The actor was so terrible that he **got booed**! I don't know how he ever got hired for the part!

TRANSLATION: The actor was so terrible that he **got a disapproving response of "Boooooooo!" from the audience**! I don't know how he ever got hired for the part!

"REAL SPEAK": The acter w'z so terr'ble thad 'e **got booed**! I dunno how 'e ever got hired fer the part!

bring the house down (to) *exp.* said of a performance that causes the audience to applaud and scream so loudly with enthusiasm that the theater (called the *house,* in theater slang) may collapse.

EXAMPLE: The music group was great! They **brought the house down**!

TRANSLATION: The music group was great! They **had the audience applauding and screaming very loudly**!

"REAL SPEAK": The music group w'z great! They **brought the house down**!

curtain *n.* refers to the time when a theatrical play begins which is as the curtain rises.

EXAMPLE: **Curtain** is in ten minutes! We need to hurry or we're going to miss the beginning!

TRANSLATION: **The beginning of the play** is in ten minutes! We need to hurry or we're going to miss the beginning!

"REAL SPEAK": **Curtain**'s 'n ten minutes! We need da hurry 'r w'r gonna miss the beginning!

Also: **curtain call** *exp.* this refers to the moment at the end of a play when the actors take their bows.

cut an album (to) *exp.* to record an album.

EXAMPLE: My music group just **cut** its first album! It's going to be sold all around the world!

TRANSLATION: My music group just **recorded** its first album! It's going to be sold all around the world!

"REAL SPEAK": My music group jus' **cud** its first album! It's gonna be sold all aroun' the world!

dark *exp.* refers to a theater when there is no performance.

EXAMPLE: The theater is traditionally **dark** on Mondays because there are performances on weekends.

TRANSLATION: The theater is traditionally **closed** on Mondays because there are performances on weekends.

"REAL SPEAK": The theeder's traditionally **dark** on Mondays b'cuz there 'er performances on weekenz.

gig *n.* a job for a musician.

EXAMPLE: David just got a **gig** playing the piano at the local bar.

TRANSLATION: David just got a **music job** playing at the local bar.

"REAL SPEAK": David jus' god a **gig** playing the piano 'it the local bar.

make the charts (to) *exp.* said of a song that has become part of the music industry's list of the most popular songs.

EXAMPLE: The love song I composed **made the charts**! I'm going to be rich and famous!

TRANSLATION: The love song I composed **has become part of the music industry's list of the most popular songs**! I'm going to be rich and famous!

"REAL SPEAK": The love song I composed **made the charts**! I'm gonna be rich 'n famous!

nose bleed section *exp.* (humorous) the cheapest seats that are furthest away from the stage and the highest in the theater (and are said jokingly to cause nose bleeds because of the extremely high altitude).

EXAMPLE: All the good seats for the concert are sold out. We could still go but we'd have to sit in the **nose bleed section**.

TRANSLATION: All the good seats for the concert are sold out. We could still go but we'd have to sit in the **cheapest seats that are really high up**.

"REAL SPEAK": All the good seats fer the concerd 'er sold out. We could still go b't we'd hafta sit 'n the **nose bleed section**.

open for someone (to) *exp.* to be the opening performance before the main event.

EXAMPLE: I wonder who's **opening for** *Madonna* tonight. I hope it's that group we saw last week. They were great!

TRANSLATION: I wonder who's **going to be the opening performance** for *Madonna* tonight. I hope it's that group we saw last week. They were great!

"REAL SPEAK": I wonder who's **opening fer** *Madonna* tanight. I hope it's that group we saw las' week. They were great!

prompter *n.* a person, not visible to the audience, who helps an actor by whispering the words of a forgotten phrase.

EXAMPLE: Larry never memorizes his parts completely. Every time he's in a play, he needs to have a **prompter**.

TRANSLATION: Larry never memorizes his parts completely. Every time he's in a play, he needs to have a **person who helps him if he forgets his lines**.

"REAL SPEAK": Larry never memorizes 'is parts completely. Ev'ry time 'e's in a play, he needs ta have a **prompter**.

scalper *n.* a person who buys tickets then resells them at a higher price (which is a common yet illegal activity).

EXAMPLE: There are no more tickets for the play. If you're willing to pay more money, we could always go to the theater the night of the play and see if we can find a **scalper**.

TRANSLATION: There are no more tickets for the play. If you're willing to pay more money, we could always go to the theater the night of the play and see if we can find a **person who buys and resells tickets at a higher price**.

"REAL SPEAK": There 'er no more tickets fer the play. If y'r willing da pay more money, we could ahweez go da the theeder the nide 'a the play 'n see if we c'n find a **scalper**.

Also: **scalp tickets (to)** *exp.* to buy tickets and resell them at a higher price.

stand-up (to do) *exp.* to perform alone as a comedian by telling funny stories to the audience.

EXAMPLE: John just started **doing stand-up** but he's already fantastic! I watched him perform yesterday and I never laughed so hard!

TRANSLATION: John just started **performing comedic monologues** but he's already fantastic! I watched him perform yesterday and I never laughed so hard!

"REAL SPEAK": John jus' starded **doing stand-up** bud 'e's ahready fantastic! I watched 'im perform yesterday 'n I never laughed so hard!

Also: **a stand-up comic** *n.* one who performs comedic monologues.

THE NEWSPAPER

Note: "The newspaper" is commonly abbreviated to *The paper* and is used by everyone!

blurb *n.* a short newspaper article.

EXAMPLE: Today I read a **blurb** in the newspaper about a new play that just opened last week. They say it's really funny. We should go see it!

TRANSLATION: Today I read a **short article** in the newspaper about a new play that just opened last week. They say it's really funny. We should go see it!

"REAL SPEAK": Taday I read a **blurb** 'n the 'paper aboud a new play th't just opened last week. They say it's really funny. We should go see it!

Synonym 1: **mention** *n.*

Synonym 2: **piece** *n.*

breaking news *exp.* important news that has just occurred, usually reported on television.

EXAMPLE: We have some **breaking news**. The war overseas has finally ended!

TRANSLATION: We have some **important news that has just occurred**. The war overseas has finally ended!

"REAL SPEAK": We have s'm **breaking news**. The war overseas 'ez fin'lly ended!

Synonym: **news flash** *exp.*

Note: This expression is also commonly used in everyday conversation when giving someone important information • *You think Bob is a nice guy? I have* ***a news flash*** *for you. He's in jail right now for breaking the law!;* You think Bob is a nice guy? I have ***some important news*** for you. He's in jail right now for breaking the law!

front page (to make the) *exp.* said of a story that is so important that it is printed on the front page of the newspaper.

EXAMPLE: Scientists think they have found a cure for cancer! The story **made the front page**!

TRANSLATION: Scientists think they have found a cure for cancer! The story **is so important that it was printed on the front page of the newspaper**!

"REAL SPEAK": Scientis' think they've found a cure fer cancer! The story **made the front page**!

funnies *n.pl.* the comic section of the newspaper containing primarily funny stories with illustrations.

EXAMPLE: Every morning before work, I read the **funnies** because it puts me in a good mood.

TRANSLATION: Every morning before work, I read the **comic section of the newspaper** because it puts me in a good mood.

"REAL SPEAK": Ev'ry morning b'fore work, I read the **funnies** b'cuz it puts me 'n a good mood.

"Hold/Stop the presses!" *exp.* "Stop printing the newspaper (because we need to add something important)!"

EXAMPLE: **Hold the presses**! The president was just shot! We need to add a story about it right away!

TRANSLATION: **Stop printing the newspaper**! The president was just shot! We need to add a story about it right away!

"REAL SPEAK": **Hold the presses**! The president w'z jus' shot! We need da add a story aboud it ride away!

op-ed *exp.* an abbreviation of "opinion-editorial" which is a story in a newspaper where a reader submits an opinion about an event.

EXAMPLE: Did you read the story in the newspaper saying how we need to get rid of all the politically correct terms in our language?! As a feminist, I'm going to submit an **op-ed** and tell them how much I disagree!

TRANSLATION: Did you read the story in the newspaper saying how we need to get rid of all the politically correct terms in our language?! As a feminist, I'm going to submit an **opinion-editorial** and tell them how much I disagree!

"REAL SPEAK": Did'ja read the story 'n the 'paper saying how we need da get rid 'ev all the polidic'ly kerrect terms 'n 'ar language?! As a feminist, I'm gonna submid 'n **op-ed** 'n tell 'em how much I disagree!

rag *n.* a newspaper filled with exaggerated stories (and often lies) in order to attract customers.

EXAMPLE: Why are you reading that **rag**? Don't tell me you actually believe the stories in there!

TRANSLATION: Why are you reading that **newspaper filled with exaggerated stories and lies**? Don't tell me you actually believe the stories in there!

"REAL SPEAK": Why 'er ya reading that **rag**? Don't tell me ya akshelly b'lieve the stories 'n there!

Synonym: **tabloid** *n.* (which refers to the size of these types of newspapers: tabloid size = 11"x17").

Note: **The tabloids** refer to all newspapers of this stye that are filled with exaggerated stories and lies.

scoop *n.* a news report that is presented first before another news agency.

EXAMPLE: John is our best reporter. He always gets the **scoop** before any other reporters.

TRANSLATION: John is our best reporter. He always gets the **news first** before any other reporters.

"REAL SPEAK": John's 'ar bes' reporder. He ahweez gets the **scoop** b'fore any other reporders.

Also 1: **scoop someone (to)** *v.* to report a news story before anyone else.

Also 2: **"What's the scoop?"** *exp.* "How are you?" "What's new to report?"

spread *n.* two facing pages in a newspaper.

EXAMPLE: Did you read the **spread** in *Variety* this morning about the new science fiction movie? They say it's the most expensive movie ever made!

TRANSLATION: Did you read the **two facing pages** in *Variety* this morning about the new science fiction movie? They say it's the most expensive movie ever made!

"REAL SPEAK": Did'ja read the **spread** 'n *Variedy* th's morning about the new sci-fi movie? They say it's the most expensive movie ever made!

Note: *Variety* is a popular Hollywood newspaper containing stories relating to the entertainment industry.

want ads *n.pl.* the classified section of the newspaper where notices for employment are placed, typically carrying the headline "Wanted" at the top.

EXAMPLE: I need to find a new job. I guess the best place to start is to look in the **want ads**.

TRANSLATION: I need to find a new job. I guess the best place to start is to look in the **classified section of the newspaper**.

"REAL SPEAK": I need da find a new job. I guess the bes' place ta stard is ta look 'n the **wan' ads**.

Teen/College Slang

THIS LESSON FEATURES 15 NEW SLANG WORDS & IDIOMS

LET'S WARM UP!

MATCH THE PICTURES

As a fun way to get started, see if you can guess the meaning of the new slang words and expressions on the opposite page by using the pictures below and following the context of the sentences.

1. I need to leave. I have to meet Dan at noon. I'll call you tonight. ***Late***.
   - ❏ It's getting late
   - ❏ I'll talk to you later

2. Hi, Steve! ***What up***? I haven't seen you in a long time!
   - ❏ How are you?
   - ❏ What's up in the air?

3. You think Bob is smart? ***Hello***! He's the dumbest person I've ever met!
   - ❏ Are you crazy?
   - ❏ Hi! Nice to see you again!

4. Anne is telling lies about me?! ***Whatever***. No one believes anything she says anyway.
   - ❏ I don't care
   - ❏ I'm glad to hear it

5. Did you see the new employee? What a ***hottie***!
   - ❏ person who perspires a lot
   - ❏ sexy person

6. I'm going to go home and ***kick it*** for a few hours.
   - ❏ relax and have fun
   - ❏ play soccer

7. I'm tired of working ***24-7***. I need to find a new job.
   - ❏ twenty-four hours a day, seven days a week
   - ❏ from midnight to seven o'clock in the morning

8. I didn't realize it was so late. I need to ***bail***.
   - ❏ stay longer
   - ❏ leave

9. If Bob thinks he's going to get an "A" on the final, he's ***tripping***! He hardly ever attended class!
   - ❏ hallucinating
   - ❏ on vacation

10. You should have seen the way Mindy ***dissed*** the teacher today! She's the most disobedient student in our school.
    - ❏ disrespected
    - ❏ disagreed with

11. Hey, ***girlfriend***! Where have you been? I haven't seen you in such a long time!
    - ❏ lover
    - ❏ friend (who is a girl)

12. I can't believe Jonathan forgot my birthday. I am ***so*** not speaking to him ever again!
    - ❏ definitely
    - ❏ very

13. Charlie was upset to discover his blind date was ***tore up***!
    - ❏ extremely beautiful
    - ❏ extremely ugly

14. When I saw Judy today, she ***was all***, "It's so good to see you!" I know that she doesn't even like me!
    - ❏ was completely
    - ❏ said

15. Did you hear the news? Susan is dating Sam? Why would she do that? He's ***like*** so weird!
    - ❏ how can I say this
    - ❏ extremely

10
11
12
14
AND SHE WAS ALL "WHAT'S YOUR PROBLEM?" AND I WAS ALL "NOTHING," AND SHE WAS ALL...
AND I WENT TO THIS LIKE CAVE THING AND SAW THIS LIKE BIG LIKE BIRD AND IT WAS LIKE...
15

AND SHE WAS ALL "WHAT'S YOUR PROBLEM?" AND I WAS ALL "NOTHING," AND SHE WAS ALL...

LET'S TALK!

A. DIALOGUE USING SLANG & IDIOMS

The words introduced on the first two pages are used in the dialogue below. See if you can understand the conversation. *Note:* The translation of the words in boldface is on the right-hand page.

SPEAKING
LISTENING

CD-B: TRACK 17

Nancy: Hey, **girlfriend**. **What up**?

Lauren: Well, you're going to think I'm **tripping**, but I think Al and Peggy are **like** dating! They've been **kicking it 24-7**.

Nancy: **Hello**! Where have you been? I found out two weeks ago. When Beth told me I **was all**, "I can't believe it!" Al's a **hottie** but Peggy's **tore up**.

Lauren: I'm **so** not speaking to her any more. Every time I say hello to her, she totally **disses** me. I don't know why he'd go out with her.

Nancy: **Whatever**. I have to **bail**. I have a class in five minutes. **Late**.

B. DIALOGUE TRANSLATED INTO STANDARD ENGLISH

LET'S SEE HOW MUCH YOU REMEMBER!
Just for fun, move around in random order to the words and expressions in boldface below. See if you can remember their slang equivalents without looking at the left-hand page!

Nancy: Hey, **friend**. **How are you**?

Lauren: Well, you're going to think I've **lost my mind**, but I think Al and Peggy are, **how can I say this**, dating! They've been **doing things together 24 hours a day 7 days a week**.

Nancy: **Aren't you aware**? Where have you been? I found out two weeks ago. When Beth told me I **said**, "I can't believe it!" Al's a **sexy guy** but Peggy's **ugly**.

Lauren: I'm **absolutely** not speaking to her any more. Every time I say hello to her, she totally **disrespects** me. I don't know why he'd go out with her.

Nancy: **I don't care**. I have to **leave**. I have a class in five minutes. **See you later**.

C. DIALOGUE USING "REAL SPEAK"

The dialogue below demonstrates how the slang conversation on the previous page would *really* be spoken by native speakers!

SPEAKING

LISTENING

CD-B: TRACK 17

Nancy: Hey, **girlfrien'**. **Whad up**?

Lauren: Well, y'r gonna think I'm **trippin'**, b'd I think Al 'n Peggy 'er **like** dading! They've been **kickin' it twen'y-four seven**.

Nancy: **Hello**! Where 'ev ya been? I found out two weeks ago. When Beth told me I **w'z all**, "I can't believe it!" Al's a **hoddie** b't Peggy's **to' up**.

Lauren: I'm **so** not speaking da her any more. Ev'ry time I say hello do 'er, she todally **disses** me. I dunno why 'e'd go out with 'er.

Nancy: **Whadever**. I 'afta **bail**. I 'ave a class 'n five minutes. **Late**.

LET'S LEARN!

SPEAKING
LISTENING

VOCABULARY

The following words and expressions were used in the previous dialogues. Let's take a closer look at what they mean.

CD-B: TRACK 18

all (to be) *exp.* to say.

AND SHE WAS ALL "WHAT'S YOUR PROBLEM?" AND I WAS ALL "NOTHING," AND SHE WAS ALL...

EXAMPLE: Jennifer was acting so strangely at the party last night. I know she doesn't like me, but when she saw me she **was all**, "How are you! I'm so happy to see you!"

TRANSLATION: Jennifer was acting so strangely at the party last night. I know she doesn't like me, but when she saw me she **said**, "How are you! I'm so happy to see you!"

"REAL SPEAK": Jennifer w'z akding so strangely 'it the pardy las' night. I know she doesn't like me, b't when she saw me she **w'z all**, "How are ya! I'm so happy da see ya!"

Synonym: **like (to be)** *exp.*

Variation: **like all (to be)** *exp.* • **all like (to be)** *exp.*

Note: The expressions *to be like* and *to be all* are so popular among teens that you'll probably hear them within your first hour of being in the United States! It would not be uncommon to hear a string of *likes* and *alls* in the same sentence. For example: *When Tessa saw me, she **was like**, "I love your new hairstyle!" and I **was all**, "Why are you being so friendly? You're always so mean to me." And she's **like all**, "No! I really like you!" So I'm **all like**, "You just want me to introduce you to my brother's friend!"*

NOW YOU DO IT. COMPLETE THE PHRASE ALOUD:
Kim walked up to me and she was all...

bail (to) *v.* to leave.

EXAMPLE: My psychology class starts in five minutes. I have to **bail**. Talk to you later!

TRANSLATION: My psychology class starts in five minutes. I have to **leave**. Talk to you later!

"REAL SPEAK": My psych class starts 'n five minutes. I hafta **bail**. Talk ta ya lader!

NOW YOU DO IT. COMPLETE THE PHRASE ALOUD:

Look at the time! I have to bail because...

diss someone (to) *v.* to disrespect someone.

EXAMPLE: Can you believe how Karen **dissed** the professor today? If Karen keeps talking to her like that, Karen is going to fail the course for sure!

TRANSLATION: Can you believe how Karen **disrespected** the professor today? If Karen keeps talking to her like that, Karen is going to fail the course for sure!

"REAL SPEAK": C'n you b'lieve how Karen **dissed** the prafesser taday? If Karen keeps talking to 'er like that, Karen's gonna fail the course fer sher!

NOW YOU DO IT. COMPLETE THE PHRASE ALOUD:

...dissed me! He/she...

girlfriend *n.* aside from meaning "the girl you are dating," it also means "friend who is a girl" and is used in greetings and conversations between two girls or women.

EXAMPLE: Hi, **girlfriend**! Do you want to go with us to the movies tonight?

TRANSLATION: Hi, **friend**! Do you want to go with us to the movies tonight?

"REAL SPEAK": Hi, **girlfrien'**! Ya wanna to go with us ta the movies tanight?

Variation: **girl** *n.*

NOW YOU DO IT. COMPLETE THE PHRASE ALOUD:

Hey, girlfriend! ...

"Hello!" *interj.* "Are you crazy?!" or more literally, "Hello! Is anyone home?!" ("home" representing your head).

EXAMPLE: You thought I went out with Rob last night? **Hello!** I wouldn't go out with him if he were the last guy on earth!

TRANSLATION: You thought I went out with Rob last night? **Are you crazy?!** I wouldn't go out with him if he were the last guy on earth!

"REAL SPEAK": Ya thod I wen' out with Rob las' night? **Hello!** I wouldn' go out with 'im if 'e were the las' guy on earth!

NOW YOU DO IT. COMPLETE THE PHRASE ALOUD:

Hello! ...

hottie *n.* sexy person (from the adjective hot meaning "sexy" in American slang).

EXAMPLE: Rick is a real **hottie**! All the girls in school want him to ask them out on a date.

TRANSLATION: Rick is a real **sexy person**! All the girls in school want him to ask them out on a date.

"REAL SPEAK": Rick's a real **hoddie**! All the girls 'n school wan'im da ask th'm oud on a date.

NOW YOU DO IT. COMPLETE THE PHRASE ALOUD:
...is such a hottie!

kick it (to) *v.* to relax and have fun.

EXAMPLE: We're going to **kick it** at Mark's house and watch television. Do you want to come?

TRANSLATION: We're going to **relax and have fun** at Mark's house and watch television. Do you want to come?

"REAL SPEAK": W'r gonna **kick id** 'it Mark's house 'n watch TV. Wanna come?

Variation: **kick back (to)** *v.*

NOW YOU DO IT. COMPLETE THE PHRASE ALOUD:
Dan and I are going to kick it at...

"Late!" *exp.* a shortened version of "See you later!"

EXAMPLE: I have to get to my history class. It starts in ten minutes. I'll talk to you tonight. **Late**!

TRANSLATION: I have to get to my history class. It starts in ten minutes. I'll talk to you tonight. **See you later**!

"REAL SPEAK": I hafta get ta my histery class. It starts 'n ten minutes. A'll talk ta ya tanight. **Late**!

Variation: **Later!** *exp.*

NOW YOU DO IT. COMPLETE THE PHRASE ALOUD:
I have to go to... Late!

like *adv.* an *extremely* popular adverb meaning "How can I say this" which is used (and typically overused, to the constant frustration of their teachers) by teens.

AND I WENT TO THIS LIKE CAVE THING AND SAW THIS LIKE BIG LIKE BIRD AND IT WAS LIKE...

EXAMPLE: That's Michelle. She's **like** my best friend in school. I've known her for two years.

TRANSLATION: That's Michelle. She's, **how can I say this**, my best friend in school. I've know her for two years.

"REAL SPEAK": That's Michelle. She's **like** my best friend 'n school. I've known 'er fer two years.

NOW YOU DO IT. COMPLETE THE PHRASE ALOUD:
David's like...

so *adv.* definitely • (lit.): extremely.

EXAMPLE: Joanne has been saying mean things about me for the past month. I'm **so** not speaking to her ever again!

TRANSLATION: Joanne has been saying mean things about me for the past month. I'm **definitely** not speaking to her ever again!

"REAL SPEAK": Joanne's been saying mean things about me fer the past month. I'm **so** not speaking ta her ever again!

Note: This is a unique usage of the adverb "*so*" among teenagers! Typically, *so* is used to emphasis an adjective such as *so tired;* extremely tired • *so happy;* extremely happy, etc. Teens use *so* to mean "definitely" and is commonly heard before the past tense of a verb (*You are **so** fired!;* You are ***definitely*** fired!) or before a phrase (*I'm **so** not shopping there again!;* I'm ***definitely*** not shopping there again!).

NOW YOU DO IT. COMPLETE THE PHRASE ALOUD:
I am so not...

tore up (to be) *exp.* to be very ugly.

EXAMPLE: Why would a great-looking guy like Dave want to go out with a girl like Betty? She's **tore up**!

TRANSLATION: Why would a great-looking guy like Dave want to go out with a girl like Betty? She's **really ugly**!

"REAL SPEAK": Why would a great-looking guy like Dave wanna go out with a girl like Beddy? She's **to' up**!

Note 2: This was originally introduced as a rhyming expression, *to be tore up from the floor up*. However, the trend in teen slang is to shorten, Shorten, SHORTEN! Therefore, this expression quickly became *to be tore up*. Next, it went through one more transformation. A southern, African-American urban accent was applied to the pronunciation, where the "R" sound is typically dropped; *to be to' up* (pronounced "tow"). It would actually be very uncommon to hear this expression with the "R" pronounced!
• See: **whore** (under **tramp**, synonym 2) *p. 48*.

NOW YOU DO IT. COMPLETE THE PHRASE ALOUD:
...thinks he's handsome, but I think he's to' up!

trip (to) *v.* • to hallucinate • (lit): to hallucinate under the influence of drugs.

EXAMPLE: If you think you can pass this class without studying, you're **tripping**!

TRANSLATION: If you think you can pass this class without studying, you're **hallucinating**!

"REAL SPEAK": If ya think ya c'n pass this class without studying, y'r **tripping**!

Variation: **trip out (to)** *exp.*

NOW YOU DO IT. COMPLETE THE PHRASE ALOUD:
I think Larry is tripping because yesterday...

"What up?" *exp.* "How are you?"

EXAMPLE: Hey, bro! **What up**? I haven't seen you around in a while.

TRANSLATION: Hey, bro! **How are you**? I haven't seen you around in a while.

"REAL SPEAK": Hey, bro! **What up**? I haven' seen ya around in a while.

Note: This is a common teen variation on the popular expression *What's up?* meaning "How are you?"

Variation 1: **"Sup?"** *exp.* a common reduction of *"What's up?"*

Variation 2: **"Wassup?"** *exp.* a common reduction of *"What's up?"*

Synonym 1: **"How's it hanging?"** *exp.* (often pronounced *How's it hangin'?*).

Synonym 2: **"What's going down?"** *exp.* (typically pronounced *What's goin' down?*).

Synonym 3: **"Word up" or "Word"** *exp.* I agree!

NOW YOU DO IT. COMPLETE THE PHRASE ALOUD:
Hey, Jack! What up? I heard that you...

whatever *interj.* an extremely common response to something you don't want to discuss any further (usually because the topic is getting annoying).

EXAMPLE:
– The only reason Sandra doesn't like you is because you get better grades than she does. She's so competitive.
– **Whatever**.

TRANSLATION:
– The only reason Sandra doesn't like you is because you get better grades than she does. She's so competitive.
– **I don't care and don't want to discuss it anymore**.

"REAL SPEAK":
– The only reason Sandra doesn' like ya 'ez b'cuz ya get bedder grades th'n she does. She's so c'mpeditive.
– **Whadever**.

NOW YOU DO IT. COMPLETE THE PHRASE ALOUD:
Diane just told me that... Whadever!

24-7 *exp.* all the time • (lit.): 24 hours a day, 7 days a week.

EXAMPLE: I think Linda and Jeff really like each other. They're with each other **24-7**.

TRANSLATION: I think Linda and Jeff really like each other. They're together **24 hours a day, 7 days a week**.

"REAL SPEAK": I think Linda 'n Jeff really like each other. They're dagether **twen'y-four seven.**

NOW YOU DO IT. COMPLETE THE PHRASE ALOUD:
I could... 24-7!

LET'S PRACTICE!

A. TRUTH OR LIE

Read the conversation each person is having on the phone, then read their actual thoughts in the bubble. Decide if the person is telling the truth or a lie and check the appropriate box.

CD-B: TRACK 19

1

I think Gerry is so sexy!

You have to meet Gerry. He's such a **hottie**!

☐ truth
☐ lie

2

Cher is the most beautiful woman I've ever seen!

You definitely wouldn't like her. She's **to' up**!

☐ truth
☐ lie

3

My girlfriend's father and I don't like each other.

We **kick it** together **24-7**! He's a great guy!

☐ truth
☐ lie

4

I hate studying!

You think I enjoy staying up all night doing homework?! **Hello**!

WAKE UP!

☐ truth
☐ lie

5

I don't have anything to do right now. I'm totally bored!

I wish I could talk with you longer, but I have to **bail**.

☐ truth
☐ lie

6

Jill totally **dissed** me as usual!

Jill's really nice. She's friendly to everyone!

☐ truth
☐ lie

B. FIND THE DEFINITION

Write the definition of the slang word(s) in boldface, choosing from the word list below.

CD-B: TRACK 20

DEFINITIONS

- ✔ to leave
- ✔ "How can I say this?"
- ✔ "How are you?"
- ✔ a friend who is a girl, and used in greetings and conversations between two girls
- ✔ sexy person
- ✔ to relax and have fun
- ✔ "See you later!"
- ✔ definitely
- ✔ a response to something you don't want to discuss any further
- ✔ "Are you crazy?!"
- ✔ to be very ugly
- ✔ to hallucinate
- ✔ to say
- ✔ 24 hours a day, 7 days a week
- ✔ to disrespect someone

1. **all (to be)** *exp.* ______________________
2. **bail (to)** *v.* ______________________
3. **diss someone (to)** *v.* ______________________
4. **girlfriend** *n.* ______________________
5. **"Hello!"** *interj.* ______________________
6. **hottie** *n.* ______________________
7. **kick it (to)** *v.* ______________________
8. **"Late!"** *exp.* ______________________
9. **like** *adv.* ______________________
10. **so** *adv.* ______________________
11. **tore up (to be)** *exp.* ______________________
12. **trip (to)** *v.* ______________________
13. **"What up?"** *exp.* ______________________
14. **whatever** *interj.* ______________________
15. **24-7** *exp.* ______________________

C. FIND-THE-WORD GRID

CD-B: TRACK 21

Fill in the blanks with the most appropriate word using the list. Next, find and circle the word in the grid below. The answers may be spelled vertically or horizontally.

BAIL	**HOTTIE**	**LATE**	**SO**	**UP**
HELLO	**KICK**	**LIKE**	**TRIPPING**	**WAS ALL**

1. You think Lisa's your friend? __________! She says terrible things about you all the time!
2. Do you want to _________ it at the beach today?
3. This movie's boring. I'm going to ___________. See you tomorrow.
4. Did you see that lifeguard? What a __________! He must exercise every day!
5. John walked up to me today and he ___________, "Do you want to go out to dinner some time?"
6. What's wrong with Karen? She's _________ really strange today. She keeps yelling at everyone.
7. I have to go study. Give me a call tonight. ___________.
8. Hi, Debbie! What _______?
9. After all the terrible things Vicki said about me, I'm ______ not speaking to her.
10. If you think I'm going to invite Bob to my party, you're _________________!

FIND-THE-WORD GRID

T	N	F	R	E	A	K	C	E	D	G	R	R	E	W	D	S	T	M	A	T
W	A	S	A	L	L	G	R	O	A	O	D	T	A	B	L	E	H	E	M	A
V	W	D	L	R	S	O	B	U	F	C	S	D	F	I	M	C	O	L	O	R
Y	T	J	T	R	E	I	A	H	L	U	E	A	O	C	E	K	T	U	V	V
E	L	O	W	K	C	K	I	C	K	T	H	E	L	O	U	S	T	N	E	E
I	I	U	O	C	O	P	L	H	O	L	A	T	R	I	P	P	I	N	G	T
Q	K	R	A	I	N	S	T	O	R	M	R	M	O	T	I	O	E	H	G	Z
U	E	N	K	I	D	L	E	R	D	H	E	L	L	O	C	W	E	S	S	D
E	U	E	W	L	A	T	E	E	R	E	C	O	G	N	I	Z	E	S	K	E
I	T	D	W	D	D	H	T	M	R	E	E	L	V	S	E	Z	O	I	S	A

More Teen/College Slang

I have to give teens **props** *(their proper credit)* for creating some **way cool** *(very interesting)* slang that really **rocks** *(is truly fantastic)*! If you're a teen or college student who doesn't know this popular type of lingo, then you're obviously **phat-free** *(dull and boring)*. But if you are familiar with the following terms, then all your **peeps** *(friends)* will think you're definitely **da bomb** *(great)*!

Note: For more slang terms and expressions used in school, take a look at *The Slangman Guide to* ***STREET SPEAK 1***, Chapter 8 *(At School)*.

ace a test (to) *exp*. to do extremely well on a test.

EXAMPLE: My math test was easy. I **aced it**!

TRANSLATION: My math test was easy. I **did extremely well on it**!

"REAL SPEAK": My math test w'z easy. I **aced it**!

Synonym: **wail on a test (to)** *exp*.

all that (to be) *exp*. to be very attractive.

EXAMPLE: Karen thinks she's **all that** ever since she got a new hairstyle! She's so pretentious.

TRANSLATION: Karen thinks she's **really attractive** ever since she got a new hairstyle! She's so pretentious.

"REAL SPEAK": Karen thinks she's **all thad** ever since she god a new hairstyle! She's so pratentious.

awesome *adj*. fantastic, great.

EXAMPLE: The movie last night was **awesome**!

TRANSLATION: The movie last night was **fantastic**!

"REAL SPEAK": The movie las' night w'z **awesome**!

Note: *Awesome* is not slang but it's included here because of its frequent use among teens.

baby / bonehead [course name] *adj*. a school course that is the lowest level or the easiest.

EXAMPLE: I'm taking **bonehead** mathematics this semester.

TRANSLATION: I'm taking **a course of the lowest level in** mathematics this semester.

"REAL SPEAK": I'm taking **bonehead** math this semester.

Note: **bonehead** *n*. a stupid person whose head is nothing but bone and no brain.

blow off something (to) / to blow something off (to) *exp*. to avoid responsibilities.

EXAMPLE: I'm going to **blow off** my homework and go to the movies tonight instead.

TRANSLATION: I've **decided to avoid the responsibilities of doing** my homework and go to the movies tonight instead.

"REAL SPEAK": I'm gonna **blow off** my homework 'n go da the movies tanight 'nstead.

See: **blow someone off (to)**, *p. 5.*

brew *n.* beer.

EXAMPLE: Sidney loves nothing more than a cold **brew** on a hot day.

TRANSLATION: Sidney loves nothing more than a cold **beer** on a hot day.

"REAL SPEAK": Sidney loves nothing more th'n a cold **brew** on a hot day.

Variation: **brewski** *n.* a variation of *brew* using the Russian suffix *-ski,* giving a fun and cheerful feeling to the word.

bro *n.* a common abbreviation of *brother*, meaning "a male friend" in slang.

EXAMPLE: Hey, **bro**! I haven't seen you in a long time!

TRANSLATION: Hey, **friend**! I haven't seen you in a long time!

"REAL SPEAK": Hey, **bro**! I haven't seen ya 'n a long time!

caf *n.* a common abbreviation of "student cafeteria."

EXAMPLE: I'm getting hungry. I'm going to run over to the **caf** and get some lunch.

TRANSLATION: I'm getting hungry. I'm going to run over to the **cafeteria** and get some lunch.

"REAL SPEAK": I'm gedding hungry. I'm gonna run over da the **caf** 'n get s'm lunch.

cheat sheet *n.* a piece of paper that contains the answers to a test that is carefully hidden so that the professor doesn't see.

EXAMPLE: The only reason Jackie passed the test is because she was using a **cheat sheet**!

TRANSLATION: The only reason Jackie passed the test is because she was using **pieces of paper that contain the answers**!

"REAL SPEAK": The only reason Jackie passed the test 'ez b'cuz she w'z using a **cheat sheet**!

chill [out] (to) *v.* to relax, to calm down.

EXAMPLE: Let's get a beer and **chill [out]** after this long day.

TRANSLATION: Let's get a beer and **relax** after this long day.

"REAL SPEAK": Let's ged a beer 'n **chill [oud]** after th's long day.

cool *adj.* (probably the oldest and still most popular American slang word!) great, fantastic.

EXAMPLE: Your new car is really **cool**!

TRANSLATION: Your new car is really **fantastic**!

"REAL SPEAK": Yer new car's really **cool**!

crib *n.* house, home

EXAMPLE: Did you see the **crib** James lives in? It's huge!

TRANSLATION: Did you see the **house** James lives in? It's huge!

"REAL SPEAK": Did'ja see the **crib** James lives in? It's huge!

cut class (to) *exp.* to avoid going to one's class.

EXAMPLE: I'm going to **cut class** today and go to a movie instead. Do you want to come along?

TRANSLATION: I'm going to **avoid going to class** today and go to a movie instead. Do you want to come along?

"REAL SPEAK": I'm gonna **cut class** taday 'n go do a movie instead. Wanna come along?

Synonym 1: **blow off class (to)** *exp.*

Synonym 2: **ditch class (to)** *exp.*

Synonym 3: **skip class (to)** *exp.*

da bomb *exp.* fantastic, great.

EXAMPLE: Our new biology professor is **da bomb**!

TRANSLATION: Our new biology professor is **fantastic**!

"REAL SPEAK": 'Ar new bio' prof's **da bomb**!

Note 1: The expression *da bomb* is actually a southern, African-American urban pronunciation of *the bomb*. Because this expression first appeared in rap music which was originated by African-Americans who commonly perform rap music with this type of accent, the accent remained as an important part of the word itself.

Note 2: This expression is not to be confused with the expression *a bomb* which means "the worst." For example: *That movie was **a bomb**!*; That movie was ***the worst***!

digits *n.pl.* telephone number.

EXAMPLE: I'd love to go out with you some time. Can I get your **digits**?

TRANSLATION: I'd love to go out with you some time. Can I get your **telephone number**?

"REAL SPEAK": I'd love ta go out with you some time. C'n I get 'cher **digits**?

dope *adj.* great, wonderful, fantastic.

EXAMPLE: The movie today was really **dope**! I'm glad I went.

TRANSLATION: The movie today was really **great**! I'm glad I went.

"REAL SPEAK": The movie taday w'z really **dope**! I'm glad I went.

drop out of school (to) *exp.* to abandon school.

EXAMPLE: After being in college for only a year, Dan **dropped out of school** to work for his father.

TRANSLATION: After being in college for only a year, Dan **abandoned school** to work for his father.

"REAL SPEAK": After being 'n college fer only a year, Dan **dropped oudda school** da work fer 'is father.

drop a course (to) *exp.* to abandon a course.

EXAMPLE: I decided to **drop** chemistry this semester. I have too many courses right now.

TRANSLATION: I decided to **abandon** chemistry this semester. I have too many courses right now.

"REAL SPEAK": I decided da **drop** chemistry this semester. I have too many courses right now.

dude *n.* • **1.** man, guy • **2.** used to signify surprise • **3.** male or female friend.

EXAMPLE 1: Who is that **dude**? I've never seen him before.

TRANSLATION: Who is that **man**? I've never seen him before.

"REAL SPEAK": Who's that **dude**? I've never seen 'im b'fore.

EXAMPLE 2: **Dude**! Did you see how fast that car was moving?!

TRANSLATION: **Wow**! Did you see how fast that car was moving?!

"REAL SPEAK": **Dude**! Did'ju see how fast that car w'z moving?!

EXAMPLE 3: Hey, **dude**! Where have you been?

TRANSLATION: Hey, **friend**! Where have you been?

"REAL SPEAK": Hey, **dude**! Where ya been?

fine *adj.* said of a very attractive person.

EXAMPLE: Did you see Norm's new girlfriend? She is **fine**!

TRANSLATION: Did you see Norm's new girlfriend? She is **really pretty**!

"REAL SPEAK": Did'ja see Norm's new girlfriend? She's **fine**!

fly *adj*. great, wonderful, fantastic.

EXAMPLE: My chemistry teacher is **fly**. She never gives us homework on the weekends!

TRANSLATION: My chemistry teacher is **great**. She never gives us homework on the weekends!

"REAL SPEAK": My chem teacher's **fly**. She never gives us homework on the weekenz!

frat rat *n*. a male student who belongs to a fraternity organization (which is a social club for male students).

EXAMPLE: I would never go out with a **frat rat**. All they ever think about is partying!

TRANSLATION: I would never go out with a **male student who belongs to a fraternity**. All they ever think about is partying!

"REAL SPEAK": I'd never go out w'th a **frat rat**. All they ever think aboud 'ez pardying!

Note: The term *frat* is a popular abbreviation of "fraternity." There is no abbreviation of "sorority," which is a social club for female students.

Synonym 2: **frat boy** *n*.

Synonym 2: **Greek** *n*. (a common term used among fraternity members – all fraternities are named after a combination of Greek letters such as Sigma Pi, Beta Theta Pi, etc.).

give it up for someone (to) *exp*. to give applause to someone.

EXAMPLE: Ladies and Gentlemen, let's **give it up for** our new school principal!

TRANSLATION: Ladies and Gentlemen, let's **give some applause to** our new school principal!

"REAL SPEAK": Ladies 'n Gen'elmen, let's **give id up fer** 'ar new school princip'l!

Synonym: **hear it for (to)** *exp*. • *Let's **hear it for** Slangman!;* Let's ***give some applause to*** Slangman!

haze (to) *v*. to subject a **pledge** *(see p. 202)* to a number of embarrassing (and sometimes painful) rituals before acceptance into the fraternity organization.

EXAMPLE: I'm thinking about joining Sigma Pi fraternity as long as they don't **haze their pledges**.

TRANSLATION: I'm thinking about joining Sigma Pi fraternity as long as they don't **subject their pledges to rituals before acceptance into the organization**.

"REAL SPEAK": I'm thinking about joining Sigma Pi frad 'ez long 'ez they don't **haze their pledges**.

Note: **hazing** *n*. the act of subjecting a pledge to a number of embarrassing (and sometimes painful) rituals before acceptance into the fraternity organization • ***Hazing** is illegal in many universities because of reported deaths as a result;* ***The act of subjecting a pledge to a number of embarrassing (and sometimes painful) rituals before acceptance into a fraternity organization*** is illegal in many universities because of reported deaths as a result.

hella *adv.* a teen variation of *Hell of a...* meaning "very."

EXAMPLE: We had a **hella** good time at Jenn's party last night.

TRANSLATION: We had a **very** good time at Jenn's party last night.

"REAL SPEAK": We had a **hella** good time 'it Jenn's pardy las' night.

Synonym: **hecca** *adv.* a variation of *Heck of a...* (which is a euphemistic version of *Hell of a...*) meaning "very."

homeboy / homegirl *n.* (originally gang slang) good friend.

EXAMPLE: Mark is my **homeboy**. We've known each other since high school.

TRANSLATION: Mark is my **friend from my hometown**. We've known each other since high school.

"REAL SPEAK": Mark's my **homeboy**. We've known each other s'nce high school.

Variation: **homey / homie** *n.*

'hood *n.* (originally gang slang) short for "neighborhood."

EXAMPLE: Hey, Dave! I haven't seen you around the **'hood** in a while. Where have you been?

TRANSLATION: Hey, Dave! I haven't seen you around the **neighborhood** in a while. Where have you been?

"REAL SPEAK": Hey, Dave! I haven't seen ya 'roun' the **'hood** 'n a while. Where ya been?

"It's all good" *exp.* "Don't get upset. Everything is fine."

EXAMPLE: I didn't know this was your girlfriend or I never would have flirted with her. **It's all good**. I'm leaving.

TRANSLATION: I didn't know this was your girlfriend or I never would have flirted with her. **Don't get upset. Everything is fine**. I'm leaving.

"REAL SPEAK": I didn' know this w'z yer girlfriend 'r I never would 'a have flirded with 'er. **It's all good**. I'm leaving.

kicking (to be) *adj.* to be fantastic.

EXAMPLE: Peggy's party was **kicking** last night!

TRANSLATION: Peggy's party was **fantastic** last night!

"REAL SPEAK": Peggy's pardy w'z **kickin'** las' night!

load *n.* the amount of courses and work one has in school.

EXAMPLE: I'm carrying a big **load** this semester. I won't have time to have any fun.

TRANSLATION: I'm carrying a big **quantity of courses and work** this semester. I won't have time to have any fun.

"REAL SPEAK": I'm carrying a big **load** this semester. I won't have time da have any fun.

Also: **overloaded (to be)** *adj.* to have more courses and work than one can manage.

mac on someone (to) *exp.* to flirt with someone.

EXAMPLE: Did you see the way Linda's boyfriend tried to **mac on** Carol at the party?

TRANSLATION: Did you see the way Linda's boyfriend tried to **flirt with** Carol at the party?

"REAL SPEAK": Did'ja see the way Linda's boyfrien' tried da **mac on** Carol 'it the pardy?

"My bad" *exp.* "It's my fault."

EXAMPLE:
– Hey! You just walked into me. Watch where you're going!
– Sorry. **My bad**.

TRANSLATION:
– Hey! You just walked into me. Watch where you're going!
– Sorry. **It was my fault**.

"REAL SPEAK":
– Hey! Ya jus' walked inda me. Watch where y'r going!
– Sorry. **My bad**.

outtie (to be) *exp.* to be leaving.

EXAMPLE: This party is boring. I'm **outtie**.

TRANSLATION: This party is boring. I'm **leaving**.

"REAL SPEAK": This party's boring. I'm **ouddie**.

Note: This is a variation on the common expression, *to be out of here* pronounced in real speak as *to be oudda here*.

peace out *exp.* good-bye

EXAMPLE: I have to get home for dinner. I'll see you tomorrow. **Peace out**.

TRANSLATION: I have to get home for dinner. I'll see you tomorrow. **Good-bye**.

"REAL SPEAK": I hafta get home fer dinner. A'll see ya damorrow. **Peace out**.

peeps *n.pl.* a slang variation of "people" used by teens to mean "friends."

EXAMPLE: My father got a job in another state, so next month we're moving. It's going to be hard to say good-bye to my **peeps**.

TRANSLATION: My father got a job in another state, so next month we're moving. It's going to be hard to say good-bye to my **friends**.

"REAL SPEAK": My father god a job 'n another state, so nex' month w'r moving. It's gonna be hard da say ga-bye da my **peeps**.

phat *adj.* great, wonderful, fantastic.

EXAMPLE: Did you see Pat's new car? It's **phat**! I can't wait to ride in it!

TRANSLATION: Did you see Pat's new car? It's **great**! I can't wait to ride in it!

"REAL SPEAK": Did'ja see Pat's new car? It's **phat**! I can't wait ta ride 'n it!

Note: This is one of those adjectives that confuse parents and teachers because it is pronounced "fat" which means "overweight," whereas *phat* means "great," "wonderful," "fantastic."

Synonym: **phat-free** *adj.* a humorous play on words because it is pronounced "fat-free" which refers to food that does not contain fat. However, in this case, *phat-free* refers to someone who is not *phat* or "cool."

Phi Beta Kappa *n.* an honorary society of college students and graduates whose members are chosen on the basis of high performance at school.

EXAMPLE: My sister is a member of **Phi Beta Kappa**. She got perfect grades in all of her courses!

TRANSLATION: My sister is a member of **an honorary society of college students and graduates whose members are chosen on the basis of high performance at school**. She got perfect grades in all of her courses!

"REAL SPEAK": My sister's a member 'ev **Phi Beda Kappa**. She got perfec' grades 'n all 'ev 'er courses!

Note: *Phi Beta Kappa* can also refer to the member of this organization. For example: *My sister is a **Phi Beta Kappa**;* My sister is a ***member of Phi Beta Kappa***.

pledge *n.* a person who has been accepted for membership in a fraternity but has not yet been initiated.

EXAMPLE: I'd like you to meet Rick. He's one of our new **pledges**. Next week, he'll be a member of our fraternity.

TRANSLATION: I'd like you to meet Rick. He's one of our new **people who has been accepted for membership in our fraternity but have not yet been initiated**. Next week, he'll be a member of our fraternity.

"REAL SPEAK": I'd like ya da meet Rick. He's one 'ev 'ar new **pledges**. Nex' week, 'e'll be a member 'ev 'ar fraternidy.

postal (to go) *exp.* to become insane and violent.

EXAMPLE: This restaurant has the worst service. If someone doesn't come and take our order soon, I'm going to **go postal**!

TRANSLATION: This restaurant has the worst service. If someone doesn't come and take our order soon, I'm going to **become insane and violent**!

"REAL SPEAK": This resterant has the wors' service. If someone doesn' come 'n take 'ar order soon, I'm gonna **go postal**!

Note: This is a humorous expression that comes from a very serious situation where a postal worker shot several other workers. This event become widely publicized so fast, that it only took a short period of time for it to be turned into an expression referring to anyone who becomes out of control emotionally.

props (to give someone) *exp.* to give someone his/her "proper" credit for an accomplishment.

EXAMPLE: I don't like the strange clothes that Cecily wears to school every day. But you have to **give her props** for not following everyone else's rules.

TRANSLATION: I don't like the strange clothes that Cecily wears to school every day. But you have to **give her credit** for not following everyone else's rules.

"REAL SPEAK": I don' like the strange clothes th't Cecily wears ta school ev'ry day. But 'cha hafta **give 'er props** fer not following ev'ryone else's rules.

rents *n.pl.* short for "parents."

EXAMPLE: Grant's **rents** just had twins! They must be so excited!

TRANSLATION: Grant's **parents** just had twins! They must be so excited!

"REAL SPEAK": Grant's **rents** just had twins! They mus' be so excided!

ride *n.* car, vehicle.

EXAMPLE: With the extra money Jeff made over the summer, he bought himself a new **ride**.

TRANSLATION: With the extra money Jeff made over the summer, he bought himself a new **car**.

"REAL SPEAK": With the extra money Jeff made over the summer, he bod 'imself a new **ride**.

rock (to) *v.* to be fantastic.

EXAMPLE: My parents bought me a new car for graduation. My mom and dad **rock**!

TRANSLATION: My parents bought me a new car for graduation. My mom and dad **are fantastic**!

"REAL SPEAK": My parents bought me a new car fer grajuation. My mom 'n dad **rock**!

Synonym: **rule (to)** *v.*

stoked (to be) *adj.* to be excited.

EXAMPLE: I'm **stoked**! I got an A on my history test!

TRANSLATION: I'm **excited**! I got an A on my history test!

"REAL SPEAK": I'm **stoked**! I god 'n A on my histery test!

sweet *adj.* great, fantastic.

EXAMPLE: I'm going to Los Angeles this summer. It's going to be **sweet**.

TRANSLATION: I'm going to Los Angeles this summer. It's going to be **great**.

"REAL SPEAK": I'm going ta L.A. this summer. It's gonna be **sweet**.

tight *adj.* great, fantastic.

EXAMPLE: Did you see Jennifer's new laptop? Dude, it's **tight**!

TRANSLATION: Did you see Jennifer's new laptop? Wow, it's **fantastic**!

"REAL SPEAK": Did'ja see Jennifer's new laptop? Dude, it's **tight**!

totally *adv.* (very popular to the point of being overused by many teens) extremely.

EXAMPLE: You like Bobby? He's **totally** weird!

TRANSLATION: You like Bobby? He's **extremely** weird!

"REAL SPEAK": You like Bobby? He's **todally** weird!

trashed (to be) *adj.* to be extremely drunk.

EXAMPLE: Give me your car keys. I'm not letting you drive yourself home. You're **trashed**.

TRANSLATION: Give me your car keys. I'm not letting you drive yourself home. You're **extremely drunk**.

"REAL SPEAK": Gimme yer car keys. I'm not letting ya drive yerself home.Y'r **trashed**.

way *adv.* • **1.** very, extremely • **2.** used to indicate agreement • **3.** used to mean "Yes, it ***is*** true!" following someone else's comment of "No way!" which means "That's absolutely not true!"

EXAMPLE 1: My home economics teacher is **way** cool. If we get done early with our assignments, she lets us leave before the end of the class.

TRANSLATION: My home economics teacher is **very** wonderful. If we get done early with our assignments, she lets us leave before the end of the class.

"REAL SPEAK": My home ec teacher's **way** cool. If we get done early with 'ar assignments, she lets us leave b'fore the end 'a the class.

EXAMPLE 2:
– Tammy is the strangest person I' ever met.
– **Way**!

TRANSLATION:
– Tammy is the strangest person I've ever met.
– **I definitely agree**!

"REAL SPEAK":
– Tammy's the strangest person I ever met.
– **Way**!

EXAMPLE 3:
– I just heard that Monica and Chandler are getting married!
– No way!
– **Way**!

TRANSLATION:
– I just heard that Monica and Chandler are getting married!
– That's absolutely not true!
– **Yes, it *is* true**!

"REAL SPEAK":
– I just heard th't Monica 'n Chandler 'er gedding married!
– No way!
– **Way**!

whack (to be) *adj.* terrible.

EXAMPLE: You failed the mathematics final? That's **whack**! What are you going to tell your parents?

TRANSLATION: You failed the mathematics final? That's **terrible**! What are you going to tell your parents?

"REAL SPEAK": You failed the math final? That's **whack**! What 'er ya gonna tell yer rents?

Variation: **whacked (to be)** *adj.*

FREEZE! THIS IS A STICK-UP!

Emergency Slang & Expressions

THIS LESSON FEATURES 15 NEW SLANG WORDS & IDIOMS

LET'S WARM UP!

READING

MATCH THE PICTURES

As a fun way to get started, see if you can guess the meaning of the new slang words and expressions on the opposite page by using the pictures below and following the context of the sentences.

1 2 3 4 BLA BLA BLA 5 6 7 8 9

1. Lie down on the ground and ***spread them***!
   ❑ run quickly
   ❑ separate your legs widely

2. Stop running away! ***Freeze***!
   ❑ look this way
   ❑ stop where you are

3. You won the lottery? ***Give it a rest***! You're such a liar!
   ❑ take a vacation and rest
   ❑ I don't believe it

4. I'm tired of you saying mean things about Carl all the time. ***Can it***!
   ❑ be quiet
   ❑ tell me more

5. That guy who walked into the bank has a gun! It's a ***stick-up***!
   ❑ very thin, powerful gun
   ❑ robbery

6. Is that a gold watch you're wearing? ***Hand it over***!
   ❑ Give it to me
   ❑ Put your hands on it

7. This is the criminal we've been looking for. ***Cuff him***!
   ❑ Hit him
   ❑ Put handcuffs on him

8. ***Get your hands in the air***! Now don't move!
   ❑ Put your hands above your head
   ❑ Put your hands at your side

9. Stay where you are and ***no funny business***! Do exactly as I say.
   ❑ no laughing
   ❑ don't do anything suspicious

10. I hear gun shots! ***Drop***!
    ❑ Move your body to the ground
    ❑ Let go of that

11. If you don't ***chill out***, you're going to get an ulcer! You need to learn how to relax.
    ❑ get cold
    ❑ calm down

12. If you don't give me your wallet right now, I'm going to ***let you have it***!
    ❑ give you what you deserve
    ❑ give you a gift

13. Stand over there! One ***false move***, and you'll be sorry!
    ❑ foolish attempt to escape
    ❑ lie

14. Show me where you keep your safe! ***Move it***!
    ❑ run
    ❑ hurry

15. ***Watch out***! He has a gun!
    ❑ Be careful
    ❑ Remove your watch

LET'S TALK!

A. DIALOGUE USING SLANG & IDIOMS

The words introduced on the first two pages are used in the dialogue below. See if you can understand the conversation. *Note:* The translation of the words in boldface is on the right-hand page.

CD-B: TRACK 22

Robber: **Freeze**! This is a **stick-up**! Take all the money from the cash register and **hand it over**. And **no funny business**. **One false move** and **watch out**! **I'll let you have it**.

Bank Teller: Okay, **chill out**! I don't have any money here. It's all in the safe.

Robber: **Give it a rest**! I know you have money in your drawer. You're asking for trouble!

Police Officer 1: **Can it**! This is the police. **Get your hands in the air**! Now **drop** and **spread them**! **Move it**!

Police Officer 2: Let's **cuff** him!

B. DIALOGUE TRANSLATED INTO STANDARD ENGLISH

LET'S SEE HOW MUCH YOU REMEMBER!
Just for fun, move around in random order to the words and expressions in boldface below. See if you can remember their slang equivalents without looking at the left-hand page!

Robber: **Stop where you are**! This is a **robbery**! Take all the money from the cash register and **give it to me**. And **don't do anything suspicious**. **One foolish attempt to escape** and **be careful of the consequences**! **I'll give you what you deserve** (meaning **"I'll shoot you"**).

Bank Teller: Okay, **relax**! I don't have any money here. It's all in the safe.

Robber: **I don't believe it**! I know you have money in your drawer. You're asking for trouble!

Police Officer 1: **Be quiet**! This is the police. **Put your hands above your head**! Now **move your body to the ground quickly** and **spread your legs apart**! **Hurry**!

Police Officer 2: Let's **put handcuffs on** him!

C. DIALOGUE USING "REAL SPEAK"

The dialogue below demonstrates how the slang conversation on the previous page would *really* be spoken by native speakers!

CD-B: TRACK 22

Robber: **Freeze**! This 'ez a **stick-up**! Take all the money fr'm the cash register 'n **hand id over**. An' **no funny bizness**. **One false move** 'n **watch out**! **A'll let cha have it**.

Bank Teller: Okay, **chill out**! I don't have any money here. It's all 'n the safe.

Robber: **Give id a rest**! I know ya have money 'n yer drawer. Y'r asking fer trouble!

Police Officer 1: **Can it**! This 'ez the palice. **Get cher han'z 'n the air**! Now **drop** 'n **spread 'em**! **Move it**!

Police Officer 2: Let's **cuff** 'im!

LET'S LEARN!

VOCABULARY

The following words and expressions were used in the previous dialogues. Let's take a closer look at what they mean.

CD-B: TRACK 23

"Can it!" *interj*. "Be quiet!"

EXAMPLE: **Can it**! If I hear so much as one more word out of you, you'll be sorry!

TRANSLATION: **Be quiet**! If I hear so much as one more word out of you, you'll be sorry!

"REAL SPEAK": **Can it**! If I hear so much 'ez one more word oudda you, you'll be sorry!

NOW YOU DO IT. COMPLETE THE PHRASE ALOUD:
Why are you talking about... like that? Can it!

"Chill out!" *interj*. "Relax!" "Calm down!"

EXAMPLE: You always let yourself get so upset about little problems. **Chill out**!

TRANSLATION: You always let yourself get so upset about little problems. **Relax**!

"REAL SPEAK": You ahweez let cherself get so upsed about liddle problems. **Chill out**!

Variation 1: **"Chill!"** *interj*.

Variation2: **"Take a chill pill!"** *interj*. (used mainly in New York).

NOW YOU DO IT. COMPLETE THE PHRASE ALOUD:
Why are you so upset about...? Chill out!

cuff someone (to) *exp.* to put handcuffs on someone.

EXAMPLE: This is the man who fits the description of the criminal. **Cuff him** and let's take him to headquarters.

TRANSLATION: This is the man who fits the description of the criminal. **Put handcuffs on him** and let's take him to headquarters.

REAL SPEAK": This 'ez the man who fits the description 'a the criminal. **Cuff 'im** 'n let's take 'im da headquarders.

NOW YOU DO IT. COMPLETE THE PHRASE ALOUD:
The police officer cuffed the guy because...

"Drop!" *interj.* "Move your body to the ground quickly!"

EXAMPLE: **Drop**! Now put your hands behind your back and keep them there!

TRANSLATION: **Move your body to the ground quickly**! Now put your hands behind your back and keep them there!

"REAL SPEAK": **Drop**! Now put cher han'z b'hin'jer back 'n keep 'em there!

NOW YOU DO IT. COMPLETE THE PHRASE ALOUD:
Drop or I'll...!

false move *exp.* a foolish attempt to escape.

EXAMPLE: Don't move! Stay right where you are. One **false move** and I'll shoot!

TRANSLATION: Don't move! Stay right where you are. One **foolish attempt to escape** and I'll shoot!

REAL SPEAK": Don't move! Stay right where you are. One **false move** 'n a'll shoot!

NOW YOU DO IT. COMPLETE THE PHRASE ALOUD:
If you make one false move...

"Freeze!" *interj.* "Stop where you are!"

EXAMPLE: Hey! Where is that guy going with my bicycle? You, there! **Freeze**!

TRANSLATION: Hey! Where is that guy going with my bicycle? You, there! **Stop where you are**!

"REAL SPEAK": Hey! Where's that guy going w'th my bike? You, there! **Freeze**!

Note: These directions are commonly given by the police when arresting a criminal.

NOW YOU DO IT. COMPLETE THE PHRASE ALOUD:
Hey! Why are you...? Freeze!

"Get your hands in the air!" *interj.* "Put your hands in the air!"

EXAMPLE: **Get your hands in the air**! As long as no one makes a move, no one will get hurt!

TRANSLATION: **Put your hands in the air**! As long as no one makes a move, no one will get hurt!

"REAL SPEAK": **Get 'cher hanz 'n the air**! As long 'ez no one makes a move, no one'll get hurt!

NOW YOU DO IT. COMPLETE THE PHRASE ALOUD:

Get your hands in the air! ...

"Give it a rest!" *interj.* "I don't believe it!"

EXAMPLE: Charles told you his family is royalty?! **Give it a rest**! He's such a liar!

TRANSLATION: Charles told you his family is royalty?! **I don't believe it**! He's such a liar!

"REAL SPEAK": Charles told ju 'is fam'ly's royalty?! **Give id a rest**! He's such a liar!

NOW YOU DO IT. COMPLETE THE PHRASE ALOUD:

You...? Give it a rest!

"Hand it over!" *interj.* "Give it to me!"

EXAMPLE: Are you hiding your purse behind your back? **Hand it over**!

TRANSLATION: Are you hiding your purse behind your back? **Give it to me**!

"REAL SPEAK": Are you hiding yer purse behin' jer back? **Hand id over**!

NOW YOU DO IT. COMPLETE THE PHRASE ALOUD:

Is that... you're holding? Hand it over!

"I'll let you have it!" *interj.* I'll give you what you deserve (either physically or verbally, depending on the context).

EXAMPLE: Stop! Give me all the money in your wallet or **I'll let you have it**!

TRANSLATION: Stop! Give me all the money in your wallet or **I'll shoot**!

"REAL SPEAK": Stop! Gimme all the money 'n yer walled or **a'll let cha have it**!

NOW YOU DO IT. COMPLETE THE PHRASE ALOUD:

If you don't give me that... I'll let you have it!

"Move it!" *interj.* "Hurry!"

EXAMPLE: I know there's a safe in here. Now, show me where you keep your money. **Move it**!

TRANSLATION: I know there's a safe in here. Now, show me where you keep your money. **Start moving**!

"REAL SPEAK": I know there's a safe 'n here. Now, show me where ya keep yer money. **Move it**!

NOW YOU DO IT. COMPLETE THE PHRASE ALOUD:

Show me where you keep your... Move it!

"No funny business!" *interj.* "Don't try anything suspicious!"

EXAMPLE: Step away from there right now and **no funny business**. You're the robber we've been looking for!

TRANSLATION: Step away from there right now and **don't try anything suspicious**. You're the robber we've been looking for!

"REAL SPEAK": Step away fr'm there right now 'n **no funny bizness**. Y'r the robber we've been looking for!

NOW YOU DO IT. COMPLETE THE PHRASE ALOUD:
I want you to... and no funny business!

"Spread 'em!" *exp.* "Separate your legs widely!" (in order to submit to a body search by a police officer).

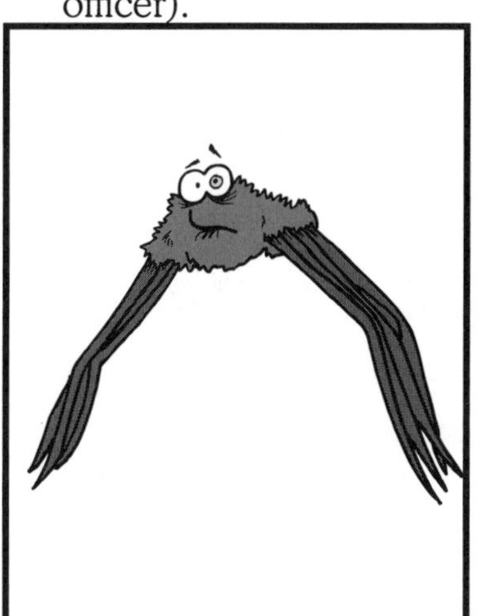

EXAMPLE: Get out of the car, put your hands on your head, and **spread them**!

TRANSLATION: Get out of the car, put your hands on your head, and **separate your legs widely**!

"REAL SPEAK": Ged oudda the car, put 'cher hanz on yer head 'n **spread 'em**!

Note: In this expression, *'em* is a reduction of "them," representing "legs." The reduction of "them" to *'em* is so common in this command that you'll probably never hear it in its unreduced form!

NOW YOU DO IT. COMPLETE THE PHRASE ALOUD:
Put your hands on your head and spread 'em! Now I'm going to check to make sure you don't have any concealed... on you.

stick-up *n.* robbery.

EXAMPLE: That man is pointing a gun at that bank customer! It's a **stick-up**!

TRANSLATION: That man is pointing a gun at that bank customer! It's a **robbery**!

REAL SPEAK": That man's pointing a gun 'it that bank custamer! It's a **stick-up**!

NOW YOU DO IT. COMPLETE THE PHRASE ALOUD:
During the stick-up, the robbers took...

"Watch out!" *interj.* "Be careful! There's potential danger about to happen!"

EXAMPLE: **Watch out**! You're about to step into a hole! That was close. You could have broken your neck!

TRANSLATION: **Be careful! There's potential danger about to happen**! You're about to step into a hole! That was close. You could have broken your neck!

"REAL SPEAK": **Watch out**! Y'r about ta step into a hole! That w'z close. Ya could'a broken yer neck!

NOW YOU DO IT. COMPLETE THE PHRASE ALOUD:
Watch out! There's a... coming this way!

LET'S PRACTICE!

A. CORRECT OR INCORRECT?

Decide whether or not the words in boldface have been used correctly or incorrectly by checking the appropriate box.

1. Would you **can it**?! I'm tired of hearing you complain all the time!
❑ CORRECT ❑ INCORRECT

2. **Cuff him**! The sleeves on that man's shirt are too long.
❑ CORRECT ❑ INCORRECT

3. **Freeze**! It's too hot in here!
❑ CORRECT ❑ INCORRECT

4. You need to get out of here now! **Move it**!
❑ CORRECT ❑ INCORRECT

5. That man just walked into the bank holding a gun! It must be a **stick-up**! Let's call the police!
❑ CORRECT ❑ INCORRECT

6. You look like you're having fun. **Hand it over**!
❑ CORRECT ❑ INCORRECT

7. We have to hurry or we're going to be late. **Spread 'em**!
❑ CORRECT ❑ INCORRECT

8. I'm going to trust you, so **no funny business**.
❑ CORRECT ❑ INCORRECT

9. I want you all to stand against the wall. **One false move** and someone is going to get hurt.
❑ CORRECT ❑ INCORRECT

10. This movie is really funny. **Watch out**!
❑ CORRECT ❑ INCORRECT

11. We're having an earthquake! **Drop**!
❑ CORRECT ❑ INCORRECT

12. If you don't stop bothering me, I'm going to **let you have it**!
❑ CORRECT ❑ INCORRECT

13. This is the police. **Get your hands in the air** and don't move.
❑ CORRECT ❑ INCORRECT

14. You look really nervous. You need to **chill out**.
❑ CORRECT ❑ INCORRECT

15. Are you tired? **Give it a rest**!
❑ CORRECT ❑ INCORRECT

B. CREATE YOUR OWN STORY

Create a short story aloud using the suggested words. You may use the words in any order in your sentence. If you need to write down your story first, that's fine!

1. **[freeze] [run] [money] [police] [cuff]**
2. **[no funny business] [move it] [jewelry] [I'll let you have it]**
3. **[stick-up] [get your hands in the air] [drop] [money]**
4. **[under arrest] [chill out] [spread 'em] [no funny business]**
5. **[watch out] [dangerous] [one false move] [move it]**
6. **[wallet] [hand it over] [one false move] [move it]**
7. **[nonsense] [I'll let you have it] [give it a rest] [watch out]**
8. **[watch out] [stick-up] [guns] [bank] [one false move]**
9. **[get your hands in the air] [can it] [hand it over] [I'll let you have it]**
10. **[freeze] [spread 'em] [drop] [gun] [chill out] [I'll let you have it]**
11. **[purse] [hand it over] [move it] [no funny business]**
12. **[freeze] [drop] [jail] [jewelry store] [chill out] [cuff]**

C. TRUE OR FALSE

Decide whether or not the definition of the words in boldface is true or false and check the correct box.

CD-B: TRACK 25

1. **"Can it!"** *interj.* "Great to see you!"
   ❑ TRUE ❑ FALSE

2. **stick-up** *n.* robbery.
   ❑ TRUE ❑ FALSE

3. **"Drop!"** *interj.* "Go to sleep quickly!"
   ❑ TRUE ❑ FALSE

4. **"Freeze!"** *interj.* "Stop where you are!"
   ❑ TRUE ❑ FALSE

5. **cuff someone (to)** *exp.* to put handcuffs on someone.
   ❑ TRUE ❑ FALSE

6. **"No funny business!"** *interj.* "Don't try anything suspicious!"
   ❑ TRUE ❑ FALSE

7. **"Get your hands in the air!"** *interj.* "Leave immediately!"
   ❑ TRUE ❑ FALSE

8. **"Chill out!"** *interj.* "You look overheated!"
   ❑ TRUE ❑ FALSE

9. **"Hand it over!"** *interj.* "Give it to me!
   ❑ TRUE ❑ FALSE

10. **"I'll let you have it!"** *interj.* "I'll give you what you deserve (either physically or verbally).
    ❑ TRUE ❑ FALSE

11. **"Spread them!"** *exp.* "Sit down!"
    ❑ TRUE ❑ FALSE

12. **"Give it a rest!"** *interj.* "Relax!"
    ❑ TRUE ❑ FALSE

13. **false move** *exp.* a foolish movement.
    ❑ TRUE ❑ FALSE

14. **"Watch out!"** *interj.* "Be careful! There's potential danger about to happen!"
    ❑ TRUE ❑ FALSE

15. **"Move it!"** *interj.* "Hurry!"
    ❑ TRUE ❑ FALSE

More Emergency Slang & Expressions

This is perhaps one of the most important sections in terms of survival! For example, if you don't understand the popular commands ***Freeze!*** or ***Hold it!*** you may find yourself in serious danger, since both commands mean "Stop!" The following slang terms and expressions were put in this list to protect you in the event of an emergency. Do make sure that you pay particular attention to the "real speak" version of the sample sentence! Sometimes the pronunciation can be just as hard to understand as the term or idiom itself and when it comes to an emergency, you need to understand the *first* time!

"Back off!" *interj.* "Stop persisting!"

EXAMPLE: Hey, **back off**! I told you I don't want to go out with you!

TRANSLATION: Hey, **stop persisting**! I told you I don't want to go out with you!

"REAL SPEAK": Hey, **back off**! I told ja I don' wanna go out w'th you!

"Cool it!" *interj.* "Calm down!"

EXAMPLE: You're making too much noise in there. **Cool it**!

TRANSLATION: You're making too much noise in there. **Calm down**!

"REAL SPEAK": Y'r making too much noise 'n there. **Cool it**!

"Cut it out!" *interj.* "Stop that!"

EXAMPLE: Why are you bothering her? **Cut it out**!

TRANSLATION: Why are you bothering her? **Stop that**!

"REAL SPEAK": Why 'er ya bothering 'er? **Cud id out**!

"Don't budge!" *exp.* "Don't move!"

EXAMPLE: **Don't budge**! A bee just landed on your arm!

TRANSLATION: **Don't move**! A bee just landed on your arm!

"REAL SPEAK": **Don't budge**! A bee jus' landed on yer arm!

"Don't fall for it!" *interj.* "Don't be deceived!"

EXAMPLE: That salesperson is lying to you to get you to buy his merchandise. **Don't fall for it**!

TRANSLATION: That salesperson is lying to you to get you to buy his merchandise. **Don't be deceived**!

"REAL SPEAK": That salesperson's lying da you da get cha da buy 'is merchandise. **Don't fall fer it**!

"Duck!" *interj.* "Lower your head because something is about to hit you!"

EXAMPLE: **Duck**! That was close. That baseball almost hit you in the head!

TRANSLATION: **Lower your head**! That was close. That baseball almost hit you in the head!

"REAL SPEAK": **Duck**! That w'z close. That baseball almost hit cha 'n the head!

"Get away!" *interj.* "Move away fast!"

EXAMPLE: **Get away**! The building is about to collapse!

TRANSLATION: **Move away fast**! The building is about to collapse!

"REAL SPEAK": **Ged away**! The building's about ta collapse!

"Get out of the way!" *exp.* "Move away from something coming toward you!"

EXAMPLE: That truck is coming toward you! **Get out of the way**!

TRANSLATION: That truck is coming toward you! **Move away**!

"REAL SPEAK": That truck's coming tord you! **Ged oudda the way**!

"[Get your] hands off!" *interj.* "Remove your hands from there!"

EXAMPLE: That's an expensive painting you're touching! **Get your hands off**!

TRANSLATION: That's an expensive painting you're touching! **Remove your hands from there**!

"REAL SPEAK": That's 'n expensive pain'ing y'r touching! **Get 'cher hanz off**!

"Halt!" *interj.* (borrowed from German) "Stop!"

EXAMPLE: **Halt** in the name of the law or I'll shoot!

TRANSLATION: **Stop** in the name of the law or I'll shoot!

"REAL SPEAK": **Halt** 'n the name 'a the law 'r a'll shoot!

"Heads up!" *interj.* "Be alert!"

EXAMPLE: There are a lot of birds in this park, so **heads up**! You certainly don't want to get hit in the head with something falling from the sky!

TRANSLATION: There are a lot of birds in this park, so **stay alert**! You certainly don't want to get hit in the head with something falling from the sky!

"REAL SPEAK": There 'er a lod 'a birds 'n th's park, so **heads up**! Ya certainly don't wanna get hit 'n the head w'th something falling fr'm the sky!

"Hold it!" *interj.* "Stop what you're doing!"

EXAMPLE: **Hold it**! I think someone is coming. Let's get out of here!

TRANSLATION: **Stop what you're doing**! I think someone is coming. Let's get out of here!

"REAL SPEAK": **Hold it**! I think someone's coming. Let's ged outta here!

hold-up (a) *n.* robbery.

EXAMPLE: All those people are holding their hands over their heads. I think it's a **hold-up**!

TRANSLATION: All those people are holding their hands over their heads. I think it's a **robbery**!

"REAL SPEAK": All those people 'er holding their hanz over their heads. I think it's a **hold-up**!

Also: **held up (to be)** *adj.* to be robbed.

"Knock it off!" *interj.* "Stop that!"

EXAMPLE: Your singing is giving me a headache. **Knock it off**!

TRANSLATION: Your singing is giving me a headache. **Stop it**!

"REAL SPEAK": Yer singing's giving me a headache. **Knock id off**!

"Look out!" *interj.* "Pay attention! There's potential danger about to happen!"

EXAMPLE: **Look out**! The door is about to close on your hand!

TRANSLATION: **Pay attention! There's potential danger about to happen**! The door is about to close on your hand!

"REAL SPEAK": **Look out**! The door's about ta close on yer hand!

"Pull over!" *interj.* "Stop your car at the side of the road!"

EXAMPLE: Driver in the white Honda, this is the police. **Pull over**!

TRANSLATION: Driver in the white Honda, this is the police. **Stop your car at the side of the road**!

"REAL SPEAK": Driver 'n the white Honda, this 'ez the palice. **Pull over**!

"Shut up!" *interj.* "Be quiet!"

EXAMPLE: Don't you ever stop talking? **Shut up**!

TRANSLATION: Don't you ever stop talking? **Be quite**!

"REAL SPEAK": Don'chu ever stop talking? **Shud up**!

Note: *"Shut up!"* is used by the younger generations to mean "You're kidding me!"

"Shut your trap!" *interj.* "Shut your mouth!"

EXAMPLE: I can't believe you would say such a terrible thing! **Shut your trap**!

TRANSLATION: I can't believe you would say such a terrible thing! **Shut your mouth**!

"REAL SPEAK": I can't b'lieve you'd say such a terr'ble thing! **Shut 'cher trap**!

Note: *Trap* (literally a device resembling a mouth with teeth, used to catch an animal) is slang for "mouth."

"Snap out of it!" *interj.* "Stop being mentally unresponsive and regain your clear thinking!"

EXAMPLE: **Snap out of it**! What's wrong with you? Are you drunk or something?

TRANSLATION: **Stop being mentally unresponsive**! What's wrong with you? Are you drunk or something?

"REAL SPEAK": **Snap oud 'ev it**! What's wrong w'th you? Are you drunk 'r something?

"Stay put!" *interj.* "Don't move from here!"

EXAMPLE: **Stay put**! I'll be back here in about five minutes to come get you.

TRANSLATION: **Don't move from here**! I'll be back here in about five minutes to come get you.

"REAL SPEAK": **Stay put**! A'll be back here 'n about five minutes ta come get 'cha.

"Stick them up!" *exp.* "Put your hands above your head!"

EXAMPLE: **Stick them up** and keep them up until I say to put them down! This is a robbery!

TRANSLATION: **Put your hands above your head** and keep them up until I say to put them down! This is a robbery!

"REAL SPEAK": **Stick 'em up** 'n keep 'em up until I say da put 'em down! This 'ez a robbery!

"Take cover!" *interj.* "Find some shelter from this danger!"

EXAMPLE: Look over there! That's a tornado coming toward us! **Take cover**!

TRANSLATION: Look over there! That's a tornado coming toward us! **Find some shelter from this danger**!

"REAL SPEAK": Look over there! That's a tornado coming tord us! **Take cover**!

ANSWERS TO LESSONS 1-10

LESSON 1 - ROGER STRIKES OUT WITH A PICK-UP LINE!

LET'S WARM UP!

1. pretending to be disinterested
2. examining you
3. reject him in a gentle way
4. ignored me
5. flirting with me
6. arranged a date for me
7. phrase meant to entice
8. fail
9. liked each other immediately
10. eager to get back into a relationship

LET'S PRACTICE!

A. COMPLETE THE PHRASE

1. checking
2. strike
3. easy
4. blew
5. hard to get
6. hit
7. rebound
8. fix
9. hit

B. CONTEXT EXERCISE

1. doesn't make sense
2. doesn't make sense
3. makes sense
4. makes sense
5. makes sense
6. makes sense
7. makes sense
8. doesn't make sense
9. makes sense

C. CREATE YOUR OWN SENTENCE (SUGGESTIONS FOR ANSWERS)

1. I think he's **checking you out**!
2. He totally **blew me off**!
3. Just make sure you don't use a stupid **pick-up line**.
4. Do you want me to **fix you up** with one of my friends?
5. I wouldn't. She's probably **on the rebound**.
6. I think she's **coming on to you**!
7. I totally **struck out**. She said no.
8. She's just **playing hard to get**.
9. We really **hit it off**!
10. Just try to **let her down easy**.

LESSON TWO - KEN POPPED THE QUESTION!

LET'S WARM UP!

1. ask you to marry him
2. dating someone much younger than she is
3. rich older man she is dating
4. They should take it to a private place
5. married
6. very much in love with
7. live together
8. got her pregnant
9. kissing
10. dating each other

LET'S PRACTICE!

A. TRUE OR FALSE

1. False
2. True
3. True
4. False
5. False
6. True
7. True
8. False
9. True
10. False

B. CHOOSE THE RIGHT WORD

1. question
2. out
3. up
4. sugar
5. Get a room
6. hitched
7. cradle
8. crazy
9. going
10. up

C. MATCH THE SENTENCES

1. G
2. B
3. J
4. C
5. E
6. H
7. I
8. A
9. F
10. D

LESSON THREE – JANE AND MIKE BROKE UP!

LET'S WARM UP!

1. B
2. H
3. J
4. E
5. A
6. I
7. D
8. F
9. C
10. G

LET'S PRACTICE!

A. WHAT DOES IT MEAN?

1. to have a romantic relationship with someone other than one's spouse or boyfriend/girlfriend
2. to end a relationship
3. to discover someone doing something inappropriate
4. to end a romantic relationship with someone abruptly
5. a woman who enjoys having a continuing sexual relationship with a married man
6. said of a marriage that is not going well
7. to reconcile one's differences
8. an abbreviation of "pre-nuptial agreement," which is a contract specifying what each person gets in the event of a divorce
9. to empty or "clean out" someone of all his/her possessions either dishonestly or in a court battle
10. a sexually promiscuous woman

B. COMPLETE THE FAIRY TALE

Once upon a time, there was a girl named Cinderella who lived in a little cottage with her stepmother and two stepsisters who were very mean to Cinderella. They made her clean the house all day long. Cinderella was especially sad today because the prince was having a big ball that evening and she couldn't go because she had nothing to wear. And this was a special ball because this is where the prince would find his princess! The prince was actually supposed to get married the previous year, but his relationship had been on the **rocks** for quite some time and it just didn't work out.

The special evening finally came and everyone, except Cinderella, went to the prince's ball. She was so sad that she didn't have a beautiful dress she could wear and through her tears she cried out, "Oh, Fairy Godmother, please help me!" Suddenly she heard a voice from behind her say, "Hello, Sweetie! I'm here to help you." Cinderella could hardly believe her eyes and said, "But...you're the tooth fairy. You don't know anything about clothes!" "True," she said. "But I can give you a lovely set of teeth made of high quality porcelain laminate veneer!" With that, she waved her magic wand over Cinderella who was now wearing the most beautiful smile in the land. And Cinderella ran off to the prince's ball.

When she arrived ,the prince couldn't believe his eyes. He'd never seen such a bright smile! He was so entranced by her grin that he insisted that they get married right away! "This is the happiest day of my life!" said Cinderella. "First, I just need you to sign this pre-**nup** stating that in the event of a divorce I get the items listed below. Just sign here..and here. Great! Now let's get married!" And they did.

They were so happy until one day, Cinderella found the prince in bed with some **tramp**! She **busted** him! It was actually his **mistress** that he had been having an **affair** with for months! Cinderella was so angry that she dropped him like a **hot potato** then and there. "I'm sure we can **patch** things up, Sweetie, Darling" said the prince. "Don't you Sweetie, Darling me!" said Cinderella. "You can do whatever you want now because we have officially **broken up**! I'm calling my attorney at Dewey Screwum and Howe and I'm taking you to the **cleaners**!"

C. CONTEXT EXERCISE

1. H
2. J
3. I
4. D
5. G
6. A
7. E
8. F
9. C
10. B

D. COMPLETE THE PHRASE

Jennifer: I just heard that Jane and Mike **broke** up because Mike was having an **affair** for the past year! She **busted** him when she walked into their bedroom and found him with some **tramp**.

Kenny: How horrible! Jane must have been so upset!

Jennifer: She sure was. She dropped him like a hot **potato** the next day! I don't think they'll ever be able to **patch** things up, either. With Jane, there are no second chances.

Kenny: Well, it doesn't surprise me one bit that he had a **mistress**. Their marriage has been on the **rocks** for a long time. I just hope they both signed a pre-**nup** or she'll end up taking him to the **cleaners**!

LESSON FOUR – TOM IS WAY OFF BASE!

LET'S WARM UP!

1. was completely unexpected
2. try hard to solve
3. unethical behavior
4. badly mistaken
5. give up
6. seduce
7. instantly
8. contact
9. behave aggressively
10. it's up to him to respond to the situation
11. surprised me
12. get revenge

LET'S PRACTICE!

A. CHOOSE THE RIGHT WORDS

1. hard
2. towel
3. left
4. pool
5. tackle
6. touch
7. score
8. off
9. threw
10. bat
11. settle
12. ball

B. CROSSWORD PUZZLE

C. MATCH THE COLUMN

1. M
2. F
3. K
4. C
5. D
6. A
7. E
8. G
9. B
10. I
11. H
12. J

LESSON FIVE – MARGE IS THE BIGGEST KLUTZ!

LET'S WARM UP!

1. True
2. False
3. True
4. False
5. False
6. True
7. False
8. False
9. True
10. True
11. False
12. True

LET'S PRACTICE!

A. I KNOW THE ANSWER, BUT WHAT'S THE QUESTION?

1. Is Ed excited about starting his new job?
2. Why is Michelle yelling at everyone?
3. Did you just hear a loud crash
4. Why are you sweating?
5. Did you make this chocolate cake yourself?
6. Why are your employees nervous around you?

B. FIND YOUR PERFECT MATCH

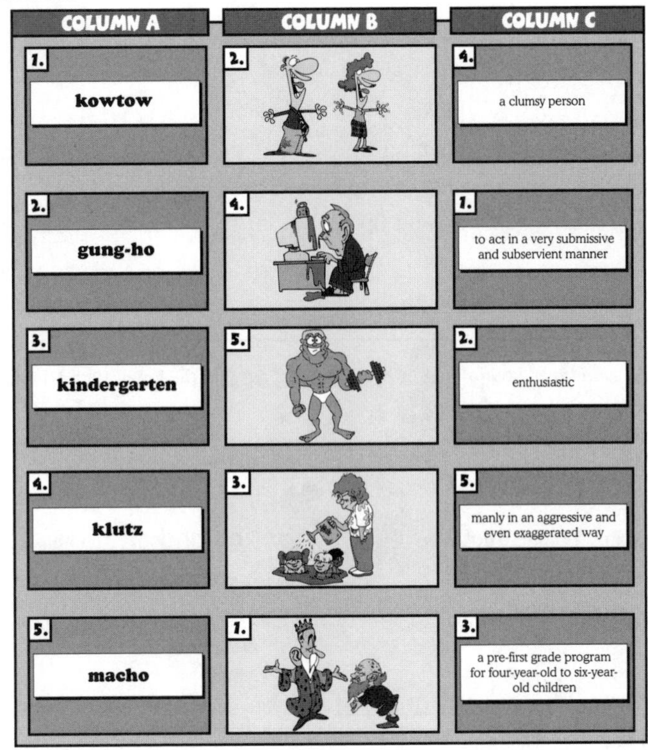

COLUMN A
COLUMN B
COLUMN C
1. kowtow
2.
4. a clumsy person
2. gung-ho
4.
1. to act in a very submissive and subservient manner
3. kindergarten
5.
2. enthusiastic
4. klutz
3.
5. manly in an aggressive and even exaggerated way
5. macho
1.
3. a pre-first grade program for four-year-old to six-year-old children

C. YOU'RE THE AUTHOR

Maggie: When I was a little girl, I had so much **angst** about going to **kindergarten**. I tried to act **blasé** about it so that my parents wouldn't be upset, but subtlety was never my **forte**, even as a child. You should have heard me screaming as we drove to the school. I had never been separated from my parents before. Also I was scared that the other kids would make fun of me because I was big for my age and a total **klutz**. I kept falling all the time!

Susan: What about your twin brother? Was he screaming, too?

Maggie: No, my brother seemed really **gung-ho** about it but looking back on it, I think he was just trying to be **macho** and not let everyone know that he was just as scared. Our parents kept telling us that it would be fun and that there would be a sense of **camaraderie** among all the kids...and they were right!

Susan: I found that, too. The worst part for me was the teacher. I'll never forget what she looked like. She wore tons of make-up and looked like she had just come from a cosmetic **boutique**! She was this **prima donna** who used to teach at an exclusive school for rich kids but had to move with her husband. She hated being at our school. She expected all the kids to **kowtow** to her. The first words that came out of her mouth were, "I am your teacher and you will do exactly as I say and nothing more." And that's **verbatim**.

Maggie: She sounds truly charming!

LESSON SIX – KAREN WENT ON AND ON ABOUT HER KNICK-KNACKS!

LET'S WARM UP!

1. repeatedly
2. crossing-ilne
3. smiling widely
4. overly decorated
5. mixture
6. in person
7. completely clean
8. little things that she has collected
9. rubber sandals
10. honest
11. talks nonstop
12. a total
13. had a casual conversation
14. lover of unhealthy food

LET'S PRACTICE!

A. THE UNFINISHED CONVERSATION (SUGGESTIONS FOR ANSWERS)

1. Yes, she was grinning from ear to ear!
2. Well, he's always been a junk food junkie.
3. Yes, I bought lots of fun knick-knacks.
4. Absolutely. He's definitely on the up and up.
5. No! It's too froufrou!

B. CHOOSE THE RIGHT WORD

1. on and on
2. span
3. flops
4. ear to ear
5. junkie
6. chatting
7. criss
8. up and up
9. knack
10. mash
11. over and over
12. out and out

C. COMPLETE THE STORY

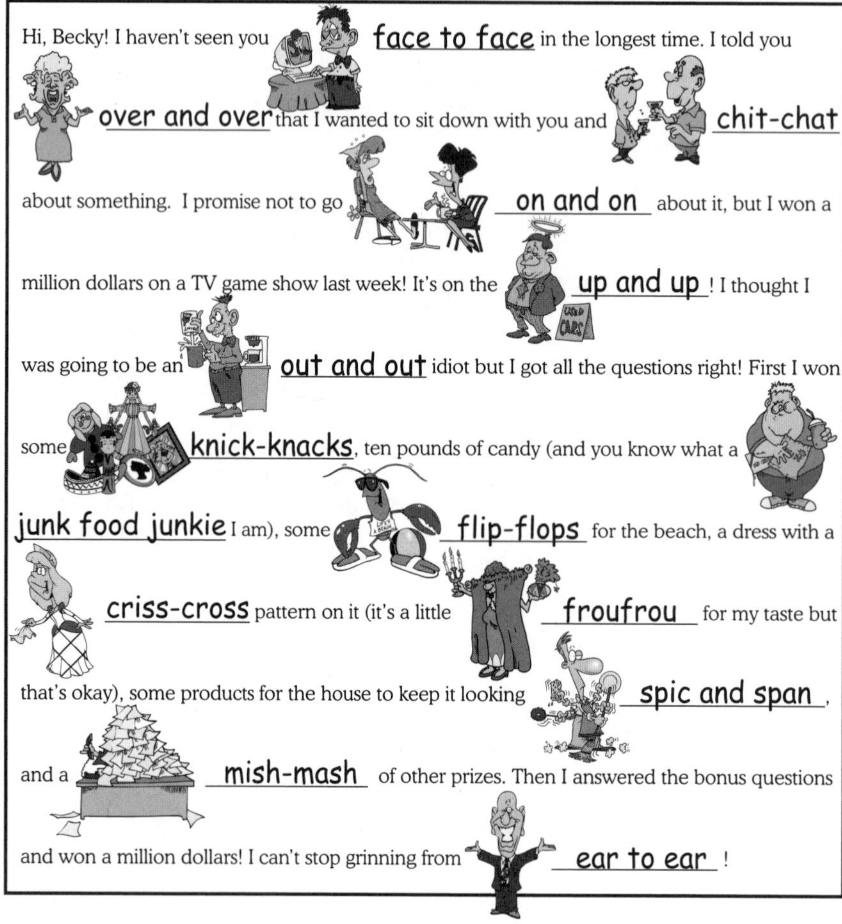

Hi, Becky! I haven't seen you face to face in the longest time. I told you
over and over that I wanted to sit down with you and chit-chat
about something. I promise not to go on and on about it, but I won a
million dollars on a TV game show last week! It's on the up and up! I thought I
was going to be an out and out idiot but I got all the questions right! First I won
some knick-knacks, ten pounds of candy (and you know what a
junk food junkie I am), some flip-flops for the beach, a dress with a
criss-cross pattern on it (it's a little froufrou for my taste but
that's okay), some products for the house to keep it looking spic and span,
and a mish-mash of other prizes. Then I answered the bonus questions
and won a million dollars! I can't stop grinning from ear to ear!

D. CREATE YOUR OWN SENTENCE (SUGGESTIONS FOR ANSWERS)

1. Because he's an **out and out** liar!
2. We've never met **face to face**.
3. Yes, she's a real **junk food junkie**!
4. Yes, we **chit-chatted** for about an hour.
5. He was **grinning from ear to ear**.
6. Because I've told her **over and over** again not to borrow my things without permission.
7. Put on my **flip-flops**.
8. It certainly was **spic-and-span**!
9. I think so. He seems like he's on the **up and up**.
10. Yes, she has hundreds of **knick-knacks** all over.

LESSON SEVEN – JENNY BECOMES A FIREFIGHTER!

LET'S WARM UP!

1. D
2. A
3. M
4. H
5. K
6. B
7. E
8. C
9. N
10. F
11. G
12. I
13. J
14. L

LET'S PRACTICE!

A. "ACROSS" WORD PUZZLE

1. The police **officer** arrested the bank robber.
2. Al is a **self-made** person. He started his own company!
3. Nancy is so funny! She should be a **comedian**.
4. The mail **carrier** just left this letter for you.
5. My mother **runs** a big company all by herself!
6. Dan is a **frosh** but he's graduating in two years!
7. The meteor missed us! **Humankind** is saved!
8. Our company has become so busy that we need to hire more **personnel** soon!

B. CROSSWORD PUZZLE

C. YOU'RE THE AUTHOR

Joe: I hear you're going to be a **frosh** next year! What kind of courses will you be taking when you start college?

David: Well, I haven't made a career choice yet. I've always enjoyed performing, so I could be an **actor**, or even a **comedian** since I love telling funny stories. But I do love traveling and as a flight **attendant**, I could help people and see the world at the same time. Or maybe I could be a **spokesperson** for the travel industry.

Joe: That's true. But I also know that you've always wanted to do something for **humankind** and one of the best ways is to become a **firefighter** or police **officer**. Actually, a mail **carrier** is probably a lot safer, except for the occasional angry dog!

David: I definitely don't want to do anything dangerous! Maybe I could become a **self-made** person like my mother and **run** my own company. I've always wanted to have my own publishing company. I just have to make sure that I get good **personnel**! That would be the hardest part. I just don't know if I'd like being in an office all day.

Joe: I've got it! Since you like to perform and also help people, why don't you become a television **anchor** and report the news! Jim Manne used to report the news for years in Los Angeles until he fell in love with his producer. Now they're **husband** and wife and live in San Diego. That could be you!

LESSON EIGHT – A BIG BREAK IN SHOW BIZ!

LET'S WARM UP!

1. True
2. False
3. True
4. True
5. False
6. True
7. False
8. False
9. True
10. True
11. True
12. False
13. True
14. True
15. True

LET'S PRACTICE!

A. & B. CREATE YOUR OWN STORY

In this section, you could have many possible answers. Remember, the more creative you are, the funnier your story will be!

C. WHAT WOULD YOU DO IF SOMEONE SAID...?

1. b
2. c
3. c
4. b
5. b
6. a
7. b
8. a
9. c
10. a

D. CREATE YOUR OWN SENTENCES (SUGGESTIONS FOR ANSWERS)

1. She just got her **big break** in **show biz**! She doing a **one-liner** in a TV show!
2. Yes, that actor is in a **sitcom**. He's a **show-stopper** in every TV **series** he does.
3. There's nothing on TV except for a **rerun** which is a total **dog**. The actors do nothing but **mug**.
4. It's a **spin-off** of my favorite **slapstick** comedy with Lucille Ball. She got her **big break** when she was only five years old!
5. Yes, I'm doing a **walk-on** in a new TV show. It's a **spin-off** of a popular comedy. This will be my start in **show biz**!
6. He's a ham **actor** in a horrible **slapstick** comedy. It's a new TV **series** where all the actors do nothing but **mug**.

E. TRUE OR FALSE?

1. True
2. False
3. True
4. True
5. False
6. True
7. False
8. False
9. True
10. False

LESSON NINE – AL AND PEGGY ARE LIKE DATING!

LET'S WARM UP

1. I'll talk to you later
2. How are you?
3. Are you crazy?
4. I don't care
5. sexy person
6. relax and have fun
7. twenty-four hours a day, seven days a week
8. leave
9. hallucinating
10. disrespected
11. friend (who is a girl)
12. definitely
13. extremely ugly
14. said
15. how can I say this

LET'S PRACTICE!

A. TRUTH OR LIE

1. truth
2. lie
3. lie
4. truth
5. lie
6. lie

B. FIND THE DEFINITION

1. to say
2. to leave
3. to disrespect someone
4. friend who is a girl, and used in greetings and conversations between two girls
5. "Are you crazy?!"
6. sexy person
7. to relax and have fun
8. "See you later!"
9. "How can I say this?"
10. definitely
11. to be very ugly
12. to hallucinate
13. "How are you?"
14. a response to something you don't want to discuss any further
15. 24 hours a day, 7 days a week

C. FIND-THE-WORD GRID

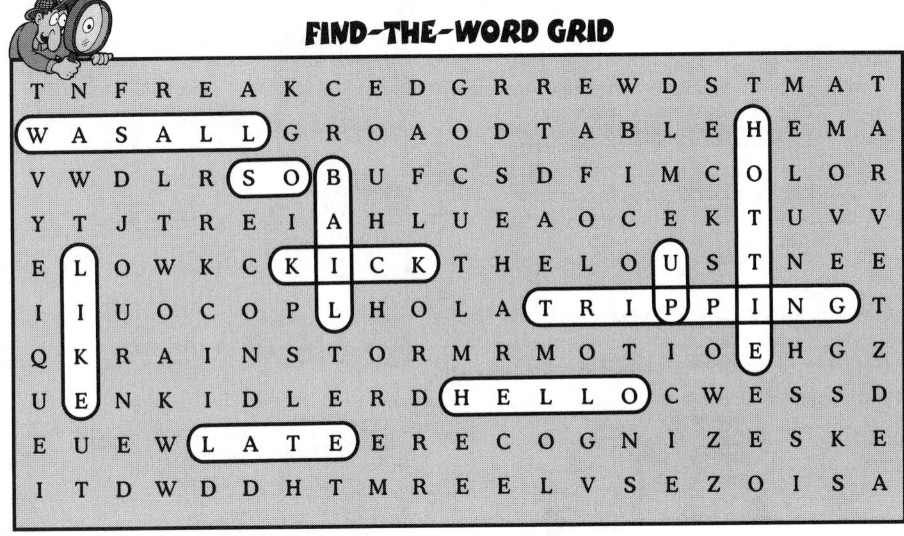

LESSON TEN – FREEZE! THIS IS A STICK-UP!

LET'S WARM UP!

1. separate your legs widely
2. stop where you are
3. I don't believe it
4. be quiet
5. robbery
6. give it to me
7. put handcuffs on him
8. put your hands above your head
9. don't do anything suspicious
10. move your body to the ground
11. calm down
12. give you what you deserve
13. foolish attempt to escape
14. hurry
15. be careful

LET'S PRACTICE!

A. CORRECT OR INCORRECT?

1. correct
2. incorrect
3. incorrect
4. correct
5. correct
6. incorrect
7. incorrect
8. correct
9. correct
10. incorrect
11. correct
12. correct
13. correct
14. correct
15. incorrect

B. CREATE YOUR OWN STORY

Make sure to use complete sentences in your story. For extra fun, try using other slang words you've leaved in previous lessons!

C. TRUE OR FALSE

1. False
2. True
3. False
4. True
5. True
6. True
7. False
8. False
9. True
10. True
11. False
12. False
13. True
14. True
15. True

STREET SPEAK 1

THE COMPLETE COURSE IN AMERICAN SLANG & IDIOMS

This book presents dozens of the most popular slang and idioms used in the U.S. as well as in many common situations such as: at a party, at the market, at the movies, on vacation, at the airport, at a restaurant, on the road, at school, on a date, and more! In addition, learn common contractions and reductions used by every native-born American!

Book: 160 pages **ISBN: 1-891-888-080 • US $18.95**

This 2-Audio CD set, ideal for ear-training, contains the dialogues used in the book, all the exercises, plus each vocabulary section, all spoken in "real speak!"

2-Audio CD set **ISBN: 1-891-888-293 • US $35.00**

This 2-Audio Cassette set contains the dialogues in the book & a selection of exercises spoken in "real speak!"

2-Audio Cassette set **ISBN: 1-891-888-307 • US $25.00**

Book and 2-CD set
ISBN: 1-891-888-250 • US $50.00

Book and 2-CD set
ISBN: 1-891-888-277 • US $40.00

STREET SPEAK 2

THE COMPLETE COURSE IN AMERICAN SLANG & IDIOMS

This book explores more popular slang & idioms, with an extra bonus – our new special section called "From The Slangman Files." This fun segment is a handy resource presenting popular slang & idioms which have been grouped in categories such as: fruits & vegetables, colors, initials, body parts, people's first names, food, clothing, numbers, and animals!

Book: 240 pages **ISBN: 1-891-888-064 • US $21.95**

This 2-Audio CD set, ideal for ear-training, contains the dialogues used in the book, all the exercises, plus each vocabulary section, all spoken in "real speak!"

2-Audio CD set **ISBN: 1-891-888-315 • US $35.00**

This 2-Audio Cassette set contains the dialogues in the book & a selection of exercises spoken in "real speak!"

2-Audio Cassette set **ISBN: 1-891-888-323 • US $25.00**

Book and 2-CD set
ISBN: 1-891-888-269 • US$50.00

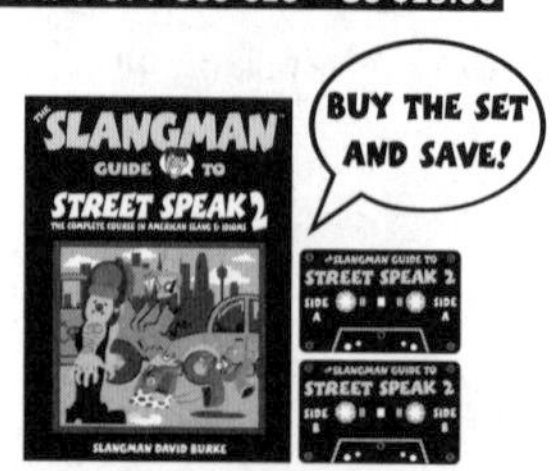

Book and 2-CD set
ISBN: 1-891-888-285 • US $40.00

STREET SPEAK 3

THE COMPLETE COURSE IN AMERICAN SLANG & IDIOMS

This book examines even more everyday slang & idioms essential for nonnative speakers! Categories include: dating, love, breaking up, hobbies, popular words & expressions taken from sports, popular teen & college slang, popular American television shows, alliterations, proverbs, being politically correct, and more!

Book: 240 pages **ISBN: 1-891-888-226 • US $21.95**

This 2-Audio CD set, ideal for ear-training, contains the dialogues used in the book, all the exercises, plus each vocabulary section, all spoken in "real speak!"

2-Audio CD set **ISBN: 1-891-888-331 • US $35.00**

This 2-Audio Cassette set contains the dialogues in the book & a selection of exercises spoken in "real speak!"

2-Audio Cassette set **ISBN: 1-891-888-34X • US $25.00**

Book and 2-CD set
ISBN: 1-891-888-560 • US $50.00

Book and 2-CD set
ISBN: 1-891-888-569 • US $40.00

DIRTY ENGLISH

A GUIDE TO POPULAR OBSCENITIES IN ENGLISH

This book is a humorous, yet academic, "course" on the most commonly used obscenities, insults, curses, and gestures used in the English language. This book is so complete, we challenge you to find a dirty word or expression that's not in it!

Book: 240 pages **ISBN: 1-891-888-234 • US $21.95**

This 2-Audio CD set, ideal for ear-training, contains the dialogues used in the book, all the exercises, plus each vocabulary section, all spoken in "real speak!"

2-Audio CD set **ISBN: 1-891-888-412 • US $35.00**

This 2-Audio Cassette set contains the dialogues in the book & a selection of exercises spoken in "real speak!"

2-Audio Cassette set **ISBN: 1-891-888-420 • US $25.00**

Book and 2-CD set
ISBN: 1-891-888-48X • US $50.00

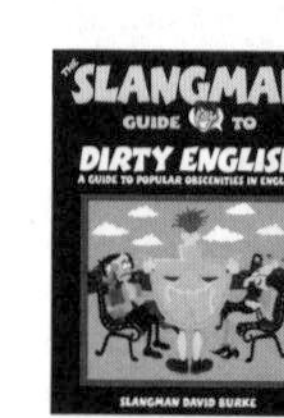

Book and 2-CD set
ISBN: 1-891-888-498 • US $40.00

PRICES/AVAILABILITY SUBJECT TO CHANGE

BIZ SPEAK 1

SLANG, IDIOMS & JARGON USED IN BUSINESS ENGLISH

Learn dozens of popular slang words and idioms used in virtually every American company. Chapters include: common abbreviations and shortcuts used in business, popular slang and idioms in the workplace, plus slang and jargon used in computer technology, Internet (World Wide Web), marketing, advertising, meetings, negotiations, and more!

Book: 160 pages **ISBN: 1-891-888-145 • US $21.95**

This 2-Audio CD set, ideal for ear-training, contains the dialogues used in the book, all the exercises, plus each vocabulary section all spoken in "real speak!"

2-Audio CD set **ISBN: 1-891-888-350 • US $35.00**

This 2-Audio Cassette set contains the dialogues in the book & a selection of exercises spoken in "real speak!"

2-Audio Cassette set **ISBN: 1-891-888-366 • US $25.00**

Book and 2-CD set
ISBN: 1-891-888-595 • US $50.00

Book and 2-CD set
ISBN: 1-891-888-609 • US $40.00

BIZ SPEAK 2

SLANG, IDIOMS & JARGON USED IN BUSINESS ENGLISH

Learn more popular slang words and idioms used in virtually every American company. Chapters include: more everyday workplace slang & idioms, plus slang & idioms used in international trade, sports terms used in business, business travel, shipping, globalization, "bureaucratese," and more!

Book: 240 pages **ISBN: 1-891-888-153 • US $21.95**

This 2-Audio CD set, ideal for ear-training, contains the dialogues used in the book, all the exercises, plus each vocabulary section all spoken in "real speak!"

2-Audio CD set **ISBN: 1-891-888-374 • US $35.00**

This 2-Audio Cassette set contains the dialogues in the book & a selection of exercises spoken in "real speak!"

2-Audio Cassette set **ISBN: 1-891-888-382 • US $25.00**

Book and 2-CD set
ISBN: 1-891-888-615 • US $50.00

Book and 2-CD set
ISBN: 1-891-888-625 • US $40.00

BIZ SPEAK 3

SLANG, IDIOMS & JARGON USED IN BUSINESS ENGLISH

This final volume includes: more everyday workplace slang & idioms, plus slang & idioms jargon used in finance and banking, human resources, business management, information technology, plus foreign words used in business, terms for being politically correct, and an important and hilarious section on common gestures to avoid at all costs in business!

Book: 240 pages **ISBN: 1-891-888-161 • US $21.95**

This 2-Audio CD set, ideal for ear-training, contains the dialogues used in the book, all the exercises, plus each vocabulary section all spoken in "real speak!"

2-Audio CD set **ISBN: 1-891-888-390 • US $35.00**

This 2-Audio Cassette set contains the dialogues in the book & a selection of exercises spoken in "real speak!"

2-Audio Cassette set **ISBN: 1-891-888-404 • US $25.00**

Book and 2-CD set
ISBN: 1-891-888-633 • US $50.00

Book and 2-CD set
ISBN: 1-891-888-641 • US $40.00

UNDERSTANDING AMERICAN-ENGLISH THROUGH AMERICAN CULTURE

HOW AMERICANS WALK, TALK, ACT, AND THINK!

It's simple. The only way to truly speak American-English like a native is to *think* like an American... to ***feel*** like an American! Hollywood native, Slangman David Burke, will give you the inside information you're unlikely to find in any other video. Included in the price of the video is:

- A full, downloadable transcript which can be found on our website, www.slangman.com
- Activities for the classroom & self-study are also available on our website such as: pair work, group activities, plus exercises for reading, writing, listening, & speaking!

20 minutes **ISBN: 1-891-888-587 • US $50.00**

SLANGMAN POSTER

The Slangman poster is perfect for the classroom! This big, colorful, 24"x36" poster demonstrates the top ten slang terms and expressions used by teens, in dating, in school, and on television. In addition, students will have hours of fun learning the updated version of *Cinderella*, complete with the most popular slang terms now being used! **ONLY US $5!**

PRICES/AVAILABILITY SUBJECT TO CHANGE

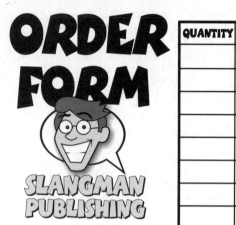

12206 Hillslope Street
Studio City, CA 91604 • USA

INTERNATIONAL:
1-818-769-1914

TOLL FREE (US/Canada):
1-877-SLANGMAN
(**1-877-752-6462**)

Worldwide FAX:
1-413-647-1589

Get the latest news, preview chapters, and shop online at:

WWW.SLANGMAN.COM

QUANTITY	ISBN	TITLE	PRICE	TOTAL
		THE SLANGMAN GUIDE TO		
		THE SLANGMAN GUIDE TO		
		THE SLANGMAN GUIDE TO		
		THE SLANGMAN GUIDE TO		
		THE SLANGMAN GUIDE TO		
		THE SLANGMAN GUIDE TO		
		THE SLANGMAN GUIDE TO		
		THE SLANGMAN GUIDE TO		
		THE SLANGMAN GUIDE TO		
		THE SLANGMAN GUIDE TO		
		THE SLANGMAN GUIDE TO		
		THE SLANGMAN GUIDE TO		
		THE SLANGMAN GUIDE TO		
		THE SLANGMAN GUIDE TO		
		THE SLANGMAN GUIDE TO		
		THE SLANGMAN GUIDE TO		
		THE SLANGMAN GUIDE TO		
		THE SLANGMAN GUIDE TO		
		THE SLANGMAN GUIDE TO		
		THE SLANGMAN GUIDE TO		
		THE SLANGMAN GUIDE TO		
		THE SLANGMAN GUIDE TO		
Total for Merchandise				
Sales Tax *(California Residents Only add applicable sales tax)*				
Shipping *(See Left)*				
ORDER TOTAL				

prices/availability subject to change

SHIPPING

—Domestic Orders—

SURFACE MAIL
(delivery time 5-7 days).
Add $4 shipping/handling for the first item, $1 for each additional item.

RUSH SERVICE
available at extra charge. Please telephone us for details.

—International Orders—

OVERSEAS SURFACE (delivery time 6-8 weeks).
Add $5 shipping/handling for the first item, $2 for each additional item.

OVERSEAS AIRMAIL available at extra charge. Please phone for details.

Name ______________________________

(School/Company) ______________________________

Street Address ______________________________

City ______________ State/Province ______________ Postal Code ______________

Country ______________ Phone ______________ Email ______________

METHOD OF PAYMENT (CHECK ONE)

❑ Personal Check or Money Order *(Must be in U.S. funds and drawn on a U.S. bank.)*

❑ VISA ❑ Master Card ❑ Discover

Credit Card Number

Expiration Date

Signature *(important!)*